Masters *of the* Sacred Page

The Medieval Book

VOLUME TWO

The Bible in the Latin West

VOLUME ONE

Masters of the Sacred Page

Manuscripts of Theology in the Latin West to 1274

LESLEY SMITH

UNIVERSITY OF NOTRE DAME PRESS
Notre Dame, Indiana

Manufactured in the United States of America

Library of Congress Cataloging-in-Publication Data
Smith, Lesley (Lesley Janette)
Masters of the sacred page : manuscripts of theology in the Latin West
to 1274 / Lesley Smith.
p. cm. — (The Medieval book ; v. 2)
Includes bibliographical references and index.
ISBN 0-268-04213-6 (alk. paper)
1. Theology—History—Middle Ages, 600–1500.
2. Theology—Manuscripts. 3. Manuscripts, Medieval.
I. Title. II. Series.

BR253 .S65 2001
230'.094'09022—dc21
2001001289

∞ *This book was printed on acid-free paper.*

Contents

Acknowledgments

I am grateful to John Van Engen and the committee of the Medieval Book series for giving me the opportunity to write this book; working with these manuscripts has been a delight.

Many friends and colleagues have helped the book take shape. I owe much to the late Leonard Boyle, Theodore Christchev, David d'Avray, Angela Dillon Bussi, Consuelo Dutschke, David Ganz, Ann Matter, Jeannette Morgenroth, Nigel Palmer, Marina Passalacqua, Susanne Simor (Verlag C. H. Beck), Patricia Stirnemann, William Stoneman, Elizabeth Teviotdale and Benedicta Ward.

It is a pleasure to acknowledge the help that so many librarians and libraries have given me. It is not simply because the Bodleian Library, Oxford, is my home base that so many of its manuscripts appear here; the library's astonishing store of riches make it an international treasure for learning. It is the least of the talents of the staff of the Duke Humfrey Reserve and the Department of Western Manuscripts that they have always managed to match book and reader. I am grateful to the Bodleian Library for permission to reproduce plates 2, 7, 11, 15, 17, 23, 24, 27, 28, and 29. Plates 12, 13, 14, 16, 19, 20, 21 are reproduced by permission of The British Library. Thanks are also due to Princeton University Libraries (pl. 1); The Beinecke Rare Book and Manuscript Library of Yale University Library (pl. 3); Kloster Engelberg (pl. 4); the Bibliothèque nationale de France (pls. 5 and 22); The Walters Art Gallery, Baltimore (pls. 6 and 18); the Dean and Chapter of Durham (pl. 8): my thanks to Roger Norris and the staff of the Cathedral Library; The Newberry Library (pl. 9); the John Rylands University Library of Manchester (pl. 10); the Österreichische Nationalbibliothek, Vienna, and Foto Leutner (pl. 25); the Biblioteca Apostolica Vaticana (pl. 26); the Master and Fellows of University College, Oxford (pl. 27); the President and Fellows of the College of the Holy and Undivided Trinity, Oxford (pl. 29); and the Biblioteca Medicea Laurenziana, Florence (pl. 30).

Martin Kauffmann has read and commented minutely on the whole text. Its felicities are his; its errors my own.

About the Author

Lesley Smith is Academic Bursar and Tutor in Politics at Harris Manchester College in the University of Oxford. After taking two degrees in Government and Political Theory at the London School of Economics, she earned her doctorate at Oxford on "Academic Commentaries on the Ten Commandments, c.1150–c.1270." Smith was a Commonwealth Scholar at the Pontifical Institute of Mediaeval Studies in Toronto and a British Academy Postdoctoral Fellow at Linacre College, Oxford.

Abbreviations

AHDLMA	*Archives d'histoire doctrinale et littéraire du moyen âge.*
CCCM	Corpus Christianorum Continuatio Mediaevalis.
CCSL	Corpus Christianorum Series Latina.
CSEL	Corpus Scriptorum Ecclesiasticorum Latinorum.
CUP	H. Denifle and A. Chatelain, *Chartularium Universitatis Parisiensis*, 4 vols. (Paris, 1889–1897).
EETS	Early English Text Society.
PL	*Patrologiae Latinae cursus completus . . .*, ed. J.-P. Migne, 212 vols. & suppls. (Paris, 1844–1864).
RThAM	*Recherches de théologie ancienne et mediévale.*
SBMA	B. Smalley, *The Study of the Bible in the Middle Ages*, 3rd ed. (Oxford, 1983).
SC	Sources chrétiennes.
Walther	*Initia carminum ac versuum medii aevi posterioris latinorum*, 2d ed. (Göttingen, 1969).

Introduction

This book is about the schools and masters of the twelfth and thirteenth centuries. Although the title may seem prosaic, it hides a history of a world turned upside down, a change in the way that knowledge itself was thought about and studied in the medieval West. The change was overwhelming, remarkably swift and, as these things will, caused an uproar among traditional thinkers. It encompassed, whether as cause or effect, all aspects of life in educated society, from book technology to the professionalization of teaching and learning. As we read of these changes today, we can recognize in them the seeds of much of our own academic life—universities, paid teachers, syllabuses for study and examination, books made for reference as well as perusal and, basic to all, the division of knowledge into a series of discrete subjects, knowable by reason and extendible by argument.

We can point to no single factor that brought this movement about. Rather, it arose from—indeed it may be seen as the epitome of—the phenomenon that Charles Homer Haskins called the twelfth-century renaissance.[1] This rebirth was fueled by the positive climatic, agricultural, demographic and economic changes that began in the eleventh century. Like the similar movements which flanked it (in the ninth century centered on the court of Charlemagne and in fifteenth-century Italy), the twelfth-century renaissance claimed to be simply a resurrection of ancient knowledge, rediscovering and restoring lost works and promoting old values in the present. Although the twelfth-century scholars were mere 'dwarves standing on giants' shoulders', in the famous dictum of Bernard of Chartres (d. *c.* 1130), with the greats of old as their guides they could see further than their illustrious teachers because they started so much higher up.

Origins tend to be vague. We rarely know the date when a famous medieval person was born, unless he or she was royal, or otherwise destined for importance from birth. But we do know when they died; by that point, they had made their mark, and the date was worth recording. Similarly, this book has, in truth, a rather vague starting date. As will become clear,

1. C. H. Haskins, *The Renaissance of the Twelfth Century*. For a new summary of thinking on the period, and bibliography, see R. N. Swanson, *The Twelfth-Century Renaissance*.

there is no exact time when medieval schools began to move toward the corporate internationalism that characterized the *studia generalia* which were the forerunners of universities. It is this change—one which for some scholars is the distinguishing mark of the twelfth-century rebirth—that I wish to chart, but although as a beginning 1100 sounds secure, it may be too neat to be entirely defensible. If key dates are needed, 1127 may well be the closest we can get to a crux. At that date, the bishop and canons of Notre Dame cathedral in Paris decided no longer to house external students (those who were not clerical members of the cathedral household) in the cathedral cloister, nor to allow masters who were not canons to teach there, in order to guard their own peace and quiet.[2] From that point on, these students and masters had to fend for themselves, and the seeds of their independence were sown: a master and students in one place is the beginnings of a college. Nevertheless, on the whole it seems best to stick to inexactitude. The date 1100 represents a convenient starting point for a book about books, since it is about the time when the first steps toward the production of an integrated glossed Bible, the *Glossa ordinaria* (plate no. 1), were being taken.

The closing date, 1274, is much more precise: the date of the death of both Thomas Aquinas and Bonaventure, scholarly contemporaries from the Dominican and Franciscan Orders. It is also the date of the Second Council of Lyons (traveling to which, Aquinas died; Bonaventure died at the Council itself); but since I mention it only after Thomas and Bonaventure, it should be clear that this book is concerned more with the people who made theology than the occasions when they made it. Patristic and medieval theology is alive with characters; their often-extraordinary personalities contributed hugely to their beliefs about God and the Creation. Many other books deal purely with theology; this one will also focus on the theologians.

The choice of the terminal date was relatively simple. This book has a companion volume (by Richard Cross) which takes the story to the fifteenth century. We chose to divide at the death of Thomas Aquinas for two reasons. Firstly, because by that date most of the institutional circumstances of theology (the university context; the course of study; how the candidates were examined, and so forth) had become relatively stable; and secondly, because after the Thomistic synthesis of the nature of theology (chiefly in his *Summa theologiae,* although there were many other works), the division between theology and philosophy became wider, and the nature of the questions asked and the way the answers are essayed takes on a rather different character. This book, then, deals with a time when there was a great deal of flux in many fields: the organization of knowledge; the organization of education; the definition of theology. By Aquinas' death, most of this was settled.

Nevertheless, in order to understand the great changes of the twelfth and thirteenth centuries, the reader will need a sketch of the background of education and learning before 1100. The twelfth-century renaissance was a change built on continuity and revival of the past. To see exactly what scholars wanted to revive and rework, we will need to know what previously existed.

2. From the cartulary of Notre Dame, Paris, cited in G. Paré, A. Brunet, P. Tremblay, *La renaissance du xiie siècle. Les écoles et l'enseignement*, p. 78. Bishops Theobald (1144–1158) and Maurice of Sully (1160–1196) reiterated this prohibition of canons renting their houses to students, *CUP*, I, no. 55.

A1. Learning in Medieval Europe up to 1100

Until relatively recently, the term 'Dark Ages' was often employed to describe the whole of the period from the Fall of Rome to the Italian Renaissance—roughly a thousand years. Although research has made it clear that such a designation is foolish, it remains true that certain parts of that period remain a little gloomy, not indeed because historians still believe that the passage of time is synonymous with progress, but because there are simply fewer survivals by which we can know some times and circumstances. Such indeed is the history of education and learning until the twelfth century; but there are a few glimmers of light, especially in Italy, where the traditions of classical education seem to have survived better than elsewhere. The Roman writer and monk Cassiodorus (d. *c.* 580) established a monastery school at Vivarium to encourage the study of both theology and secular learning. His *Institutes of Divine and Secular Learning*[3] set out a program of education based on the Bible and the seven liberal arts. His thesis was that secular learning could contribute to the proper understanding of the works of God in the Bible—a theme that will recur in the works described in this book. Cassiodorus had a list of 'set books'—those necessary for a complete education. Since books were in short supply, and under threat from warfare and the uncertain politics of the time, he set his monks to copy whatever they could find. This was a crucial step, since it paved the way for a monastic tradition of copying literature, of whatever sort, in order to preserve the knowledge of the past. Ironically, it is largely only via the copies made in monasteries that we know a great deal of the pagan classical literature of which many Christians so disapproved.

Some lights were flickering elsewhere. Those we know of come from the Irish-Northumbrian axis; Bede (d. 735), working in his Northumbrian monastery of Wearmouth-Jarrow, produced magisterial books on the interpretation of the Bible, on the calculation of time and on cosmography, as well as his famous *Ecclesiastical History of the English People.*[4] Although his works were influential, Bede was very much a lone star, working on his own, as far as we know, without a school or pupils. Yet we know that his northern monastery had direct links with Rome[5] and, moreover, he may possibly have felt the influence of the school that Archbishop Theodore (d. 690), originally a Greek monk, established in Canterbury.[6] But the importance of Northumbria is clear still in the eighth century when Alcuin, master of the cathedral school at York, was invited by Charlemagne to be tutor to his royal household.[7]

3. Cassiodorus, *Institutiones. Divine and Human Readings,* trans. L. W. Jones.

4. Bede, *Historia ecclesiastica,* ed. and trans. B. Colgrave and R. A. B. Mynors; historical notes, commentary, and bibliography by J. M. Wallace-Hadrill.

5. For example, Bede writes of John the Archchanter being sent from Rome by Pope Agatho to teach the monks the correct observance of the liturgy of the Roman Church (*Historia ecclesiastica,* IV.18); or again, the Codex Amiatinus (the oldest extant manuscript of the complete Latin Vulgate Bible) was made in Wearmouth-Jarrow between about 690 and 700, and sent to Rome as a present for Pope Gregory II.

6. See B. Bischoff and M. Lapidge, *Biblical Commentaries from the Canterbury School of Theodore and Hadrian.*

7. For the episode according to two Carolingian commentators, see *Einhard and Notker the Stammerer. Two Lives of Charlemagne,* trans. L. Thorpe: Einhard, p. 79, Notker, p. 94.

Alcuin set up a palace school and library which was the core of the 'Carolingian Renaissance', and which lasted until the death of Charlemagne's grandson, Charles the Bald.[8] The Carolingians were canny rulers, so their thirst for learning (as patrons, even if they were not very successful pupils themselves) found its way to the ends of the Empire, as part of a determined political program. Charles the Bald's school at Laon, or in nearby Quierzy, was home to a remarkable group of learned Irishmen, including the grammarian Martin of Laon, and John Scot Eriugena (d. *c.* 877), linguist, translator of Greek theology and, eventually, an original and learned theologian and cosmologist himself.[9]

Irish-Northumbrian monks made another mark. From the late sixth century onward, men such as Columbanus, Boniface and Willibrord traveled as missionaries to continental Europe. They established monasteries such as Luxeuil, Corbie, Fulda and Bobbio which built traditions of learning (or at least of copying books). These monasteries flourished in the Carolingian period; they set up schools which, from the evidence which remains, were sometimes rather elementary, but which did at least keep some sort of education and scholarship alive in the West. Moreover, they established a custom that monasteries might hold schools and that to be learned meant association with the Church; and they ensured that monastic libraries were repositories of ancient treasure, which later scholars were to mine. They were the foundation on which the twelfth-century revival was to build.

A2. The Early Curriculum to 1100

The basis of all study was the seven liberal arts, the heritage of the materials and ethos of the classrooms of the later Roman Empire.[10] Arts teaching had a long history, but the system used in the Middle Ages had been laid out between 400 and 439 by Martianus Capella in his *Marriage of Mercury and Philology* (*De nuptiis Mercurii et Philologiae*). Although still a commonly read text in the twelfth century, Martianus' schema had been subordinated to that of Anicius Manlius Severinus Boethius (d. *c.* 524), who clarified the standard division of the seven arts into the *trivium* (grammar, rhetoric, dialectic) and the *quadrivium* (arithmetic, music, geometry, astronomy), and who had written or translated many of the books used as standard texts in arts teaching.

The *trivium* gathered together the arts concerned with words and language. It was studied first. Latin grammar was the basis of all study; no matter what vernacular language the stu-

8. For Charles, see J. Nelson, *Charles the Bald;* more generally, R. McKitterick has written or edited several recent volumes on the Carolingian renaissance, e.g., *Carolingian Culture: Emulation and Innovation;* see also n. 9.

9. See J. J. Contreni, *The Cathedral School of Laon from 850 to 930: Its Manuscripts and Masters* and *Carolingian Learning, Masters and Manuscripts.* For Eriugena, see J. J. O'Meara, *Eriugena;* an up-to-date bibliography may be found in J. J. Contreni and P. P. O Niill, *Glossae divinae historiae: The Biblical Glosses of John Scottus Eriugena.*

10. See generally D. Wagner, *The Seven Liberal Arts in the Middle Ages.*

dent spoke, Latin was the international language of education and the educated. Rhetoric was the art of correct expression or persuasion. Dialectic was verbal argument and logic. Each had its own textbooks. In grammar, throughout the Middle Ages, the key texts were the *Ars minor* (or *De partibus orationis ars minor*) and *Ars maior* (or *Ars grammatica*) of Aelius Donatus (fourth century), and the *Institutiones grammaticae* of Priscian (fifth–sixth century). These texts had their Christian continuation in Isidore of Seville's *Etymologiae* (no. 12). The necessary texts for rhetoric were even older, centering on Cicero's *De inventione* (which was the most copied classical text in manuscript[11]) and the pseudo-Ciceronian *Rhetorica ad Herennium* (the third most copied text). These texts had no rivals, but were sometimes supplemented by the fourth book of Boethius' *De differentiis topicis.* Rhetoric posed a problem for Christian scholars, such as Augustine, who had been trained in this Roman art of persuasive speaking and writing. Should Christians use profane learning in the service of their faith? Partly in response to this dilemma, Augustine wrote *De doctrina Christiana* (no. 9) as an alternative course of study. The final trivial art, dialectic, was provided with a constellation of texts. Boethius had translated Aristotle's *Categoriae* and *De interpretatione* as well as Porphyry's *Isagoge*, and added his own *De differentiis topicis* and *In Ciceronis topica.* To this basic list might be added the *De definitionibus* of Marius Victorinus (fourth century).

Boethius was also heavily represented in the books of the *quadrivium*, whose arts were united by their reliance on number. His *De arithmetica* and *De institutione musica* were the core of arithmetic and music, as had been his translation of Euclid's *Elements* for geometry. Long before the twelfth century this translation was lost, and geometry had to use texts in compendia of the arts, such as Martianus Capella. This was true in astronomy as well, although Calcidius' translation of Plato's *Timaeus* and Bede's works on reckoning time came to be added to the list.

Nowhere was the curriculum in arts exactly the same: teaching depended on the teacher. Neither were the seven arts studied for their own sakes, precisely. A few schoolmasters might become specialists in one particular subject, but their pupils generally were studying in order to take up a career, or to move on to the study of the Bible. In his *De Trinitate*, Boethius, following Aristotle, divides speculative (as opposed to practical) knowledge into three parts, natural science, mathematics and theology.[12] Without possessing Aristotle's works on the natural sciences, the first part of this triad could be not so much taught as sketched; not until the recovery of the works of Aristotle and the Arab natural scientists in the twelfth and thirteenth centuries could the study of physics (i.e., natural science) become a reality. Mathematics was pursued via the *quadrivium.* We can only piece together theological teaching from extant works. It does not seem to have been uniform; there was nothing similar to the seven arts to guide teachers. Apart from the books of the Bible, there was no curriculum other than what could be copied from the *De doctrina Christiana*, and it is difficult to reconstruct what students were taught. Moreover, we need to remember that, for most, the purpose of teaching

11. B. Munk Olsen, 'The Production of the Classics in the Eleventh and Twelfth Centuries'.

12. Boethius, *De Trinitate* (*Opuscula sacra* I), c. 2, in *Boethius. The Theological Tractates. The Consolation of Philosophy*, trans. H. F. Stewart, E. K. Rand, and S. J. Tester, pp. 8–9.

theology was never 'objective' but rather, in order to instruct and build up faith. The existence of Bibles and psalters with marginal glosses suggests that individual books were expounded line by line. The content of these glosses varies from the exposition of unfamiliar words to allegorical interpretations of large chunks of text. Glosses such as those thought to be from the school of Theodore and Hadrian at Canterbury seem rather dry: it is hard to know how they were used in the classroom. Longer and more sophisticated Bible commentaries, such as those by Bede or Haimo of Auxerre (d. *c.* 875), are more obviously interesting and easier to understand as building up faith; but whether and how they were used in teaching is difficult to say. They are more likely to be the fuel of individual monastic reading. On anything more than an elementary level, scriptural study at this time seems likely to have been individual and tailor-made. It relied on reading the works of the early Church Fathers, especially Jerome for biblical commentary, Augustine for questions of doctrine, and Ambrose and Gregory for spiritual development and pastoral care. Their writings were known more through compendia of extracts grouped by author or by subject than by full copies of the works themselves.

For all of this, we cannot know if early medieval works debating particular issues (such as those on the Eucharist by Paschasius Radbertus and Ratramnus of Corbie [no. 14]) were used at all in teaching or were simply (as seems more likely) the preserve of a very few specialists working at a high level. Whether more than a handful of his contemporaries read and understood the works of John Scot Eriugena must be open to doubt. Instead, elementary teaching on doctrine used Boethius' *Opuscula sacra*, five short works focusing mainly on the nature of the persons of the Trinity and their relationship.[13] Below this, the simplest theological teaching consisted of reading and expounding the psalter, the liturgy and the Creed.

During this early period, then, theology was not well defined, but included whatever might pertain to a deeper knowledge of God and the Christian faith. Curricula depended on the preference of individual masters, but would most likely begin with easy instruction in the liturgy, and the psalms, followed by expositions of the Creed and a choice of books of the Bible. Boethius would be studied to answer questions about the nature and persons of God. More advanced students would go on to *florilegia* of extracts from the Fathers. The detail would depend on why the student was learning—the curriculum would surely be different in monastic houses where the pupils were novice monks, to early cathedral schools where the pupils would be taking up 'secular' careers. All in all, since the number of students overall was not large, those who progressed beyond simple Bible study must have been few. Finally we should remember that literacy was valued and used by Carolingian government and in secular affairs.[14] It was at this time that script, which had become cramped and difficult to read, was consciously reformed. In its clarity and simplicity, the Caroline minuscule that was created still forms the basis of all 'Roman' scripts today.

13. *Boethius. The Theological Tractates.*

14. For some uses of literacy in Carolingian government and society, see R. McKitterick, *The Carolingians and the Written Word* (Cambridge, 1989).

B1. The Context of Learning, 1100–1200

These individual monastic schools continued to have life as long as their parent institutions survived and made provision for them, but the fame of any of them was dependent on the reputation of the scholars who taught or studied there. The schools were not themselves large or established; generally, they depended on a small staff whose monastic vocation took precedence over their scholarship. So the prestige of each school rose and fell in accordance with the personnel associated with them. Bec, for instance, an abbey in Normandy, is famous as the home of Lanfranc and Anselm, both of whom became archbishops of Canterbury in the eleventh century. They came to Bec from Italy; when they had gone, the abbey school did not retain its eminent position.

The situation was similar in the schools established in association with cathedrals, such as those in Paris, Laon, Reims or Chartres—old Roman centers taken over by the Carolingians, whose bustling economies could support the comparative luxury of education. The schools were staffed by cathedral personnel and offered education to students from the diocese, as long as they could afford it.[15] Like monastery schools, most depended on the fame of one or two masters, such as Gilbert the Universal of Auxerre. Very few schools were large or rich enough to achieve greater permanence and attract students from further afield. Chartres' cathedral school was brought to prominence by the year 1000 by Fulbert, its chancellor. It had its heyday in the late eleventh and the first half of the twelfth centuries, in particular under the brothers Bernard and Thierry. The extant writings of the Chartrian masters suggest that the program of study there was wider than that of most other schools, especially in the fields of cosmology and natural science, which they added to the usual liberal arts and theology.

The importance of Chartres in the history of the twelfth-century revival has been much debated.[16] Some scholars claim that Chartres was the pre-eminent twelfth-century school; others believe its influence to have been much more limited, not different from others of its size, but better known to us simply because of the description of his time there by its famous student, John of Salisbury. This is not the place to rehearse those arguments, but we do need to be clear that Chartres was not some sort of proto-MIT, full of modern, skeptical scientists working in a secular environment, without thought of God. In addition to Bernard, whose glosses on the *Timaeus* are extant, and his brother Thierry, who was particularly known for the *Heptateuchon*, a guidebook to the liberal arts, the scholars of Chartres included Bishop Ivo (no. 16) whose work was primarily on theology and canon law; Gilbert de la Porrée, a biblical exegete of brilliance; and the grammarian (an old-fashioned specialty by the twelfth century) William of Conches, who was a pupil of Master Bernard. Even those who wrote on natural

15. 'Although a school was an ancient part of a cathedral's equipment in the service of the diocese of which it was the centre, the obligation for every cathedral to have a school seems first to have been expressed in general legislative form by Gregory VII in 1078' (R. W. Southern, *Scholastic Humanism and the Unification of Europe*, 1: *Foundations*, p. xviii, n. 1). Southern also cites a letter from a German student remarking on the strangeness of William of Champeaux offering his teaching without charge, see ibid., p. 202 (= *Biblioteca rerum Germanicarum*, ed. P. Jaffe, 6 vols. [Berlin, 1864–73], 5, p. 286).

16. Southern, *Scholastic Humanism*, ch. 2, with bibliography.

science and astronomy did so within a solidly Christian worldview. They studied the stars not, indeed, in order to disprove the existence of God, but to understand how God brings order to the chaos of the universe. By gathering knowledge of all that was around them, and by fashioning it into an orderly form, they could participate in the creative work of God, and understand the Creator's mind more fully.

It is not clear when the cathedral school of Notre Dame in Paris was founded, but it probably dates back at least to the Carolingians.[17] It was certainly not immediately pre-eminent and vied for the best scholars and teachers with cathedral and monastery schools elsewhere. But from the time of the reign of the first Capetian monarch, Hugh (d. 996), Paris had been the official capital of France (or at any rate the portion of it ruled by Hugh).[18] Its political and economic importance helped it grow in size so that, by the beginning of the twelfth century, there were several establishments offering higher education in or around the city.[19] A student like John of Salisbury, journeying to the Paris schools from his native England, in the first half of the twelfth century, could hear masters lecture at Notre Dame, the Petit-Pont, Mont Ste-Geneviève, at the schoolrooms on the Ile de France, and, after 1108, at the new free school at the abbey of St Victor, founded by William of Champeaux, the most famous teacher of the day. [20]

The first schools at Notre Dame (which were the first in Paris) were in the cathedral 'cloister'. This was not a monastic-style cloister, but an enclosure of houses to the northeast of the church where the canons and cathedral staff lived. Some of these, like William of Champeaux, who was archdeacon of the cathedral, held classes themselves. Others rented rooms in their houses to independent masters to teach there.[21] Until 1127 students at these schools lived alongside the canons; but in that year a decree of the bishop, Stephen of Senlis, banned external students (those who were not cathedral clerics) from living in the cloister (although he also built a new episcopal palace on the Ile complete with large lecture hall).[22] The schools moved to the pavement (*parvis*) in front of the cathedral, and to the south of it, toward and

17. A. L. Gabriel, 'The Cathedral Schools of Notre-Dame and the Beginning of the University of Paris'.

18. For the development of the Capetian monarchy, see E. Hallam, *Capetian France 987–1328* and J. Dunbabin, *France in the Making 843–1180*.

19. The city of Paris was geographically small, so that, for instance, the abbeys of Ste-Geneviève and St Victor were both outside the city until Philip II rebuilt the walls in 1211; A. Friedmann, *Paris, ses rues, ses paroisses du moyen âge a la révolution*, describes the process, with maps.

20. John of Salisbury, *Metalogicon*, ed. C. C. J. Webb, 2, c. 10; and for his account of William, Peter Abelard, 'Historia calamitatum', pp. 58–62. For William and St Victor see n. 14. Unlike other non-secular schools, the Augustinian school at the abbey of St Victor was open to all students, not just those of its own order. There were other monastery schools in or around Paris at St Denis, St Maur des Fossés, and St Germain des Prés; see S. Ferruolo, *The Origins of the University. The Schools of Paris and Their Critics, 1100–1215*, p. 17 and Gabriel, 'The Cathedral Schools', p. 44.

21. There was no single, central organization. Each unit of master plus students was reckoned as a school; hence the coinage, 'the school*s* of Notre Dame'.

22. Southern, *Scholastic Humanism*, commentary to pl. 2 (a useful map of medieval Paris); *Cartulaire de l'Eglise de Notre-Dame de Paris*, ed. B. Guérard (Paris, 1850), 1, p. 339, quoted in Gabriel, 'The Cathedral Schools', p. 42.

onto the Petit-Pont, and across to the green spaces on the south (or left) bank of the Seine, opposite the cathedral, taking over the disused churches of St Julien-le-Pauvre and St Séverin. This area is still known as the Latin Quarter, after the language of the schools. The arts masters moved even further out to the south, beyond the city walls to Mont Ste-Geneviève, outside the civil and episcopal jurisdictions.

Apart from the Augustinian canons of St Victor, the teachers at these establishments were 'secular' theologians, grammarians, or whatever, which is to say that, although they were clerics, they did not belong to a monastic order.[23] Although scholarship was still pursued by monks, notably by Bernard of Clairvaux (no. 4) and Rupert of Deutz (d. 1129/30), and monasteries continued to provide primary-level education, the twelfth century marks a decisive shift toward 'secular' schools, generally located in or near the local cathedral.[24] By the middle third of the twelfth century, the confluence of a group of masters in Paris, led by Peter Comestor, Peter the Chanter and Peter Lombard (see nos. 3, 24, 18), had established Paris decisively as a major European center for education and as pre-eminent in the study of theology. Its position was cemented in 1200 when the French king Philip II Augustus gave the scholars and masters of Paris certain privileges, designed to attract them to the city and keep them there.[25]

These privileges mostly referred to the masters' and students' legal position. Since the Paris schools were based on monastic and cathedral education, the students and teachers of theology were all 'clerks in holy orders', that is, at least tonsured as sub-deacons, although they never needed to take the higher orders of deacon or priest. Technically, this left them subject to ecclesiastical rather than civil jurisdiction. Just as scholars at a monastic school would be subject to the abbot, so those at a cathedral school like Notre Dame were the responsibility of the local bishop. The scholars were keen to continue this privilege (known in England as 'benefit of clergy'). Church law was sometimes thought to be more lenient than civil law, but, more importantly, it meant that the scholars could keep themselves separate from the rest of the town and manage their own affairs. As we shall see, the scholars were simultaneously (and ultimately successfully) trying to establish their independence from the bishop of Paris and become responsible to the pope alone.

Philip Augustus decreed that the scholars were immune from civil jurisdiction and subject only to the bishop. Moreover, the city provost and civil authorities had to swear to uphold the scholars' rights and to inform on anyone they saw harming a scholar or his interests in any

23. Since such men followed a Rule of life they were known as 'regulars' as opposed to the non-monastic 'seculars'.

24. At a synod in Rome in 1078, Gregory VII had ordered that 'all bishops make provision for the teaching of the arts of letters in their cathedrals': J. D. Mansi, *Sacrorum conciliorum . . . collectio*, vol. 20 (Venice, 1775), col. 509. Canon 18 of the Third Lateran Council, held under Alexander III in 1179, stated that each cathedral had to employ a master or grammarian to teach the clerks of the church and poor students for free. Lateran IV (1215) added that each metropolitan church (which did not include Notre Dame as it was not the central church of the diocese) had to employ a theologian to train priests and others in *sacra pagina* (canon 11). See *Decrees of the Ecumenical Councils*, ed. N. P. Tanner: Lat. III, c. 18, I, p. 220; Lat. IV, c. 11, I, p. 240.

25. See *CUP*, I, no. 1; and, generally, P. Kibre, *Scholarly Privileges in the Middle Ages.*

way. Philip's reasons for supporting the scholars are not spelled out. Probably, he had two motives: first, since the civil authorities were not royal officers, Philip's support of the bishop's men and the masters strengthened rivals to the civil powers; secondly, at least from the time of Philip I (r. 1059–1108), Capetian monarchs took much interest in learning and scholarship. The Capetians wanted to promote their claim that they were descendants of Charlemagne's dynasty, and by supporting a school they were following in Carolingian footsteps. Further, they seem genuinely to have believed that association with learning and scholarship would help glorify their capital city, which they promoted as a worthy successor to the ancient capitals of Jerusalem and Rome.[26] Thus, although Philip II's grant of 1200 is the first extant set of privileges we know, it was almost certainly only a restatement of the situation which had prevailed in the twelfth century, but which the civil authorities had been unwilling to recognize.

* * *

What were the early twelfth-century schools like? We cannot give entirely clear answers, since little material evidence exists for much of their procedure. There are no extant statutes regulating the schools, and we must reconstruct from accounts like those of Peter Abelard[27] or documents where 'masters' of Paris are cited as witnesses or signatories, telling us that a particular position was recognized and given a name. Moreover, the Paris scene was a rich mixture: apart from the independent masters, there were schools at the cathedral, at the abbey of St Victor and at Ste-Geneviève. At least until the charter of 1215, which we will consider later, what was important to the schools was not the place or buildings, but the masters who were teaching. Classrooms were often basic, with a magisterial chair (hence our modern word 'chair' for a professorship) and students perhaps on benches or sitting on straw at the master's feet. Thus it was that the street where the arts masters concentrated was called the 'rue de fouarre'—in Latin, *vicus stramineus*—or street of straw.[28]

Student lodgings and dormitories, and the eventual establishment of colleges and nations of students, are subjects beyond the scope of this work, but they have been extensively written about elsewhere.[29] This independence from fixed buildings and administration gave the masters a great deal of power over the local community and the civil government, since the schools brought in a lot of revenue to Paris. The threat of a university strike (with the masters simply

26. See, e.g., S. Ferruolo, 'Parisius-Paradisus: The City, Its Schools, and the Origins of the University of Paris'.

27. G. Post, 'Parisian Masters as a Corporation, 1200–1246'.

28. *CUP*, I, intro. p. xvii; Gabriel, 'The Cathedral Schools', p. 58.

29. On colleges: H. Rashdall, *The Universities of Europe in the Middle Ages*, 1, pp. 497–539, gives an account with a bibliography of early sources. The earliest college record is of the College of the Dix-Huit in 1180 (*CUP*, 1, intro. no. 50 and L. Thorndike, *University Life and Records in the Middle Ages*, pp. 21–22); and see the college's reformation by William of Auvergne in 1228 (pp. 31–32). Astrik Gabriel has written extensively on early colleges, e.g., 'The Cathedral Schools' and *Student Life at Ave Maria College, Mediaeval Paris*. On Nations: Rashdall, *Universities*, 1, pp. 298–320; P. Kibre, *The Nations in the Mediaeval Universities*.

packing their bags and going to another town) was used a number of times, notably by the Oxford masters in 1209, when they mostly decamped to Cambridge; by the annoyed students of Bologna who went off to Padua in 1222; and by the masters who left Paris in 1229, calling principally at Toulouse, Angers, Reims, Orléans and, indeed, Oxford and Cambridge.[30]

We do not know how the early Paris schools were regulated. At first it seems as though students came and went as they pleased, paying individual masters as they heard them, and moving from one master to another, following subject-matter, reputation, or simply fashion. There was as yet no 'degree structure' and no requirement to stick to one school or the other. Students talk of 'hearing' masters, which meant, as far as we can tell, hearing them lecture on a particular book of the Bible (in the case of theology) or on one of the liberal arts textbooks. We know almost nothing of 'qualifications' at this stage. If Abelard is typical (and where Abelard is concerned this is always a big if—but John of Salisbury gives a similar impression), some students simply hung around the schools, listening to masters and engaging in debate, until either money ran out or they went home and took up a job, perhaps in a local noble or ecclesiastical household (for which a very good reference was that they had 'been to the schools of Paris') or, if they wanted to pursue an academic career themselves, they simply set up shop on their own. Those working inside the city boundary of Paris needed the authorization of the chancellor or *scholasticus* of the cathedral. Since Ste-Geneviève was outside the city wall in the twelfth century, the masters teaching there did not need such permission—an attractive situation for many. It seems that the chancellors attempted to charge for issuing such permissions (known, from the time of Pope Alexander III [1159–1181] as a 'license to teach' [*licentia docendi*]), for this practice is forbidden at a council in 1138, and later by the Third Lateran Council of 1179. Indeed, Lateran III stated that the chancellor was *obliged* to give a license to teach to any qualified person.[31] Ironically, the independent arts masters of Ste-Geneviève must have taken up the same habit and charged for issuing licenses. Certainly by 1223 this had become an accepted custom, for Pope Honorius III warned the chancellor of Notre Dame not to interfere in their doing so.[32]

It has been suggested that the main reason Abelard was considered such an *enfant terrible* by the scholarly 'establishment' was that he dared to start teaching *sine magistro*, 'without a master'; but whether this means that he did not have the patronage of an established master, or that he did not have some sort of formal license to teach, is unclear.[33] It is most likely that there was a type of swearing-in ceremony, when masters testified that students had heard certain courses and reached a particular level of competence; but we have no early evidence for this. It seems probable that students registered with a particular master and became

30. See Rashdall, *Universities*, 1, pp. 334–37; 2, pp. 10–11; 3, pp. 276–78.

31. Gabriel, 'The Cathedral Schools', pp. 44, 50; Rashdall, *Universities*, 1, pp. 280–83; Southern, *Scholastic Humanism*, p. 219. Abelard claims ('Historia Calamitatum', p. 65) that teaching in and around Paris brought him wealth as well as fame.

32. Gabriel, 'The Cathedral Schools', p. 50.

33. See Paré, Brunet, and Tremblay, *La Renaissance*, pp. 67–68.

part of his stable of pupils.[34] We do not know how the overall shape of a student's course was monitored—some courses must have had prerequisites. Written examinations should not be expected. In this, as in most other levels of medieval society, oral testimony and the swearing of oaths were the norm. Students would swear publicly that they had fulfilled the necessary requirements; masters would hear them go through their paces, and then swear publicly that they had reached the expected standard. Oral teaching and examination were the usual medieval method. There was no simple 'degree'; the 'license to teach' was only useful for those who wished to pursue an academic career. As today, most students came to learn and then leave, going to other sorts of job.

The position of the masters was complicated by the difficult moral problem of whether or not one could charge for lectures on theology, since it was a sin not to inform other people about God and salvation. Teachers with ecclesiastical benefices were funded by the Church;[35] but for those without, the problem was acute. Custom and need eventually dictated they could take honoraria from wealthy students, and poor masters could charge fees as well. In his commentary on Genesis, Stephen Langton (d. 1228) notes, 'thus it is clear that masters are allowed to take goods from students and even to ask for them'.[36] The moral issue is addressed by Peter the Chanter, among others, who came to a compromise about hiring out sitting space in the rooms where lectures were held.[37]

Who were the masters? Although Paris was the center of theological study, masters were certainly not restricted to Frenchmen. John Baldwin has calculated that between 1179 and 1215, three-quarters of the masters came from outside the French royal domain.[38] In fact, the twelfth century is a remarkable period for internationalism in careers. A monk like Anselm might be born in Aosta in Northern Italy, study at Bec in Normandy, and end his career as archbishop of Canterbury in England. This was not unusual. Few of the famous names of the schools were French: Peter Abelard was Breton, Hugh of St Victor was a Saxon, Robert of Melun and, probably, Andrew of St Victor were English, and Peter Lombard is self-explanatory. Such internationalism is one of the keynotes of the growing schools. Originally, schools in the main provided for scholars from their locality. In the later twelfth century, the prestigious schools became known as *studia generalia*, places of general study. General, in this case, did not mean

34. Southern suggests that the pattern was for arts students to have one main master but simultaneously to attend other masters' lectures; in theology students had a series of masters consecutively (*Scholastic Humanism*, p. 221).

35. See the bulls *Quia nonnullis* (1215), *CUP*, i, no. 22 and *Super specula* (1219), *CUP*, 1, no. 32; the latter gave selected students leave of absence from their benefices in order to study theology, for up to five years with pay, 'to bolster the teaching of theology and to counteract the lucrative sciences of law and medicine'. See generally, L. E. Boyle, *Pastoral Care, Clerical Education and Canon Law 1200–1400*.

36. Quoted in Rashdall, *Universities*, 1, p. 471, n. 2; see also G. Post, 'Masters' Salaries and Student Fees in the Mediaeval Universities'.

37. See J. W. Baldwin, *Masters, Princes and Merchants: The Social Views of Peter the Chanter and His Circle*, 1, pp. 124–27.

38. J. W. Baldwin, 'Masters at Paris from 1179 to 1215: A Social Perspective'; R. W. Southern, 'The Schools of Paris and the Schools of Chartres'; and A. L. Gabriel, 'English Masters and Students in Paris during the Twelfth Century'.

that students could study a wide variety of subjects there, but rather that students could come 'generally'—from far and wide—to hear the masters. This anti-parochialism is one of the tenets that mark out a university, and it is a mark of the continuing development of the late twelfth-century schools.

B2. The Curriculum, 1100–1200

Medieval learning was based on the exposition of authoritative texts. This was, perhaps, a reflection of a biblically based religion: since God had written a book about Creation, there was a cultural supposition that books and texts formed the basis of knowledge. If God had a textbook, then human learning should follow suit.

Twelfth-century scholars knew that God had revealed many things to the ancients, and what needed to be done, as a beginning, was to retrieve and ponder on what had been given already. A select group of savants, the Latin (and Greek, as their works became available) Fathers of the Church, principally Augustine (no. 9), Ambrose (no. 11), Gregory the Great (no. 10), Jerome (no. 6), Gregory of Nazianzus, Gregory of Nyssa, John Damascene, John Chrysostom, John Cassian and (selectively) Origen, were regarded as authoritative thinkers whose interpretations of the Bible and Christian tradition could be cited as orthodox statements or used to bolster principles of argument. Over time, some more recent 'moderni', such as Bernard of Clairvaux (no. 4) and Anselm of Canterbury were cautiously added to the list, although the custom was that, whereas the older authors were cited by name, the newer thinkers were always quoted anonymously. These additions to the select list of authorities are more interesting than they might seem, since they signal a shift in mentality from believing that truth was to be found in past revelation to thinking that God might continue to reveal knowledge into the present. The 'giants' of Bernard of Chartres might have been given much more to begin with, but even the 'dwarves' were not simply repeating old material—they too could know more about the world.

It is not entirely clear whether Bernard's dwarves and giants are to be understood as modesty or pride, for the twelfth-century scholars who were describing themselves as dwarves were also formulating new ideas about the real worth of humanity in the eyes of God:

> The animals express their brute creation
> By head hung low and downward looking eyes;
> But man holds high his head in contemplation
> To show his natural kinship with the skies.
> *He* sees the stars obey God's legislation:
> *They* teach the laws by which mankind can rise.[39]

39. Quoted and trans. in Southern, *Scholastic Humanism,* pp. 30–31.

This reworking of Ovid by Bernard Silvestris (d. *c.* 1159) takes the Roman poet's fiction for modern fact. Humans could begin to look beyond the disgrace of the Fall to the dignity of the Incarnation. If they were made in God's image, they might then dare to aspire to God's knowledge.

Since we live in an age which feels it has little to learn from the past, and where ideas need to be new to be seen as worthwhile, it may be hard for us to understand why ancient texts were so important, and tradition so valued. The answer depends on the twelfth-century attitude to knowledge. Medieval scholars believed that all knowledge came from God, who was omniscient. To seek knowledge was to participate in God's revelation of Godself to humanity. Much of this knowledge had already been vouchsafed to human beings in the work of the Christian Church Fathers and, as it became more and more known through travel and translation, the writings of Arab and, through them, ancient Greek philosophers and scientists, in particular Plato and Aristotle. The tradition of learning was much more continuous in the Middle East and Islamic Spain, but not until the twelfth-century revival of interest in learning were these sought out in any systematic fashion and made available to Latin scholars, although the non-Christian content of these works was increasingly problematic to theologians.

In fact, twelfth-century scholars did far more than merely accept the tradition (Latin *traditio* = handing over) of past scholarship. Tradition is never in reality so straightforward; for the exchange relies not only on what the past is prepared to hand on but also on what the present is prepared to pick up. Additionally, in this case, it depended on what could be salvaged from the books, learning and practical techniques that had been lost after the Fall of Rome and the Western Empire to the Goths in 476.

As we saw earlier, the basis of the curriculum was the seven liberal arts. In the twelfth century, some new texts were added to the earlier books, in particular, the *new logic* (*logica nova*) of Aristotle (the *Sophistici elenchi, Analytica priora, Analytica posteriora* and *Topica*) was added to the works of old logic (*logica vetus*) of dialectic. Geometry and astronomy benefited from the rediscovery of Greek texts, like Euclid's *Elements* and Ptolemy's *Almagest.* Contemporary authors also added texts to these disciplines, such as Hugh of St Victor's *Practica geometria* and (in the early thirteenth century) John de Sacro Bosco's *De sphera.*

These were the books of the old subjects of arts. The new schools were beginning to teach the ancient professions as separate higher subjects: law (divided, by now, into canon or Church law, and civil or Roman law), medicine and the study of sacred scriptures or theology. Until the mid-twelfth century, these too had few textbooks: law used the legal codes promulgated by the Emperor Justinian (d. 565), the *Corpus iuris civilis;* medicine had only scraps of works by the ancient Greek doctors, Galen and Hippocrates; theology, of course, rested on the Bible. The increased number of schools and scholars in the twelfth century, alongside a genius for collection and collation that was a feature of much that happened during the century—a thirst to make ordered sense of the world, as God did at the Creation—led directly to a need for new books.

Although the teaching of the seven liberal arts of the *trivium* and *quadrivium* became the basis for arts teaching in the medieval schools, this sort of syllabus was regarded as only a preliminary (hence our word 'trivial') to the serious study which took place in the 'higher faculties' of theology, medicine and law. Around the 1140s and 1150s, top masters produced new books for students and teachers. Law, which needs always to be up-to-date, and medicine, looking for new methods, were the prime movers in this enterprise.[40] Their positive attitudes to novelty and innovation were at odds with the more conservative stance of theology. In law, the new textbook was the *Concordance of Discordant Canons*, usually known as the *Decretum*, by Gratian.[41] In medicine, there was a flock of translations from the Greek and Arabic (Galen *Tegni*, Hippocrates *Prognostics*, Johannitius *Isagoge*, etc.), producing the compendium of works which came to be known as the *Articella*. In theology there was a variety, reflecting the breadth of the subject, since each addresses a different facet. The *Ordinary Gloss* on the Bible (no. 1) rather pre-dated these others; it dealt with the foundations of biblical interpretation through the eyes of the Fathers; the *Historia scholastica* of Peter Comestor (no. 3) was an aid to understanding the biblical world from a more literal point of view; the *Verbum abbreviatum* of Peter the Chanter (no. 24) addressed ethical questions; and *Four Books of Sentences* by Peter Lombard (no. 18) took theological questions arising from the Bible out of their scriptural context and tried to solve them using the opinions (*sententiae*) of the Fathers.

The production of these texts, their use and the attitude of scholars toward them is one of the major themes of this book. To sketch an answer here to how they were used in the curriculum of the schools (indeed, to *form* the curriculum of the schools) requires us to look back at the scholarship of the monasteries. Typically, the sort of writing and thinking that took place in the cloister was based on monastic *lectio* (reading) and *ruminatio* (deep consideration). Monk-scholars read their text, whether it be a biblical book or a work of, say, Augustine, from beginning to end. It was a slow, careful process that aimed at depth rather than breadth.[42] As he read, the monk ruminated—chewed the cud as a cow does its grass, many times and in several stomachs—until he was ready to write down his exposition of the text. The results of his thought would be a piece of considered and careful scholarship, also to be read slowly from end to end and digested by the reader.[43]

Such at least is the theory. In fact, the picture is less clear-cut. Just as much as the products of the schools, the works of the cloister depended a good deal on the intended audience. When monk-scholars were writing for the edification of their fellow monks or novices, they wrote the sort of contemplative exegesis described above. But often their ideas about scripture and theology were contained in letters or tracts in answer to queries posed by their various correspondents inside and outside the cloister (e.g., Anselm, *Letters* and *Meditations*), or in

40. See B. Smalley, 'Ecclesiastical Attitudes to Novelty c. 1100–c. 1250'.

41. For Gratian, see J. Brundage, *Medieval Canon Law*, with good bibliography; Southern, *Scholastic Humanism*, ch. 9. S. Kuttner has written much of the standard material on canon law this century: see, e.g., his *Harmony from Dissonance: An Interpretation of Mediaeval Canon Law*. The standard edition of the *Decretum* is A. Friedberg, *Corpus Iuris Canonici*, 1.

42. Note, for example, Benedictine legislation about the length of time that books should be borrowed from a monastery library; see Lanfranc's rules, based on those of Cluny, in E. A. Savage, *Old English Libraries*, pp. 101–102.

43. For a description of monastic patterns of reading, see J. Leclercq, *The Love of Learning and the Desire for God*, pp. 18–22.

manuals of advice (e.g., Bernard of Clairvaux, *De consideratione*) or, as often, single works in response to burning issues of the day (e.g., Lanfranc, *De corpore et sanguine Domini*, Rupert of Deutz, *De voluntate Dei*). Just like the 'secular' schoolmen of the twelfth and thirteenth centuries, monk-scholars considered the study of the Bible to be the necessary prerequisite for further consideration on topical questions of practical morals or Christian doctrine. What happens, then, as the secular schools of the twelfth century become more organized, numerous, and specialized, is not a sea change in the nature of orthodox doctrine itself—nothing written in 1200 or even 1274 would have been foreign to Augustine—but a change in the amount of work produced and in its place in intellectual culture: where was theology to belong in the scheme of learning?

What, indeed, was theology? In the *Didascalicon*,[44] a sort of handbook for how to go about studying, Hugh of St Victor (no. 17) sets out how knowledge (*philosophia*) is ordered. He draws heavily on Boethius, who had in turn been influenced by Plato. First of all, we must note that it does not mean to Hugh what it means to us. 'Knowledge (*philosophia*) is the love of that Wisdom which, wanting in nothing, is a living Mind and the sole primordial Idea or Pattern of things',[45] which is to say that the intention of knowledge, thus defined, is 'to restore within us the divine likeness, a likeness which to us is a form, but to God is his nature. The more we are conformed to the divine nature, the more do we possess Wisdom'.[46] Hugh's *philosophia* divides into four branches of knowledge: theoretical or speculative, practical or moral, mechanical or that concerned with labor, and logical or linguistic. Logical knowledge was covered by dialectic; mechanical knowledge is divided into seven trades or crafts; practical or moral knowledge we will return to; but theoretical knowledge is where we must start, since Hugh subdivides it into Boethius' triad of mathematics (the quadrivial subjects), natural science (or physics), and theology.

Hugh begins by insisting that each constituent part of knowledge must be given its due; thus, we need to build our knowledge from the arts upward, going from the simple to the difficult. There is a distinct order for good learning; it is not enough just to plunge in wherever, willy-nilly. Next, he looks at what is needed for study; Hugh insists on order, on discipline and on humility as among the most important skills, and he gives a practical list of some of the books which are most useful and necessary for students. At this point, however, halfway through the work, Hugh changes gear and spends the second half of the book explaining the study of sacred scripture. This is to say the least unexpected, because it is the first time in the work that sacred scripture has been mentioned. It does not appear in his ordering of *philosophia;* and yet Hugh now proposes to spend half his space on it. His reasoning becomes clear: the study of sacred scripture *is* theology; and since it leads on to morality, i.e., the category of practical knowledge, it is the basis of this branch of learning as well.

44. Hugh of St Victor, *Didascalicon*, trans. J. Taylor (New York, 1961).

45. *Didascalicon*, bk. 2, c. 1.

46. Ibid.

What does Hugh mean by sacred scripture? He gives a careful definition. In another of his works, *On Scripture and Sacred Writings* (*De scripturis et scriptoribus sacris*)[47] and in the *Didascalicon*, Hugh lays out what to study and how to do it:

> Sacred Scriptures are those which were produced by men who cultivated the catholic faith and which the authority of the universal church has taken over to be included among the Sacred Books and preserved to be read for the strengthening of that same faith.[48]

In the *De scripturis*, Hugh divides sacred scriptures into Old Testament and New Testament. Following Jewish practice learned from Jerome, he further divides the Old Testament into Law, Prophets and Writings. The New Testament is similarly divided into three: the first group contains the Gospels; the second the Pauline and Catholic epistles, Acts and the Apocalypse; and the third group includes the writings of the Fathers.[49] But when he addresses the schema of sacred scripture again in the *Didascalicon*[50] Hugh repeats the division and extends it slightly. The third group now includes the Decrees of the Church Councils, the writings of the Fathers (mentioning by name Jerome, Augustine, Gregory, Ambrose, Isidore, Origen and Bede), and finally the writings of 'many other orthodox authors'. Hugh has thought this through:

> In these groups most strikingly appears the likeness between the two Testaments. For just as after the Law come the Prophets, and after the Prophets the Hagiographers [i.e., the 'Writings' or historical books], so after the Gospel come the Apostles, and after the Apostles the long line of Doctors. And by a wonderful ordering of the divine dispensation, it has been brought about that although the truth stands full and perfect in each of the books, yet none of them is superfluous. These few things we have condensed concerning the order and number of the Sacred Books, that the student may know what his required reading is.[51]

For Hugh, it seems, the Decrees of the Councils (specifically Nicaea in 325, Constantinople in 381, Ephesus in 431, and Chalcedon in 451, i.e., the Councils which defined the canon of scripture during, and just after, Jerome's lifetime), and the writings of certain Doctors are on a par with the Epistles and Gospels. The *De scripturis* is quite clear that these others are not in the canon of the Bible, but Hugh knows that the canon is not without its problems: there are

47. Hugh of St Victor, *De scripturis et scriptoribus sacris*, in *Opera Omnia.*

48. *Didascalicon*, bk. 4, c. 1.

49. *De scripturis*, c. 6: On the order, number, and authority of the books of sacred scripture. On the contents of the Law, Prophets and Writings see *Didascalicon*, bk. 4, c. 8.

50. *Didascalicon*, bks. 4–6.

51. *Didascalicon*, bk. 4, c. 2. Hugh, like most medieval writers, uses 'Doctors' where we might say 'Fathers', which is an uncommon term in the scholastic period. The all-encompassing 'Sancti' (holy men) is another common term for patristic (and later) authorities.

differences between the Greek and Hebrew canons of scripture, after all. Hence he remarks that certain Old Testament books are not accepted by all Christians and yet are still read and used: sacred scripture is then able to be more than a set list of biblical books.[52]

Where did Hugh get this extended idea of sacred scripture, and why did he hold it? The notion is very close to what Jerome implicitly does in his *Catalogue of Catholic Writers.*[53] Jerome lists 135 Christian writers, giving short biographies and bibliographies of each. The list begins with St Peter, encompasses the New Testament writers, the questionably orthodox Origen (his entry, no. 54, is very long and careful), early translators such as Hilary (no. 100: 'he translated *ad sensum* a commentary on Matthew and a treatise on Job from Origen's Greek'), and ends with Jerome himself. He lists his own accomplishments, in a long entry, in some detail: 'I rendered the New Testament faithfully from the Greek. I translated the Old Testament from the Hebrew'. Jerome seems to be almost explicitly declaring that there is no distinction between the New Testament writers, St Peter and his own contemporaries.

Jerome, then, may be a possible source for Hugh's idea of New Testament, but why might he make this unusual division at all? What Hugh is, in fact, describing is a kind of glossed Bible, with a base text of Old and New Testaments and the addition of patristic and ecclesiastical interpretation. What Hugh's distinction does is to give a more theoretical justification for such glossed books. They are acceptable and authoritative because they are all writings (the canon of scripture as well as the Fathers and others) which have been given the approval of the Church as a whole—those books which 'the authority of the universal church has taken over to be included among the Sacred Books'.[54] Canon law is the product of the Councils and its inclusion can be justified because it too is the considered opinion of the Church acting in concert. The work of individual theologians (or even specific works of individual writers, in a case like Origen) is accorded this authoritative status when taken up by the Church and promulgated as useful and true for the building-up of knowledge and faith. What begins as individual opinion becomes the received wisdom of the whole Church. Hugh, then, is taking the doctrine of continuous revelation seriously.

Why is Hugh so careful to set out what is effectively the theory behind the practice of glossing scriptural texts? Here we must look to questions of method rather than canon. Judged by their writings, it seems that the scholars at St Victor, and Hugh in particular, were consciously holding a bridge position between two methodological extremes. One side (sometimes unhelpfully termed 'monastic scholarship', because it was the position held by Bernard of Clairvaux) believed that all knowledge was simply an adjunct to theology and that all theology was based on biblical exposition, and the rewards of such study were not to be found in this world. The other pole (sometimes called 'scholastic', since its exponents were teachers in the new schools) thought theology should be studied in much the same way as any other subject, using

52. *De scripturis*, bk. 6: 'Haec tamen scripta patrum in textu divinarum scripturarum non computantur, quemadmodum in veteri test. (ut diximus) quidam libri sunt qui non scribuntur in canone, et tamen leguntur, ut sapientia Salomonis etc.'

53. *Catalogus de catholicis scriptoribus* or *De viris inlustribus*, ed. E. C. Richardson (Leipzig, 1896); for ease of access I used Oxford, Bodleian Library, MS e Mus. 31, fols. 181^{v}a–215^{r}a.

54. *Didascalicon*, bk. 4, c. 1.

the tools of grammar and dialectic, as if it were nothing more than an ordinary subject, and as though the answers that emerged could be viewed as dispassionately as statements about, say, the triangle. Chief among the latter group was Peter Abelard.

Abelard was someone who left few people unmoved. His forceful personality made him the focus of intense feelings among his contemporaries, and these feelings go some way toward obscuring our view of his place in the history of the schools.[55] Nevertheless, it is clear that in his eventful life he produced work which pushed the endurance of some religious men, such as William of St Thierry and Bernard of Clairvaux, to the limit. Abelard's early training and teaching career were in logic, and though he turned to theology later in life, he never lost that basic approach to any problem, whatever the questions involved. Bernard argued that Abelard was reducing theology to the level of the arts, making it just one subject of study among many.[56] Certainly, however Abelard's interest in theology may have started, he finished his career as a committed practitioner. His position was not one of reason versus faith, as it may sometimes be portrayed, but of reason employed in the service of faith: I understand in order that I might believe. Abelard used his reason to try to illuminate the enigmas of faith. It is probably true to say that it was less the doctrines he espoused than the methods he employed, which so enraged his opponents, aggravated as they were by his edgy personality.

Abelard wrote a key work, the *Sic et non*. In the prologue, he describes his purpose as being to present the problems of theology using the method of doubting and inquiry. He identifies particular questions (that is, propositions open to doubt[57]) on theological matters, lays out opinions for (*sic*) and against (*non*), but does not try to answer them. The work reads like an excellent source book for teaching and argument. Ironically, this approach was not really new; Abelard seems to have based himself on Augustine's methodology in the *Quaestiones in Heptateuchum* and the *De doctrina Christiana*.[58] In fact, of course, this method was very much the way any logical person would think about a problem; what was daring in Abelard was to write down the working on paper as it applied to questions of theology. Exposing the working was controversial because it suggested that the solutions to such theological questions were somehow uncertain, that they rested on the knife edge of human reason. Shockingly, it implied that the solutions were as open to the mechanical workings of the *trivium* as a problem in grammar. From being an exposition of sacred scripture for the edification and salvation of the student, theology in Abelard's hands was in danger of becoming a technical specialty with its own abstruse language and workings.

55. On Abelard, see M. T. Clanchy, *Abelard: A Medieval Life;* D. E. Luscombe, *The School of Peter Abelard;* and J. Marenbon, *The Philosophy of Peter Abelard,* all of which have good bibliographies.

56. 'He (Abelard) who, while he disdains to be ignorant of nothing of all the things which are in the heavens above and the earth below, except for the words "I do not know", sets his face to the heavens and examines the heights of God; and returning to us he brings back ineffable words which it is not allowed to men to speak. And while he is prepared to use reason on all things, even those which are beyond reason, he dares to go both against reason and against faith. For what is more against reason than to try to transcend reason by reason. And what is more against faith than to be unwilling to believe whatever he cannot attain by reason?' (Bernard of Clairvaux, *Ep.* 90, *PL* 182:1055).

57. Boethius, *In topica Ciceronis, PL* 64:1048B.

58. B. Smalley, '*Prima Clavis Sapientiae:* Augustine and Abelard'.

Abelard's *sic et non* attitude brought him trouble; but the procedure was too useful in the context of the schools not to be taken up. His pupil, Peter Lombard (d. 1160 [no. 18]) took up and extended the *Sic et non* in his *Four Books of Sentences*, which became the greatest single textbook of the medieval theologians. As well as his old master, it seems that the Lombard had read and digested Gratian's *Decretum* (*c.* 1142).[59] This came from that other higher subject which had already made its way into the schools—law.

The renewed study of law seems to have begun seriously in Bologna in the second quarter of the twelfth century. It was fueled by the legal practice (and perhaps teaching) of Irnerius, and Gratian's pioneering book, whose formal title, *Concordance of Discordant Canons*, tells succinctly what he envisaged it to be. Law is by nature argumentative: it lays down rules, and so it must determine whether or not those rules have been broken. To do this it may subdivide the circumstances of the case—the rules apply to circumstance *x*, but this is slightly different, it is circumstance *y*, and so the rules do not apply. Alternatively, it may attempt to cover all possibilities by detailing a situation minutely, breaking it down into its constituent parts. In cases where the law is not clear, it may need to argue back and forth until one side wins. Further, none of the laws or the decisions is lost; they become written into the existing law, or taken up in the existing custom, and applied in future circumstances, or need to be contended with in future cases. These skills, of division and subdivision, of argument about a question using case law or custom, and of the addition of the outcome to the stock, were taken up into the study of theology, and were the bones of the scholastic method.

The scholastic method has three tenets. Firstly, it is authoritative, proceeding by the use of the opinions of established authorities. These were primarily the Bible, the Fathers, the decrees of canon law, and some more modern writers, just as Hugh of St Victor details. Ideally, the questions on which the method is to be used come from these authoritative texts, and particularly from the Bible. The questions multiplied as the number of students and the limits of what was suitable expanded. Secondly, the method was argumentative. Like the proceedings in law, it moved by putting the case on one side, then on another, with the authorities as witnesses; then, after a judgment for one of the sides, it answered the points of the opposition, one by one. Finally, the method was additive. When a question had been asked or a point raised in a particular context, it had to be included in all subsequent questions and arguments, and answered by masters who afterward addressed the same issues. It was a system that believed in the building-up of truth; nothing could be thrown away since all might contribute to the elaboration of knowledge. The method solved a problem for academic theologians, at Paris and elsewhere. They were fighting for respectability against bigger and richer university faculties of lawyers and physicians. If they were to be taken seriously as scholars, they had to adopt some of the same practices; the *Sentences* made it easy for masters to teach theological issues point by point, and to examine their students in the same way.

So, did the schools study 'theology' where monks had studied 'Bible'? It is a fallacy, but a surprisingly hardy one, that monastic writers wrote biblical exegesis that simply expounded

59. Brundage, *Medieval Canon Law*, ch. 3; Southern, *Scholastic Humanism*, ch. 9; but see also J. T. Noonan, 'Gratian Slept Here: The Changing Identity of the Father of the Systematic Study of Canon Law', who questions the general identification of Gratian as a Camaldolese monk from Bologna.

the text, and that all this changed with the advent of the schools when scriptural study disappeared and the identification and solution of separate 'questions' (*quaestiones*) was the only way of working. This is much too simplistic to be true; it ignores both the known syllabuses of the schools and the extant works of schoolmen (or those we know they wrote by repute); and it neatly sidesteps a lot of pre-scholastic writing. However, it is certainly true that, throughout the period of the early schools, increasing numbers of problematic questions were extracted from biblical and patristic texts and debated in the classrooms; simply sitting and listening to a teacher expounding a scriptural (or other) text for its own sake became less and less popular. There are a number of reasons for this, and we will address them in the next section.

The movement was by no means universally approved of, and the argument between the 'monastic' and 'scholastic' groups was not quickly settled. Walter of St Victor (d. after 1180), taking a position rather outside the Victorine tradition, condemned the introduction of arts methods as inimical to theology. He characterized Peter Abelard and Peter Lombard as two of the 'Four Labyrinths of France', whose work confused the issues instead of leading to clarity.[60] Stephen, abbot of Ste-Geneviève and bishop of Tournai (1192–1203), wrote to the pope protesting against these new ways of learning, especially public disputation of theological doctrine: 'the indivisible Trinity is cut up and wrangled over in the trivia'.[61] The essential reason for study had been lost: 'scriptural studies have lapsed into a state of confusion in our time, for students applaud nothing but novelties and the masters are more intent on glory than on doctrine.'[62]

Part of the reason for the change, however, goes back to the purpose of study. For monastic scholars the purpose was clear: the study of theology or sacred scripture was an essential element in their vocation, and was intended to aid their salvation. With the spread of schooling this was bound to change. Even though, in order to be a student in a medieval university, one had to be a clerk in holy orders, one might choose to go no further in the Church. As the Church became a useful and rewarding career, simply another profession like law or medicine, then study could be seen as just a qualification on the career ladder. Some bishops, such as the Oxford theologian and bishop of Lincoln, Robert Grosseteste (no. 28) or his Paris contemporary William of Auvergne, continued to write pastoral theology while they held office; but other, less gifted men kept theologians to do the work for them; or they simply turned to the Paris masters to provide the answers.

This development from vocation to career starts early. Hugh of St Victor details three motivations of students who wish to study sacred scripture:

> There are some who seek knowledge of the Sacred Scripture either in order that they may gather riches or in order that they may obtain honours or acquire fame. . . . There are still others who delight to hear the words of God and to learn of His works not because these bring them salvation but because they are marvels. . . . There are others, however, who

60. Walter of St Victor, *Contra quatuor labyrinthos Franciae*, ed. P. Glorieux.

61. Stephen of Tournai, *Ep.* 251, *PL* 211:517; trans. Thorndike, *University Records*, pp. 22–24.

62. Ibid.

> study the Sacred Scriptures precisely so that . . . they may forthrightly demolish enemies of the truth, teach those less well informed, recognize the path of truth more perfectly themselves, and, understanding the hidden things of God more deeply, love them more intently.[63]

Although there is no doubt that the masters themselves were motivated by love of learning, it seems unlikely that the same can be said for all of their students. Whether, too, the love of learning was joined to the desire for God, to borrow Jean Leclercq's phrase, even in the case of every master, we cannot be entirely sure. In a society where Christianity was ubiquitous, and where, although skepticism existed, it was something of an underground activity, one might perhaps make one's living as a teacher of theology or scripture in the same unthinking way as people might now become investment bankers or financial consultants, without thinking of the capitalist system of morals which underpins their working lives.

C1. The Context of Learning, 1200–1274

By 1200, the masters of Paris had taken on a loose corporate identity[64] and their schools were recognized all over Europe as the most important center for the study of theology. Paris joined Salerno (in medicine) and Bologna (in law) in the top rank of *studia* in the higher faculties—that is, the faculties which went beyond the preliminary study of the arts. Initially, Paris also taught law, but the teaching of civil law was prohibited by Pope Honorius III in 1219,[65] apparently at the behest of Philip Augustus who did not want French customary law infected with the competing ideas of codified Roman law. They may also have hoped that students would not be tempted from the study of theology into the much more lucrative profession of law.

As other *studia generalia* developed in the thirteenth century, it was possible to study theology elsewhere, notably in Oxford. The papal curia established its own *studium* in 1245; and the Mendicant Orders of Franciscans and Dominicans set up their own *studia* in major cities throughout Europe. But all of these were founded on Parisian lines, as far as theology was concerned. Paris led the way and others followed. Certainly until 1274 there were few significant differences between the curriculum of Paris and Oxford; and so I shall concentrate on describing developments in Paris.[66]

As we have seen, the kernel of the Paris *studium* was the schools which had grown out of the cloister school of Notre Dame, which was the responsibility of the bishop and his official, the

63. *Didascalicon*, bk. 5, c. 10.

64. G. Post, 'Parisian Masters as a Corporation, 1200–1246'.

65. *CUP*, I, no. 32.

66. Readers wishing to follow up the story elsewhere may refer to A. B. Cobban, *The Medieval English Universities;* W. J. Courtenay, *Schools and Scholars in Fourteenth Century England;* G. Leff, *Paris and Oxford Universities in the Thirteenth and Fourteenth Centuries;* Rashdall, *Universities*, vol. 3; *The History of the University of Oxford. 1: The Early Oxford Schools*, ed. J. I. Catto (Oxford, 1984).

chancellor. As the schools grew, the bishop and chancellor still thought they could and should control them. The masters had other ideas, and cleverly they worked on substituting the more distant pope for the bishop and his chancellor, finally achieving virtual independence from their local overlords in the early thirteenth century, when the series of decrees by Honorius III regarding the university marked the papacy's assumption that it controlled the schools. We have already noted Alexander III intervening to stop the chancellor charging for the *licentia docendi* and ordering that the license must be given to anyone who was qualified; further, Honorius protected the right of Ste-Geneviève, outside the city, to issue licenses too. In fact, the cathedral clergy must have recognized that they could not ignore those who were teaching elsewhere since, from the episcopate of Maurice of Sully (1160–1196), bishops of Paris began to appoint important masters to the chancellorship, recognizing a link between Notre Dame and the other schools.[67]

The masters were right to be wary, lest they find themselves regulated by outsiders.[68] They worked to constitute themselves into a guild, in much the same way as other craftsmen and women were members of self-regulating, trade closed-shops. The higher degrees fulfilled the same function for masters as apprenticeships and masterpieces did for manual crafts. We have no definite date for the formation of a masters' guild in Paris before 1208, but they are recognized tacitly as such in various documents from about the 1140s. In 1200, King Philip II granted his charter of privileges to the *masters*, but not to any *studium* or 'university' as a whole (the charter was reiterated by Louis IX in 1229). The masters' customary privileges were officially recognized in a series of letters of Pope Innocent III between 1208 and 1216.[69]

Successive popes were supporters of the schools; they saw in the Paris masters a theological think-tank to advise them on doctrine and morals. The first official statutes were granted to the masters and scholars in 1215 by the papal legate, Robert Courçon, an act which effectively put the university under papal protection.[70] For the next sixteen years the bishop of Paris and his chancellor strove to regain control over the university: they did not want to lose control over theology in the city and wanted the prevailing standards to be theirs; and they were also loathe to lose the money they gained from fees, as well as the leverage with the merchants and lodgings-keepers of the city that attracting such a big constituency gave to the schools. The masters finally won in 1231 when Pope Gregory IX's bull *Parens scientiarum Parisius* (Paris, parent of the sciences) established their supremacy over the cathedral and its officers.[71]

67. Gabriel, 'The Cathedral Schools', pp. 51–56, with references.

68. Medieval *studia* divided loosely into two types: those in the north of Europe, like Paris, were universities where the masters arranged the syllabus, regulations, administration and so forth; those in the south, such as Bologna, tended to be universities where the students dictated terms and hired the faculty. Southern, *Scholastic Humanism*, pp. 312–13, remarks persuasively that lawyers were always financially independent of their teaching, so the students had to organize to enforce their rights; at Paris, the theology masters who depended on teaching for a living had to enforce *their* rights against the students.

69. G. Post, 'Parisian Masters as a Corporation, 1200–1246', p. 424; I have relied on Post for much of this section.

70. *CUP*, I, no. 20.

71. *CUP*, I, no. 79.

Successive popes continued Gregory's policies, so that by 1261 privileges included exemptions from summonses outside Paris, the right to have their own seal (thus definitively giving the *studium* the status of a legal corporation, a 'universitas'), the right to tax members for their own purposes, the right to expect non-university members to safeguard their papal privileges, and freedom from excommunication without papal consent.

What was it like to be a theology student at this time? Although Robert Courçon's charter was not introduced until 1215, it is likely that in many respects it simply legalized what was already happening. Courçon does not detail everything that need be done, suggesting that much was already customary; but as is so often true, we cannot be definite about rules and procedures. Similarly, the regulations for the faculties given in *Parens scientiarum Parisius* of 1231 leave much unspecified. Other documents are likewise vague, so that we cannot produce more than a sketch of university life around 1235.[72]

Students went to university earlier than they do today, probably at about the age of fourteen, when they entered the arts faculty to do a preliminary degree, and became bachelors of arts. The arts degree took about six years, and there was a minimum age for a lecturer in arts of twenty-one. At this point, some students could specialize in arts, and go on to higher degrees in the subject. More chose to enter one of the other higher faculties: theology, law and medicine. The course for a theology master was long and arduous according to Courçon's statutes, taking at least six years to listen to lectures and another eight years as a junior teacher. The course lengthened throughout the thirteenth century, eventually taking about sixteen years in all. The minimum age for a 'regent' master (a fully qualified teacher) in theology was thirty-five. Students were supervised by masters who, at each stage, had formally to swear that the student was competent to continue. At each stage, the student seems to have had to undergo a kind of *viva voce* or oral examination. The faculty was made up of the regent masters who held chairs.

A student began the course in theology by hearing lectures on the Bible for four years, followed by two years on the *Sentences* of Peter Lombard. The *Sentences* had been introduced as an integral part of his course by Alexander of Hales (d. 1245). Already influential, it became, with the Bible, the essential textbook for the theology course, and was included in the prescribed books listed in *Parens scientiarum Parisius.* Within ten years, the *Sentences* was also the standard of doctrine; masters judged their theological positions vis-à-vis the solutions given by Lombard.[73] After hearing the *Sentences,* if the student was deemed to have progressed successfully, he was allowed to start lecturing on the Bible, and proceeded to lecture cursorily as a biblical bachelor (*baccalarius biblicus*). Cursory (*cursorie*) lectures involved superficially glossing the text according to the letter, explaining difficult words and phrases and summarizing

72. Our vagueness about the exact curriculum and course is shown by the differing accounts of it that can be found in modern authors, each of which gives a slightly varying description of what was done and when. This may, of course, reflect a contemporary latitude about what course any one student had to follow.

73. So strong was Peter Lombard's influence that Albert the Great could write, 'Which position, however, I do not believe, but I will uphold it because the Master of the *Sentences* does.' (Quod tamen ego non credo, licet sustineam propter *Magistrum.*) *In II Sent.* d. 24 a. 1 sol.

the narrative. This stage continued for one year on the student's own choice of one or two biblical books. When this was finished, he became a bachelor of the *Sentences* (*baccalarius sententiarius*) and spent two years lecturing on Peter Lombard's text. If he completed this stage, the student became a formed bachelor (*baccalarius formatus*) and for another year or two had to take part in public disputations on set questions and quodlibetal questions, that is, questions on 'whatever' (*quodlibet*) topic he or his masters chose to address, as well as delivering a university sermon (although this seems only to have come in after *c.* 1250). Only after this did he become eligible to be a regent master, one of the 'reigning' chairs in theology, a position he had to hold for a further two years, lecturing on the Bible *ordinarie* (that is, according to both literal and spiritual senses), in order to become a complete master: *magister in sacra pagina.* The number of regent masters was limited by statute in 1207 to eight and expanded to twelve by 1231,[74] but it is not clear that the supply exceeded the demand. The theology course was long and difficult, and few, in any case, wished to go on to the very end. As far as we can judge, many students came to hear part of the course, but did not, or could not, stay till the end. In the period before the first statutes of 1215, we have no idea how people were deemed to have done enough to qualify; nor, indeed, what they qualified *as.* The *masters* were teachers, or rather, schools' lecturers; what people got who were not going on to lecture is not at all certain. Certainly, unless one were intending to teach at a *studium* as a profession, there was no point in staying to the end; an episcopal or noble employer might well be happy with a man who had several years of higher education behind him, without having bothered to get the license to teach theology.

The school year began by the Feast of St Remi, on 1 October, with breaks for Christmas and Easter and a summer vacation limited by *Parens scientiarum Parisius* to one month. Sundays and saints' days were free, and some days were set aside for extraordinary disputes, such as quodlibets. A school day started early with a regent master's lecture, followed by a lecture by a bachelor of *Sentences.* Theology masters lectured later in the morning than masters of arts so that the former could come to hear the latter's teaching. The afternoons had 'ordinary' (*ordinarie*) lectures and disputes. Extra or 'cursory' (*cursorie*) lectures by bachelors of the Bible or the *Sentences* (who had to teach as the next stage in their degree) could take place at any time, apart from certain holidays, when masters were not teaching.

Just as the secular masters were beginning to flex their muscles and establish their privileges, the situation was radically changed by the arrival at Paris of students from the newly founded Franciscan and Dominican Orders of mendicant friars. The Dominicans came to Paris in 1217, settling first near Notre Dame, but moving soon to their permanent home in the rue St Jacques, at the gate on the main road out of the city to the south. Honorius III arranged for a secular master, John of St Albans, to teach them. He was followed by another secular,

74. The number of chairs was limited to eight in 1207 (*CUP,* I, no. 5). This was still the case in 1218 (*CUP,* I, no. 17), but it rose to twelve in 1254 (*CUP,* I, no. 230). According to Glorieux, 'L'enseignement au moyen âge. Techniques et méthodes en usage à la Faculté de Théologie de Paris, au xiiie siècle', (at p. 97: but he gives no reference), of the original eight chairs, three were reserved for canons of Notre Dame; of the twelve chairs of 1254, three were for canons of Notre Dame, six were for seculars, and three for Mendicants (two Dominicans and one Franciscan).

John of St Giles, but in 1229 the Dominican Roland of Cremona became a master and brought his chair with him to St Jacques. The next year, John of St Giles joined the Dominicans himself, giving the Preachers two chairs of their own. In less than twenty years, they became a dominant force in Paris theology, and their *studium* was open to all students.[75]

The Franciscans arrived in Paris about 1220, and were slower off the mark than the Preachers; but by 1227 they too had their own school at the Convent des Cordeliers, by St Germain des Prés. Their first chair came around 1236–37 when an already famous master, Alexander of Hales, publicly took the Franciscan habit and moved his teaching chair to their school. It was not long before his Franciscan pupil, John of La Rochelle, was also a master.

Both orders wanted education for pastoral work since they were charged by the pope with preaching and hearing confessions. The Dominicans had a special interest in rooting out heresy, so they needed to be theologically sophisticated. At first, the secular masters were welcoming; but clashes occurred when they felt that the Mendicants put their vocation as friars before their loyalty to mastership and the schools. The masters' suspicions were probably justified. During the suspension of teaching in 1229, the seculars accused the Mendicants, justly, of strikebreaking. The two groups could never have entirely similar needs: the secular masters relied on the schools for their living; the Mendicants were ploughing a different furrow.

The situation was resolved temporarily by an increase in the number of regent masters to twelve, so that Mendicant masters could be accommodated without loss to the seculars. Moreover, they brought to Paris a large number of new students. Mendicant students followed almost the same curriculum as secular students but, since they had had elementary theological training before they came to Paris, they were allowed to begin at a higher level and give ordinary lectures as biblical bachelors, instead of only cursory ones. From about 1230 until the end of the century, the majority of famous names among the masters came from within the Mendicant orders. The older, monastic orders, such as the Benedictines, who had their own halls of residence at Paris but not their own schools, sent their monk-students to the friars for education.[76]

It may well have been the influx of friars that kept the theology faculty from becoming just another professional school, with teachers whose interests did not stray outside the technical confines of their discipline. That such a narrowing of purpose was a real possibility may be seen from thirteenth-century writings describing the ideal master, which reflect anxiety that such a course might be pursued.[77] Sometime between 1236 and 1241 an Oxford master denounced those theologians who neglect real wisdom for philosophy. Vincent of Beauvais (d. *c.* 1264) and Humbert of Romans, Dominican Master-General (d. 1277), both warned masters against indulging in the wrong sort of hypothesizing when they were teaching. Teaching had to be done with the intention of discovering the truth, not just for the sake of idle speculation and curiosity and finding fault with others. Humbert details eight major things to avoid: bold-

75. Regulations for Dominican students: *CUP*, I, no. 57.

76. A tradition which continues in Oxford today: the Benedictine candidates for the priesthood from St Benet's Hall go to the Dominicans at Blackfriars for some of their tuition.

77. A. L. Gabriel, 'The Ideal Master of the Mediaeval University'.

ness; too much humility, which is really false pride; ostentation in dress and manner; wanting to win rather than to find the truth; an unwillingness to change one's mind; attempting to confuse those of another opinion; prolixity; and exaggerated inquiries, i.e., not knowing when to stop, but going on and on to no proper purpose. Discussions of the ideal master stress that teaching theology is not just a matter of what someone knows. The master must also be of good character, with a 'combination of profound learning and excellent virtue';[78] he needed the wisdom to secure salvation for himself and his students; and above all he had to set an example of charity. Bernard of Clairvaux would never have needed to be taught such lessons. What had happened to theology that such injunctions had to be written down?

C2. Theology, 1200–1274

The inclusion of theology among the higher faculties of the *studium generale* changed the way that theology was thought about. This is partly because the universities taught more than just theology. Theology was always a minority sport; law, medicine, and arts had more takers, made more money. But despite its high ideals, as a university subject theology had to conform to the same criteria as the other faculties in order to be respected. This led theologians into a quandary: how could a subject about an essentially unknowable God, about faith, be taught in the same way as one which specialized in hard fact, such as law? The problem intensified. During the thirteenth century, *studia* became examination-based. Whether this move was what the masters wished, to ensure that their students were reaching certain standards, or whether they were pushed in this direction by either the students or their prospective employers, who wanted to know that they were getting people with a measurable qualification, is unclear. It was probably a combination of both. In a subject like law, determining how to test knowledge was not really a problem. But theology had to be sure where (and if) academic study ended and faith began. The increasing availability of new translations of the works of Aristotle heightened the tension. Aristotle's logical and scientific works were a cornerstone of the arts curriculum; but the theology faculty was forbidden by the pope, in 1210, to study his natural scientific or metaphysical works or those of his Arab commentators.[79] Robert Courçon renewed the ban in 1215, and it was reiterated in 1231 by Gregory IX. Aristotle was fascinating because he had written about almost everything, and he used a method based on observation and reason; but his non-Christian view of the world seemed to threaten some of the assumptions of Christian doctrine. For scholars seeking to restore and re-deploy the revealed knowledge of the past, he looked (ironically) like a godsend. Moreover, many of the students in theology had studied arts in Paris before going on to the higher discipline. In

78. Ibid., p. 9.

79. *CUP*, I, no. 11. In fact, the weight of the prohibition seems to be directed against Amaury de Bene and David of Dinant, who had apparently taught heretical doctrines, based on Aristotle. Amaury's body was ordered to be exhumed and reburied in unconsecrated ground. After these orders, the prohibition against Aristotle seems almost an afterthought.

the arts faculty, knowledge of Aristotle was a basic, key requirement. How could anyone believe that theology was a serious subject for study if it could not accommodate him? The prohibitions simply could not keep him out. Soon, accredited and respected scholars like William of Auxerre, Philip the Chancellor, Alexander of Hales and William of Auvergne brought Aristotelian ideas into their theological writings.

Aristotle had described a coherent and comprehensive non-Christian world, and he did so with a systematic method that students in the arts were keen to emulate. He proceeded by logic, using a series of *categories* (who, what, where, when, etc.), and, above all, he had a rational vision of the world: *everything* could be discovered by the application of human reason to observation of the world. This chimed with twelfth-century notions of the possibilities of human dignity and reason, but it was a challenge to those tenets of theology that had to be taken on faith.

Long before the scholastic discussions of the thirteenth century, theology had been divided into parts. Clarembald of Arras (d. after 1170), for example, thought there were two kinds: that which was susceptible to evidence and reason; and contemplative theology which covered 'perception of the divine being . . . without the help of created matter'.[80] Aristotle appealed to and expanded this twelfth-century passion for definition and division with his sectioning of knowledge into 'sciences', each science being a self-contained system with given principles, 'given' in that they were unproveable within any one science (as premises are, by definition), but out of which reason could produce further conclusions. Following the *Sentences* commentary of Alexander of Hales, all such commentaries imitated Lombard in discussing the status of theology as a branch of knowledge. After William of Auxerre's *Summa Aurea* (no. 20), masters asked whether or not theology was a 'science'.[81] The common view, based on Augustine, followed Roland of Cremona: 'theology (*sacra doctrina*) is not itself either an art or a science, in the sense that philosophers mean art or science; but it is something more noble, namely, wisdom'.[82] His solution stood as the norm until Thomas Aquinas, working entirely within Aristotelian metaphysics, affirmed that theology was the science of those truths which cannot be known by unaided reason.[83] The first principles of this science were the articles of faith, not *known* as such (or indeed, knowable) but simply believed by the Christian. Thomas admits, following earlier masters like William of Auvergne, that such first principles cannot be proved for those (like Jews or Muslims) who do not believe them; but once they

80. N. Häring, *The Life and Works of Clarembald of Arras. A Twelfth-Century Master of the School of Chartres*, p. 70.

81. See the examples in M.-D. Chenu, *La théologie comme science au xiiie siècle*, including William of Auxerre, *Summa Aurea*, ed. J. Ribaillier, 4 vols. (Paris & Grottaferrata, Rome, 1980–1987) bk. 4, tr. 5, c. 4, qu. 3 (mistakenly numbered 1 by Chenu): 'Just as other sciences have their principles and conclusions, thus even theology has its principles and conclusions. And the principles of theology are the articles of faith. For faith is an argument, not a conclusion'.

82. 'Hec autem (doctrina sacra) non est ars proprie vel scientia secundum quod philosophi loquuntur de arte et scientia, sed quiddam nobilius, scilicet sapientia' (Roland of Cremona, *Summa*, prologue, q. 2; quoted in Chenu, *La theologie comme science*, p. 61n.).

83. *Sancti Thomae de Aquino. Summa theologiae*, 2.2.1.4; 2.2.1.5.

have been accepted, all doctrine can be reasoned from them.[84] The affirmation of the articles of faith as first principles was a reaction to the thoroughgoing Aristotelianism of Aquinas' contemporaries, such as Siger of Brabant and Boethius of Dacia, arts masters who followed Aristotle so completely into his given principles as to find themselves concluding, with him, that the world was eternal and there was a single, unified intellect in the cosmos, in which all others participated (no. 22). Such ideas were heretical, although they seemed to be proveable by reason, and they were condemned by the bishop of Paris, Stephen Tempier, in 1270.[85] This seems to have sent a shock through the arts masters, since, after a meeting of the faculty, they passed a statute forbidding arts masters from publicly discussing theological questions.[86]

Thomas' opinion was not entirely agreed upon immediately.[87] Definitions of theology did, however, become tighter (and to some degree less interesting) in the fourteenth century; but most thirteenth-century masters still saw themselves as part of an enterprise wider than what we might call strictly academic or dogmatic theology (a phenomenon we can observe among theologians even today). Indeed, the word 'theology' was not commonly used. The more usual terms were *sacra scriptura, sacra pagina* or *sacra doctrina;* on completing the theology faculty degree a student became a 'master of the sacred page' (*magister in sacra pagina*). At this date, then, rather than inquiring further into definitions of 'theology', we should do better to decide of what *sacra pagina* consisted.

Old-fashioned purists like Roger Bacon (d. ?1292) complained of the way that students in theology were skipping the arduous basics of the Bible to read only the easy summaries of Peter Comestor; they preferred argument about theological problems, like those posed by Peter Lombard's *Sentences*, to contemplation on theological mysteries.[88] But Bacon is missing the point; he has no sense of what the scriptures must do to survive in the *studia.* He himself was a Franciscan and did not need qualifications to earn a living; but he is in danger of mistaking his own motives for study with those of the run of students. And he has forgotten that it is difficult to the point of impossibility to examine a student on an extended piece of biblical exegesis or contemplative theology. The candidate may well exhibit all sorts of logical and linguistic skills along the way, as well as biblical knowledge, but it is hard to mark him on them. For that purpose, a single question, 'disputed'—argued for or responded against—much better exhibits one's marshaling of knowledge, powers of reason, rhetoric, quick thinking and presentational skills. In fact, these skills were as useful for a Dominican preaching in the street or debating with a Muslim as for a budding court official or papal diplomat.

In terms of schools and examinations, there was only so far that one could go with exegesis. The study of the Bible was in principle infinitely extensible, but in practice there were only

84. *Summa theologiae*, 1.1.8 resp.: 'If, however, an opponent believes nothing of what has been divinely revealed, then no way lies open for making the articles of faith reasonably credible'.

85. *CUP*, I, no. 432.

86. *CUP*, I, no. 441.

87. See, for example, the reiteration of Stephen Tempier's condemnations in 1277: *CUP*, I, no. 473.

88. *Fr. Rogeri Baconis. Opera quaedam hactenus inedita*, ed. J. S. Brewer, pp. 328–30. A. G. Little, 'The Franciscan School at Oxford in the Thirteenth Century', pp. 808–809, has Bacon on Robert Grosseteste's biblical regime.

so many ways of taking a particular passage without repetition. Even by the time of Alan of Lille (d. 1203) interpretation had a bad name. His famous saying, that exegesis has a wax nose which can be manipulated as one pleases,[89] suggested that one could go just so far and no further. Those scholars who remained more interested in biblical exegesis than in theological questions began to look at adding different sorts of material to the stock. Men like Andrew of St Victor (no. 15) and Nicholas of Lyra turned to Jewish scholars and scholarship for help with the literal meanings of texts, and scholars began further to explore the theory of exegesis and interpretation to be clear that they knew what they were doing and why.[90]

Sacra pagina, far from narrowing to questions of dogmatic theology, in the thirteenth century had as wide a remit as ever, with each of its facets producing a separate genre of writing. An anonymous late twelfth-century author of a logical treatise provides us with an interesting example of a topical dispute:

> What is dialectic? Dialectic is the art of arts and the science of sciences, because it alone permits us to know and to make manifest the unknown. Contra. Theology is the art of arts and the science of sciences, therefore dialectic is not. Response. Dialectic is the art of arts and the science of sciences because without it no art can be mastered.[91]

In contrast, however, the Fourth Lateran Council of 1215 authoritatively stated another position: 'The art of arts is the governance of souls.'[92] The Council wished to make it clear to students and teachers alike that the point of the study of theology was the pastoral care (or 'cure') of souls, implicitly stating that this skill could be taught in the schools, as though it were one of the liberal arts. Lateran IV was not inventing something new,[93] but its reiteration of the importance of teaching *sacra pagina* in the context of care for the laity provided the impetus for a wealth of writings meant for clergy who were working solely in the parishes. The teaching of the *studia* was not to be confined there, or to become esoteric: it must be put to the service of the whole Church.

It would be tidy to say with Grabmann,[94] that some theologians were involved in 'pure theology' while others concentrated on practical morality; but it would not be correct. Especially for the Mendicants, such a division could never hold true. Bonaventure, for example, a Franciscan scholar who became head of the order, wrote biblical exegesis, a *Sentences* commentary,

89. Alan of Lille, *De fide catholica*, 1.30, *PL* 210:333.

90. See A. J. Minnis, *Medieval Theory of Authorship: Scholastic Literary Attitudes in the Later Middle Ages*, and Minnis, A. B. Scott with D. Wallace, *Medieval Literary Theory and Criticism c. 1100–c. 1375: The Commentary Tradition;* P. D. W. Krey and L. Smith, *Nicholas of Lyra: The Senses of Scripture* (Leiden, 2000).

91. L. M. de Rijk, ed., *Logica modernorum*, 2, p. 418. I am grateful to Joseph Goering for drawing my attention to this passage.

92. Lateran IV, canon 27: Tanner, *Decrees*, 1, p. 248.

93. For example, canon eleven of the Council, which repeats previous enjoinders to each metropolitan church to employ a canon theologian who would teach 'the sacred page and those things known to pertain to the care of souls' (Tanner, *Decrees*, 1, p. 240).

94. M. Grabmann, *Die Geschichte der scholastischen Methode*, 2, pp. 476–501, divides Paris theologians into the 'biblical-moral' and the 'practical'.

contemplative mystical theology like the *Six Wings of the Seraphim* or the *Itinerarium mentis*, issue-based treatises such as the *Apologia pauperum*, and practical works such as the Narbonne Constitutions. Such variety was also true of secular scholars; after all, 'secular' in this context meant simply someone not attached to a religious order, rather than someone who was not an ecclesiastic. Seculars had many of the same concerns as Mendicants, especially if, as often, they held high-level ecclesiastical office in conjunction with, or after, their teaching posts. William of Auvergne (d. 1249), for example, master and bishop of Paris, wrote a handbook for preachers and a work on holding multiple benefices as well as treatises on the Trinity and the soul.

Although there was no single textbook of pastoral care for teaching in the schools, there were other occasions such as disputations when theologians could discuss relevant issues. There was no requirement as to what the subjects of their publicly debated questions might be. Leonard Boyle has shown that Thomas Aquinas used these occasions for much more than 'pure (speculative) theology'.[95] Moreover, as well as lecturing and disputing questions, masters were expected to preach to university audiences. Scholastic sermons survive in enormous numbers. Joseph Goering has suggested that there is scarcely a manuscript containing a miscellany of scholastic theological writings that fails to include at least one sermon.[96]

* * *

Histories of the medieval *studia* and of the meaning of 'theology' depend heavily not only on those texts and books which have, by chance, come down to us, but often to a surprising extent on what has been edited and published by modern scholars. This has a tendency to skew the evidence since sets of theological questions and *summae* generally held more interest to nineteenth- and twentieth-century scholastically trained historians, who were often themselves members of religious orders. Long, repetitive biblical commentaries or sketches of sermons and manuals of pastoral care seemed not to hold the same fascination. The imbalance is being redressed to some extent by more recent scholarship.[97] Yet we are still in danger of thinking that, by the mid-thirteenth century, one conception and facet of theology held sway, and that what we would call systematic theology was all-conquering. Certainly, such theology was important in the medieval schools, but their vision of theology was broader

95. L. E. Boyle, 'The Quodlibeta of St Thomas and Pastoral Care', *The Thomist* 38 (1974): 232–56; repr. in Boyle, *Pastoral Care*, no. 2.

96. J. Goering, 'Teaching the Art of Arts', paper given at *Learning Institutionalized*, a conference held at the University of Notre Dame, Ind., Sept. 1992. (Partial proceedings published as *Learning Institutionalized*, ed. J. Van Engen, [Notre Dame, 2000]). Goering notes that scholastic sermons have been relatively neglected, because of the form in which they have come down to us, and because they rarely contain any striking theological innovations. This is precisely the point: they offered the opportunity for the orthodox presentation of theology in practical form.

97. For sermons, see L.-J. Bataillon, *La prédication au xiiie siècle en France et Italie;* D. L. d'Avray, *The Preaching of the Friars;* d'Avray and N. Bériou, *Modern Questions about Medieval Sermons.* For pastoral care, see Boyle, *Pastoral Care;* J. Goering, *William de Montibus (c. 1140–1213). The Schools and the Literature of Pastoral Care.*

than ours. *Sacra pagina* had a much wider compass, never straying far from the Bible and always with the needs of the wider Church in mind. After all, the *secunda secundae*—that part of Thomas Aquinas' *Summa theologiae* which looked at the questions of practical morality—was copied independently of the rest and enjoyed the widest circulation. At least for the period treated by this book, the masters of the sacred page saw their subject as much wider and deeper than our own need for neatness and division, inspired by Aristotle, might wish us to conceive of 'theology'.

D. The Texts: Books as Reflectors of Change

The texts and manuscripts in this selection reflect this wide conception of theology—*sacra pagina*—in the life of the schools before 1274. I have tried to put together a standard and typical set of books which a university theologian would have at his fingertips in the mid-to-late thirteenth century. Obviously, a theologian such as William of Auvergne, who died in 1249, would not have had Bonaventure's *Apologia pauperum*, written in 1267; but he would have known all of the texts included here which were written before or during his lifetime. All of them were standard—famous, useful texts, which remained the staple diet of theological masters until at least the end of our period. Theologians after William might add more books, but they were unlikely to subtract any. This is partly to do with the success of these texts themselves—each has a niche which it fills superbly well—but it is also due to the medieval habit of addition, which we have already discussed.

The texts cover all facets of Hugh of St Victor's description of the study of sacred scripture. Section one, 'The Bible as Theological Tool', contains the Bible and its offshoots—the *Ordinary Gloss*, biblical commentaries, a concordance, and Bible reference works like the *Historia scholastica*. Section two, 'Sources', looks at the non-biblical side of Hugh's sacred scripture, including the Fathers, canon law, and some more 'modern' authors whose works were standard works of reference. Section three, '*Sentences* to *Summae*', looks at the development of dogmatic theology, with texts that are issue- or *quaestio*-based, and order their biblical and extra-biblical source material by problem rather than by text. Section Four, 'Theology Made Accessible', presents works that considered the world outside the theology faculty syllabus—practical or moral theology which transformed the conclusions of the masters in their schools and took them to the working world.

Thus, although the gathering of texts in this book represents a collection which Thomas or Bonaventure might themselves have used, it does not, probably unlike the bookshelves of a modern theologian, contain only or even mostly contemporary works. The wide range of the texts, in date as in topic, reflects the all-encompassing mind of the twelfth- and thirteenth-century masters.

Merely to describe the works themselves would not be complete without demonstrating their context in contemporary manuscripts. Alongside the development of the schools went developments in book technology. Having been largely the preserve of monastic libraries, manuscript books moved with their secular masters into other hands. Since learning was text-based, students needed the texts their masters prescribed. In law, particularly, students needed copies of Justinian and Gratian at least—the essential reference tools of their would-be trade. Descriptions and illustrations of the Bologna law schools show students at desks following along in their textbooks as the master lectures. In theology it was probably not quite the same; but many of the texts we now know, especially commentaries on the *Sentences* and reports of questions and disputations, come down to us through student *reportationes*—official lecture notes, taken down live and, ideally, later corrected and approved by the master.

The flourishing schools of Paris meant the book trade was big business. The masters stepped in to regulate the sale of parchment and booksellers' practices, much as they regulated the prices of bread and lodging. Street names such as the *rue des parcheminiers* (parchment-makers), by the university church of St Severin, tell their own story. We have reports of booksellers' shops on the *parvis* in front of Notre Dame; this area became the hub of book production and decoration.[98] Manuscripts were labor-intensive and library provision was slight until Robert de Sorbonne's foundation of a college for poor scholars, around 1257. Although it began with few books, the Sorbonne library became 'possibly the best in Paris'.[99] Students who could not afford to buy ready-made books (text books were available off-the-peg, but many medieval books were bespoke copies) could avail themselves of the ingenious *peciae* system (no. 19), whereby books could be hired in sections for copying.[100]

Not only did the new schools and their curricula mean there were not enough books to go around: the needs of teaching and examination meant that the old style of book was inadequate too. A book intended to be read straight through, from start to finish, needs nothing more than a bookmark. A book which deals with a host of different topics commented on by a bevy of authorities needs an index, running heads, and marginal reference signs to indicate which master is responsible for which opinion. Books were not just to be *read*, they were to be *used*. When the Dominicans came to Paris, their house full of students provided the work force for a series of innovations in the look and layout of books that we now think of as classically 'scholastic'. Theirs was not the first of the great changes in medieval book manufacture—that honor must go to the changes in layout that ensured the success of the Ordinary Gloss (no. 1)—but the numbers involved in the book trade of the schools meant that the friars were working in a milieu eager for their skill.

As well as typical texts of the period, then, I have selected a cross-section of theological manuscript production. The reader will find the brilliant layout of the Gloss, books made for monasteries, Paris 'red-and-blue' decorated textbooks, friars' tiny pocket-books (they

98. R. H. Rouse and M. A. Rouse, *Manuscripts and Their Makers: Commercial Book Producers in Medieval Paris 1200–1500*, 2 vols. (Turnhout, 2000). Also, see their 'The Book Trade at the University of Paris, ca. 1250–ca. 1350', and 'The Commercial Production of Manuscript Books in Late-Thirteenth Century and Early-Fourteenth Century Paris'.

99. *CUP*, I, no. 448. R. H. Rouse, 'The Early Library of the Sorbonne', p. 45.

100. J. Destrez, *La Pecia dans les manuscrits universitaires du xiiie et xive siècle;* and see Thorndike, *University Records*, pp. 112–17 (Paris = *CUP*, I, no. 530) and 166–68 (Bologna).

needed small books for their itinerant preaching), and books made for the wealthy. None of the manuscripts was made later than the last quarter of the thirteenth century, so not only the texts but the books themselves are what medieval theologians would have physically known and used. The reader will be able to spot the inclusion of such items as running heads, reference signs, diagrams, subject headings and, that wonderful guarantee that at least one person has looked at the text, readers' notes. In order to cram more text onto less parchment, the use of abbreviations becomes more common during this period and writing was often diminutive; it is no coincidence that spectacles were invented in the late thirteenth century! [101]

Each entry which follows includes a short codicological description of the book as object, as well as the main material concerning the work and its context. Since they were entirely handmade, no two medieval books are alike. The physical book can tell us a great deal about the text, its milieu and its reception. We are fortunate indeed in having not only the texts on which our subjects worked, or which they wrote themselves, but the very books they worked in. The history of no medieval subject can be properly written without recourse to the materials it produced. The history of the theology of the schools would be incomplete without the 'sacred pages' themselves in front of us.

101. A sermon preached by Giordano da Pisa in 1305 suggests spectacles were invented about twenty years previously: J. S. Neaman, 'Magnification as Metaphor', 120.

List of Plates

C. *Sentences* to *Summae*

D. Theology Made Accessible

The Bible as Theological Tool

one

The *Ordinary Gloss* (*Glossa Ordinaria*)

Princeton, University Libraries, Grenville Kane Collection, MS 2, fol. 36^r
France; first third of twelfth century

Medieval theology was founded on texts. Its primary texts were the Old and New Testaments of the Bible, thought to be the revealed Word of God. But, as Hugh of St Victor explained (*Didascalicon*, bk. 4), the New Testament was more than the biblical books: it included the writings of the Fathers, canon law, the decrees of the Church Councils, and even some 'modern' authorities. With the development of schools of theology, the plain Bible text became less useful to teachers and students than one surrounded by the explanations of its most important commentators.

The first glossed Bibles probably grew from marginal notes made by individual owners for their own use; but at the beginning of the twelfth century, one particular version emerged as the standard edition, with the glosses surrounding the biblical text. This Bible (including Jerome's prologues: no. 6) with commentary is known as the *Ordinary Gloss*. Numerous manuscript copies of the standard version were produced from around 1130 to about 1250, containing in effect a digest of the opinions of all the important patristic commentators and occasionally selected 'moderns' on any given text. Jerome, on whose translation the *Gloss*'s Bible text is based, is also a major source of the individual glosses, along with Ambrose (no. 11), Augustine (no. 9), Bede, Cassiodorus, Gregory the Great (no. 10), and Origen, although many others, especially Carolingian authors such as Hrabanus Maurus, may also appear. Not all sources are used for each biblical book: the editors of the *Gloss* carefully selected what seemed most fruitful.

How the *Gloss* developed is not entirely clear. By about 1490, it was a commonplace that the Carolingian scholar Walafrid Strabo was the compiler of the *Gloss*, but recent scholarship prefers to credit the Psalter, Pauline Epistles and (perhaps) the Gospel of John to Anselm of Laon (d. 1117), and the Pentateuch, Jeremiah, (perhaps) Joshua to 2 Kings, and the Minor

PARCHMENT: i (paper) + 66 + ii (paper) fols.; page 270 x 180 mm; biblical text 160 x 60 mm; overall text 160 x 150 mm; biblical text 19 lines; one scribe. Red initials with red and brown penwork to begin chapters in main text. Underlining and markers in red as reference signs to join text and gloss.

From the Benedictine abbey of St Martin, Aubazine, Central France (*ex libris*, fol. 66ᵛ); in private ownership since the Revolution, until bought by Princeton from Grenville Kane in 1946.

CONTENTS: fols. 1ʳ–66ᵛ Gospel of Luke, with *glossa ordinaria*, beginning imperf. ch. 7:2.

A very typical early copy.

Prophets to Gilbert of Auxerre, 'the Universal'. Anselm's brother, Ralph, may have assembled the gloss on Matthew. The compiler(s) of the other glosses remain a mystery.

The *Gloss* was taken up by two famous twelfth-century Paris masters, Gilbert of Poitiers (d. 1154) and Peter Lombard (no. 18). Peter wrote commentaries on the Psalter and Pauline Epistles which were incorporated into the *Gloss* as standard (a version known as the *Magna glosatura;* Gilbert's version is known as the *Media glosatura*). The perfecting of the characteristic layout, apparently in Paris in the twelfth century, made it the biblical reference tool *par excellence.*

The *Gloss* was printed in many early versions, the first by Adolph Rusch of Strassburg (1480–81). From the 1495 edition, it was printed together with the *postillae* of Nicholas of Lyra. An increasing number of interpolations in texts printed after 1500 make them unreliable witnesses to the twelfth-century versions, but demonstrate its continuing popularity. The adjective *ordinaria* was not added to the general term *Glossa* until the fourteenth century.

The *Gloss* was always too big to be contained in one volume (and indeed, this was generally true of Bibles before the thirteenth century); rather, it appeared as sets of single books or groups of books. The manuscript shown here contains only the Gospel of Luke and its *Gloss.* This page shows the beginning of chapter 15 (note the chapter number added later as a Roman numeral in the right margin). It is very typical of its sort, with marginal and interlinear glosses surrounding a double-spaced, double script-sized central text. Each capital letter in the marginal glosses denotes the beginning of a new gloss. Sometimes (although not here) the authority quoted is named. Using the *Gloss* required a high level of biblical knowledge, as is shown by a marginal comment with a quotation from Luke (right margin, fourth gloss, lines 3–4) which begins: 'Dīc̄ g.° Mai⁹ gaudiū erit i.c.s.u.p.p.a.q.s.xc.viiii.iustis.q. n.i.p.' i.e., 'Dicit ergo: Maius gaudium erit in celo super uno peccatore penitentiam agente quam super nonaginta novem iustis qui non indigent penitentia.' [He (Christ) says: there will be more rejoicing in heaven over one sinner who repents than in ninety-nine just men who have no need to repent = Lk 15:7.]

Quis ex uob. h. dedicas in supiorib; ablegare negligencia. uitare arrogancia.
De uoem sume. selarib; occupacionib; n teni. caduca n pferre ppetuis. s; qs fragili
tas humana firmu neqd intanto seli lubrico tenere

uestigiu. i ad ius errorem
remedia t medic de mons
trat. iudex spe uenie non
negat. Vn scs lucas tres
ex ordine pabolas ponit.
ouis. dragme. filii.

Oim. Angelica natura l suma
btudine existente qsi re
liqd. du seipsu exinaniuit.

Hum x. cruci brachia ft.
I lle pecca mea deposui. in
illa nobit patibuli ceru
ce requieui.

F Oues pastor cui nos oms
centesima portio sum.
Dimittit. qs roat creatur
nus peunte hoie erat im
minut. querit uita h
omine. ut suma itegret.

Vicini. qs clitate uisionis ei
fruunt. i nota qd n dic
ogratulamini oui inue
te. s; m. qs gaudiu ei
uita nra.

Angli qs roales gaudent
de reconciliato s hoie.
qd accendit nos ad pbita
te ut agam qd illis gra
tu sit. q rassectare pa
trocinium. i offensam
timere debemus.

Sinaga. xviiii. iustis q n
errauerit. nec idigt peni
tencia. angli intelligunt.
mai uidr i pios iustifica
re. q iustos errare. i oseruare

audiendi audiat. Erant au

Qui publica uectigalia exi

tem appropinquantes ei publica

git. t oducunt. i qui lucrii seli pnegocia sequr.

ni. i peccatores ut audirent illu.

Duplicit errant. qs se iustos putant cu sint supbi. i illos reos cu iam penitea(n)t.

i murmurabant pharisei. i

Quasi. gtri:

scribe dicentes. Quia hic pecca

legi q hoc phibet.

tores recipit. & manducat

cu illis. & ait ad illos parabola

ista dicens. Quis ex uob ho qui

ht centu oues. i si pdiderit

In his

una ex illis nne dimittit no

In celo. qd desertu ab hoie peccante.

Diu p pdi

aginta noue in deserto. i uadit

cacionem uocat.

Querens.

ad illa que perierat. donec inuem

Se huma

at illa. & cu inuenerit ea. impo

na natura suscipiens peccata nra ipse portauit.

nit in humeros suos gaudens.

Reparato hoie. ad celu pastor redit. ibi angloz coros inuenit.

& ueniens domu. conuocat ami

q amici. qs instabilitate sua uolutate ei omne custodiunt.

cos. i uicinos dicens illis. Con

gratulamini m. qr inueni oue

mea que perierat. Dico uob. qd

celo

ita gaudiu erit in celo sup uno pecca

Quia no solu iusti pinertia peccare s; etia
peccor psollertia pot resipiscere. pt eiec
tione in fatuitate salutis ois penitencium
mt ad missa de scribr. q ad audiendu
uerbu dei appropinquantes. non solum
ad colloquidum. s; i ad uescendu recepti
st. Vn dedignant pharisei. qs falsa iusti
cia n opassione. s; de dignoe habet. S;
qs eg. erant ita ut se egros nescirent quenusq
agnoscerent. celestis medic padigma obi
cit. q meoz corde uulnus tumore pmit
dicens. Qis ex uob ho.

Quia centenari nus pfect e. d centu
oues. i. pfectu num habuit. cu an
gloz i houi. subam creau. s; una pit.
qn ho pascua uite peccando dereliquid. F

Non ne dim. qsi. o murmatis qs peccores
recipio. s; ego n ueni. nisi ut aberran
tes colligam. sic un qsq; urm aberran
te ouem reducere laborat.

iustoz nus intelligit. In una oue pec
catoz. Vn alibi. Non ueni uocare ius
tos s; peccores. dic g. Mai gaudiu erit
i. c. s. u. p. p. a. q. s. xc. viiii. iustis. q n
i. p. qs ut cotidie expim. q illicita n omi
sert. iureb; licitis sepe sibi usu pbent.
ad celestia anxie n anelant. i qs securi st.
ad bona agenda pigri remanent.
Erit au peccor pluq; facit. Mai g. s.
deco qm destante iusto. Vn dux in
plio. pl cu militem dilig. q pt fuga re
uersus. hoste fortit pmit. q eu q nq
fug. ne nq fortit egit. S; i st qda
iusti de qb; tm e gaudiu. ut eis nullo
penitetes ppom possit. q si n sit sibi ma
loz osci. tn licita respuunt. i oib;
se humiliant. qntu g gaudiu e. si hu
milit plangit iust. cu gaudiu sit.
si qd male gessit plang iniustus.

BIBLIOGRAPHY

Biblia latina cum glossa ordinaria, facsimile reprint; T. Gross-Diaz, *The Psalms Commentary of Gilbert of Poiters;* C. de Hamel, *Glossed Books of the Bible and the Origins of the Paris Booktrade;* B. Smalley, 'Glossa Ordinaria'.

TWO

Herbert of Bosham, *On Peter Lombard on the Psalms*

Oxford, Bodleian Library, MS Auct. E inf. 6, fol. 119ʳ
Made probably in Paris, 1173–77

Because of their place in the liturgy, their usefulness for personal devotion, and their enormous variety of imagery and emotional voice, the Psalms were the most popular book of the Bible. Although they were included in the early twelfth-century *Gloss*, the commentary found there was quickly superseded, first by that of Gilbert de la Porrée and then, magisterially, by that of Peter Lombard. In order to distinguish them, these three are known as the *parva*, *media*, and *magna glosatura*, respectively.

The Psalter itself was known in three translations, the Roman, Gallican and Hebraic, all attributed to Jerome, although his link with the first (that of the Old Latin Bible) is dubious. The Gallican psalter is his 'Vulgate' translation; he made the Hebraic version directly from the Hebrew text, but it remained largely the preserve of scholars. The astonishing manuscript we see here gives both Gallican and Hebraic texts for comparison, along with Peter Lombard's commentary with interpolations by Herbert of Bosham.

Herbert was a pupil of Peter Lombard (no. 18) and Andrew of St Victor (no. 15) who became secretary and companion-in-exile of Archbishop Thomas Becket. Apart from the additions he made to Lombard's psalter commentary, Herbert wrote a full commentary on the literal sense of the psalms, utilizing Hebrew scholarship (he was one of the first Englishmen to learn the language). He also wrote a Life of Becket after Thomas' martyrdom.

This is the second part of a two-volume set. In the preface to the first volume (Cambridge, Trinity College, MS B. 5. 4), Herbert tells us that Becket asked him to make this book when they were in exile at Pontigny, probably for him to present to the monks of Canterbury. However, the present dedication (with portrait) to William of Sens suggests that Becket was dead before it was completed, and Herbert changed the recipient to the archbishop in whose diocese

PARCHMENT: i (paper) + i (parchment) + 142 (foliation misses no. 27) + i (paper) fols.; page 470 x 325 mm; text 2 cols., each 315 x 80 mm; 52 lines; ruled in lead-point; one very competent scribe. Profusely decorated; size and complexity of the initials reflects the importance of the text they introduce. Palette of gold, pale blue, orange, pale green, pink and white. Originally included marginal drawings of theological subjects, now excised except on fol. 21^{v}.

In Christ Church, Canterbury, probably by the end of the 12th c.; given in 1616 to the Bodleian by the sons of Richard Colfe, prebendary of Canterbury, in memory of him.

CONTENTS: fol. i^{v} preface by Herbert of Bosham for William, archbishop of Sens; 1^{r}–139^{v} psalms 74–150 in two versions, with the *magna glosatura* of Peter Lombard, and interpolations by Herbert of Bosham; 140^{r}–41^{v} separate notes on other psalms.

A gorgeous book, yet with great scholarly value.

he and Thomas had lived in exile, and whom he perhaps hoped might provide him with an ecclesiastical living.

Herbert probably wrote this manuscript himself; the decoration seems to be a product of the earliest professional (lay) illuminators in Paris. The spectacular layout, incorporating very early use of running heads, chapter numbers, and a hierarchy of script and initial sizes, aids the reader in his search through the text. Each page has two columns themselves divided into six parts:

Running title: psalm no. in Roman numerals, in red and blue.

1. References to New Testament quotations cited in commentary text; notes to other references (e.g., Augustine). N.T. preceded by ***L(iber)*** with chapter number and first few words of lemma. (Excised) theological drawings.
2. Patristic authors cited, e.g., Aug. (Augustine), Cas. (Cassiodorus). Names alternating in red and blue, identified by quotation marks (two vertical or horizontal dots), here and in commentary text. Duration of quotation marked by vertical line.
3. References to other psalms occurring in the commentary. References in the form S^{a} = supra (before this psalm) or I^{a} = infra (after), followed by number and first line.
4. Hebraic version of the psalms.
5. Gallican version of the psalms. Text written double size, on alternate lines.
6. Peter Lombard, *Magna glosatura* with Bosham interpolations. Lemmata to psalms underlined in red. Titles in red. Quotation marks (double dots) linking text with reference (col. 2).

This description is of the left-hand column of any page; right-hand columns run in the order 4 5 6 3 2 1. The shape of the three reference columns is static, but the three text columns change shape, depending on the ratio of the size of commentary to psalm text at any point; sometimes the commentary takes over the space of all three text columns. The outer margin on both sides contains decorators' and rubricators' instructions.

On this page, we can particularly notice a small portrait of Augustine in the margin. He points to a quotation claiming to be from his works, and says 'Non ego'—not me! In a very

.i. xpc pus in cruce. pea in celo exaltatus. a q ros gre descendit in syon .i. in eccliam. et e sens. Ita e illud bonum: sic ros hermon .i. gra x. p⁹ us in cruce. pea in celo exaltati. qui ros descendit in monte syon .i. in eccliam. Non enim in uno e ecclia: n ei gra. Ide sigcat hic syon: qd sup barba et hora uestimti. Id u ros hermon: qd sup unguentum. s. gra. p qua fit cohabitatio. Qui enim in uno e sn tote caritatis s: sunt inqetum iumentum in iunctura. qd non tralhit & turbat. Odiosi enim s. molesti s. turbulenti s. anxietate sua ceteros turbant. et querut quid sinistri de aliis dicant. hu et murmurant de quib; dr in libro ihu filii syrac. Precordia fatui rota carri: fenum portat et semp murmurat. hu tales s qui relinquunt in mola. in agro. in lecto. qui in uno corpe solum n s. Lecti u assumunt. qui in unum sunt corde. Vl ita. hermon: mons pascualis e. sic et mons syon. Per hermon g sigcant gts. que pabulum ubi receperut. et e. Ita e hoc bonum: sic ros hermon .i. gra qm in gts receperunt. qui pus descen. in mon. syon .i. sr iudeos. Vt p hermon qui in ptr anatha: accipiunt peccatores. p syon: ecclia. Ros e tenuis aqua: un ita gminat. et sigcat gram qua peccatores ouituntur. Ros g e .i. hermon: e ros gre. qui peccatores mittit in bo. qui ros: des. in mon. syon. qm illi hoc rore rigati: ouitunt ad eccliam. que eos recepit et e s. Ita e illud bonum: sic ros hermon .i. gra mittens peccatores. qui descen. i mo. sy. .i. quo illi ouituntur ad eccliam. sequitur.

4 Qm ibi mandauit dns bndicti one. uitam usq; ieternum.

Qm illic mandauit dns benedictionem: et uitam usq; in seculum.

5 Qm illic .a. id bonum e et iocundu habitare in unum: qm illic .i. in fribus qui habitat in unum. mandauit dns benedictione. hic .i. pcepit ut hic benedicerent deum. Concordes enim benedicunt deum. Discordes non. 6 Nam in discordia: non e uera benedictio. quia si lingua sonat: cor silet. et mandauit .i. promisit: uitam. in futuro duraturam. usq; in seculum .i. in eternum.

Ecce nunc benedicite do. Tyrl. Canticu graduu.

Ecce nunc benedicite dominum: omnes serui dni.

Canticum graduum.

Ecce nunc benedicite dnm: omnes serui dni.

Quintus decimus gradus e caritas dei. et e iste tertius ps de caritate dei. de qua hic agit. sic supra de caritate proximi. n q alia gra sit qua diligit ds: et alia qua proximus. s; cp diuisos actus ht ipa uirtus: et diuisa diliguntur ea. Iuit. monet: ad diligendu dm. Modus. Byptite e. Primo: inuitat plat bndicere dnm. Scdo: optat bndici. ibi. Benedicat. Monens g ad bndicendum: Ecce. demonstratiuale e: et qb; fiat. faciat hanc demonstratione. determinat. uos s iu dni. os adunati in unum. ne s. tot gradib; ascensis. ut ne .i. in hoc tepe. in his ad uisis: bndicite dnm. Vd dico:

Stantes in domo dni: in atriis domus dei nostri.

Qui statis in domo dni.

Qui statis. .i. psuatis. in domo dni .i. in penetralibus. s. maiores et pfectiores: in ecclia. et uos et qui statis in atriis domus dei nri .i. i ingssu. s. incipientes. Sunt enim in hac domo: diuisi statuum ostentes. Et nota qd ait: statis. n sedetis. q2 suorum: no e sede in domo dni. ut de eisde accipit et p domum intelligt ecclia: p atria latitudo caritatis. In caritate enim que extendit usq; ad inimicos latitudo e: in odio angustia. a. d. uos bndicite: qui statis .i. pseuatis in do. dni .i. in ecclia. et q statis in atriis dom dei nri .i. i latitudine caritatis ubi nullus angustiatur. et

In noctib. .i. in aduersis

In noctibus

In noc

scholarly fashion, Herbert never alters Peter Lombard's text, even when he finds fault; he merely, as here, adds his own correction alongside.

BIBLIOGRAPHY

Smalley, *SBMA*, ch. 4.vi; *eadem*, *The Becket Conflict and the Schools;* C. de Hamel, *Glossed Books of the Bible and the Origins of the Paris Booktrade;* M. Gibson, T. Heslop, and R. Pfaff, *The Eadwine Psalter;* N. Pain, *The King and Becket*, fig. 5, p. 144.

three

Peter Comestor, *Historia scholastica*

New Haven, Yale University, Beinecke Rare Book and Manuscript Library, MS 214, fol. 130^{r}
Abbey of Mont-Saint-Quentin, N. E. France; 1229

It was probably only after he resigned his teaching post at the cathedral school of Notre Dame that Peter Comestor produced his *Historia scholastica*, the *School Histories* with which he became immediately synonymous. Peter had not become an overnight sensation: he was chancellor of Notre Dame and head of its school; but this book made him simply 'Master of the *Histories*' in the same way that Peter Lombard was 'Master of the *Sentences*'.

Although 'Comestor' ('Eater') may be a joke about the thoroughness with which he digested the Scriptures, it is also a family name in the Champagne region which seems likely to have been Peter's home. An Augustinian canon and dean of Troyes, he went to Paris, where he heard and admired Peter Lombard (no. 18) and, soon after 1164, was made chancellor. Retiring from teaching (but not the chancellorship) in 1169, he went to live at the Augustinian abbey of St Victor, where he died and was buried around 1180.

Peter had produced other works, but nothing as successful as the *Historia:* his years of experience bore fruit and retirement gave him the time to write. The dedication to William, archbishop of Sens, allows us to date the composition between 1169 and 1173. The *Historia* is an exposition of the Bible, firmly grounded in the literal sense. Peter was fascinated to explain all of the practical matter of the Scriptures. To Jewish and Christian chronology and events, he added material from pagan authors, making the whole a kind of world history of wide-ranging interest. Modern readers need to remember that, aside from local chronicles, medieval people had virtually no existing history of the world other than the Bible, which was thought to be literally true as well as allegorically meaningful. History and sacred history were one and the same. But then, as now, many of the references to ancient people, materials, measurements, or places were mystifying; Peter set out to explain them as fully as contemporary knowledge would allow, using Holy Land topography and archaeology, and Hebrew etymology, in an attempt to be comprehensive.

PARCHMENT: iii (parchment) + 203 + iii (parchment) fols.; page 450 x 305 mm; text 2 cols., each 315 x 85 mm; 47 lines; ruled in crayon; one scribe. Corrections and short marginal notes in 13th-c. hands. Highly decorated, including (fol. 2^{r}) a miniature of Comestor presenting his book to William of Champagne, archbishop of Sens. Many historiated and decorated initials with gold. Minor initials in red or blue, with blue or red flourishing.

Given to the abbey by 'Petrus' (fol. 1^{r}). Privately owned since the Revolution until presented to Yale, 1954.

CONTENTS: fol. 1^{r} title-page in orange and blue; 2^{v}–180^{v} Peter Comestor, *Historia scholastica* (some text missing at 2 Kings and 1 Samuel); 181^{r}–203^{r} Peter of Poitiers, *On Acts* (here attributed to Comestor).

Much has been made of Peter's Jewish sources. He was probably born near and educated in Troyes, a Champagne fair town which also housed the famous rabbinic school of Rashi (*Ra*bbi *Sh*lomo ben *I*saac; d. 1105). Did Peter's knowledge stem from direct contact with the learned Jews of Troyes? Alas, it seems that he could have gathered most of his material from Jerome and other patristic writers, mediated especially through that known Hebraeophile, Andrew of St Victor (no. 15). Since Andrew was still alive when Peter was writing, Peter followed contemporary convention and did not mention borrowings from him by name; but the Victorines in general, and Hugh (no. 17) in particular, were certainly among his greatest influences, and his work reflects the Victorine tradition of theology firmly rooted in the study of Scripture.

So pervasive was the *Historia* as a textbook that scholars of the stature of Hugh of St Cher (no. 8) wrote commentaries on it, and Roger Bacon complained that students no longer read the Bible, just the *Historia*. Peter of Poitiers (no. 19), Comestor's successor at Notre Dame, added *Acts* to the original text which only went as far as the Gospels. Frequently, as in this manuscript, this too was attributed to Comestor himself. Peter of Poitiers also added a pictorial version of the *Histories* (the *Compendium Historiae*), detailing the genealogy of Christ from Adam, which was often included in copies of the *Historia* or produced as independent, scroll-shaped 'wallcharts' for classroom use.

This page shows the beginning of the book of Judith, including a historiated initial (with detail corresponding closely to the text) of Judith decapitating Holofernes and handing the head to her servant to put in her shoulder-bag. Judith begins with a long scene-setting description of Holofernes and Nebuchadnezzar (here Nabugodonosor), which Peter efficiently compresses to bring the story up to Judith's entrance. This page alone encapsulates almost seven chapters of the biblical text.

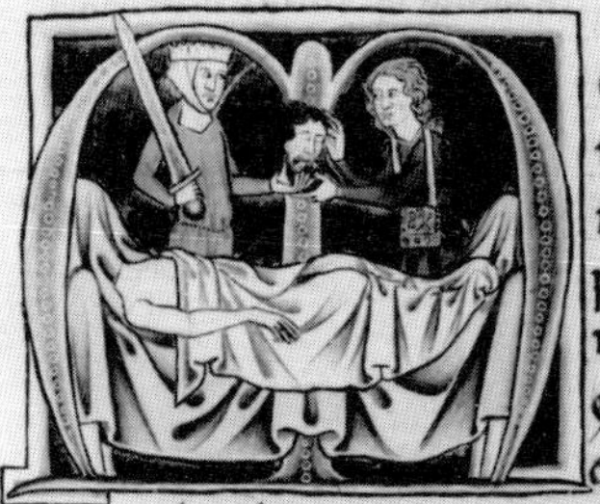

ortuo autem cyro
quidam arphaxath
medus metbatha
nis surrexit et re
parauit eam et
muniuit eā in
expugnabiliter.
quasdam partes
medie sibi conciliians ut tandem toti me
die imperaret. Nabugodonosor uero rex
assyriorum qui regnabat in niniue. anno
xii. regni sui obtinuit arfaxath in campo
regaui. qui est inter eufraten et tygrum. Hic
est cambisses cui pater adhuc uiuens nini
uem et regnum assiriorum concessit. et
nabugodonosor. cognominauit. Hic mor
tuo patre. xii. illius regni annum agebat.
nam in regno monarchie non nisi. viii.
annis regnauit. Qui postquam factus ē
monarchus exaltatum est cor eius et mi
sit ad omnes qui habitabant in cilicia et
damasco. et libano. et carmelo. galilea. et
samaria. et usq; in ihe̅rl̅m. exigens ab eis
tributa longe grauiora quam patris sui.
qui omnes uno animo contradixerunt. Tunc
iratus rex iurauit per thronum suum. q̄d
defenderet se de omnib;. Igitur anno. xxvi.
regni sui precepit oloferni principi mili
tie. ut egrederetur ad regiones illas et
nulli hominum uel munitionum parcer̄
oculus eius. qui egressus est cum exerci
tu. et operuerunt faciem terre sicut lo
custe. Qui cum uastasset ciliciam et meso
potamiam et madianitas. miserunt ad eū
principes prouinciarum dicentes. Desi
nat indignatio tua circa nos. ueni no
bis pacificus et utere seruitio nr̄o sicut pla
cuerit tibi. Et descendit de montib; cum
uirtute magna. et obtinuit omnes ciuita
tes. et destruxit eas. et omnes deos terre
exterminauit. Sic enim preceperat nabugo
donosor. ut ip̄e solus deus diceret ab his na
tionibus qui potuissent olofernis potentia
subiugari. Et audientes filij isr̄l timuer̄t
ualde ne similia faceret in ihe̅rl̅m et in
sanctuario dei. et miserunt in terminis terre
p quos poterat iter ēē in ihe̅rl̅m et munie
runt angusta uiarum et humiliauerunt
se coram domino ad exhortationem eliachim
sacerdotis filij ihu. filij iosedech. uel forte alt̄
quem ip̄e ibi mittebat ad exhortationē filio
rum isr̄l in montib;. Et operuerant sacerdo
tes altare domini cilicio. et ipsi in cinere et
cilicio offerebant holocausta et clamabant
ad dominum. Nuntiatum oloferni quod
filij isr̄l parassent se ad resistendum. et mon
tium itinera conclusissent. et uocauit duces
amon et moab dicens. Quis est p̄p̄l̄s iste q̄
montana obsidet? aut que est uirtus eorum.
Tunc achior dux filiorum amon. respondit.
replicans ei quomodo primo uenisset p̄p̄l̄s
ille de chaldea per mesopotamiam in terram
chanaan ~~est~~. cumq; descendissent in egyptū.
reduxerat eos deus eorum in terram promis
sam. qui cum placatus erat eis. nemo po
terat eis resistere. Cum uero irritabant
flagellabat eos. quia deus odiens erat
iniquitatem. Super autem reduxerat eos
in ihe̅rl̅m de seruitute. cui tradiderat eos p̄p̄t
peccata sua. et nunc obtinebant montana
hec. Et addidit achior. Perscrutare si deus eor
offensus est eis et poteris eos expugnare. alio
quin non preualebis eis. Et iratus olofer
nes dixit. Ut ostendam tibi quia non est d̄s
nisi nabugodonosor. ex hac hora illorum p̄p̄l̄o
sociaberis. ut cum illis pariter pereas. Tunc
precepit holofernes seruis suis. ut ducerent
eum in betuliam. ante quam castra metat̄
fuerat. Cumq; traherent eum fundibalarij
egressi sunt aduersus eos. et timentes liga
uerunt achior ad arborem et recesserunt.
fundibalarij uero soluentes eum statuer̄t
eum in medio seniorum et p̄p̄l̄i. Miserant q̄
dem de ihe̅rl̅m in betuliam duos sacerdotes.
et principem oziam de tribu symeon. Cumq;
exposuisset eis achior quare transmissus
ēēt ab holoferne ad eos. recepit eum ozias in
domum suam. Factum est autem ut inue
niret holofernes ductum aquarum que
influebant ciuitatem. particulas que
ebibebant aquam de alueo per latentes rimulas
aq̄ duct9. ī̄ interrupto aq̄ ductu abstulit ei aquā. Erant au
tem non longe a muris fonticuli quib; fur
tim ciues utebantur. ad refocillandum

BIBLIOGRAPHY

Petrus Comestor. Historia scholastica; I. Brady, 'Manducator and the Oral Teachings of Peter Lombard'; S. Daly, 'Peter Comestor: Master of Histories'; S. Lacks, 'The Source of Hebrew Traditions in the *Historia Scholastica*'; A. Landgraf, 'Recherches sur les écrits de Pierre le Mangeur'; E. Shereshevsky, 'Hebrew Traditions in Peter Comestor's *Historia Scholastica*'; B. Smalley, *The Gospels in the Schools c. 1100–c. 1280.*

four

Bernard of Clairvaux, *Sermons on the Song of Songs*

Engelberg (Switzerland), Stiftsbibliothek, MS 32, fol. 2[v]
Made at Engelberg under Abbot Frowin (verse, fol. 3[r]); mid-twelfth century

The foundation of medieval theology on a relatively few authoritative texts, added to scholastic custom, led to numerous treatises being written on the same topic or text. Nevertheless, some works were reckoned to be classics of interpretation. Such was Bernard's commentary on the Song of Songs, a series of eighty-six exegetical homilies which he wrote in the latter part of his life, from 1135 to his death in 1153 (by which point he had reached only the beginning of chapter 3). Perhaps monks and schoolmen were simply relieved that such a magisterial work had been written on such a problematic book, for it provided them with solutions to difficult questions. More likely, the issues that the Song raised were of lesser interest to university masters, since they were hard to fit into the syllabus; but the Song continued to have influence for contemplatives and spiritual writers as a text for devotion.

The Song has always posed a problem. Why is such a blatantly sexual poem, a paean to physical love, found in sacred Scripture? Was it not an immoral celebration of the flesh? What could such a text teach believers about the love of God? For Jewish interpreters, such as those of the Targum, the poem describes the love of God for Israel. Christian exegesis took over this understanding with few changes, simply making the lovers Christ and the Church—a shift made easier since *ecclesia* (church) is a feminine Latin noun. The most important early Christian interpreter of the Song was Origen (*c.* 185–*c.* 254), a scholar from Alexandria, who wrote a commentary and two homilies on the text. His opinion, that the bride and bridegroom signified the union of the soul and the Word, remained the standard, along with the common allegory of the marriage of Christ and the Church, until the twelfth century when the person of the Virgin Mary was added (by Bernard and Rupert of Deutz [*c.* 1075–1129]) as a 'type' of the Church. This addition gives us a layering of images, with Mary taking three allegorical parts as Christ's mother, lover and spouse, and is typical of the medieval ability simultaneously to appreciate multiple meanings.

PARCHMENT: 177 fols.; page 320 x 230 mm; other details unavailable. Decorated and plain colored initials.
CONTENTS: fols. 2r–177v Bernard of Clairvaux, *Sermons on the Song of Songs* nos. 1–82.

Bernard had been a member of the new Cistercian Order (founded 1115) and founder-abbot (1118) of their house at Clairvaux in Burgundy for about twenty years when a Carthusian friend, Bernard of Portes, asked him to write on the Song of Songs. It was a perfect vehicle for Bernard's gifts, combining the fruits of his monastic rumination on the Bible with his belief in the exalted place of physical humanity in the Creation, typified by his adoration of Mary, the human mother of God. Above all, it allowed him to write on his favorite theme: love. He did not tie himself to the letter of the biblical text, but used it as a starting point to dilate on the Christian life, interior and exterior, moving—and this is crucial—from his own experience, whether as a contemplative monk or as an ecclesiastical dignitary, to universal truths about the love of God in the Trinity and in the world. Bernard's emphasis on the importance of one's own experience—often previously discounted as the trivia of this fleeting world—was a crucial step toward the opening up of theology to human reason and the scientific movement of the thirteenth-century schools (not all of which would have been to his liking). His immense reputation for holiness, combined with an astonishingly strong personality, lent Bernard an authority scarcely less massive than that of the early Fathers. His works were regarded as modern classics.

This page is the beginning of the book. The extraordinary frontispiece depicts Christ and the Church (who wears a prelate's mitre) as bridegroom and bride—*sponsus* and *sponsa*—setting the interpretive parameters for what is to come. The picture tells the reader how to interpret the Song text: it emphasizes the tender and intimate love of Creator and Creature; and it shows the importance of the human Church, which is thought fit to stand alongside her Lord.

The verse above the figures reads: 'Coniugis in morem permiscetur per amorem/Ecclesiae Christus. perit hinc dolor et quoque fastus.' [Christ is mingled with the Church through love, in the manner of a spouse. By this, sorrow and pride are both destroyed.] Both carry speech scrolls. Christ quotes from the Song text (2:1) 'Ego fios campi' [I am the flower of the field]; the Church answers 'Dilecte mi rep[re]hen[di] te' [My love, I have caught you!].

Underneath the picture, a later hand has added the *ex libris* of the library of Engelberg: Bibliothecae Angelo Montana.

Coniugis in morem per miscetur per amorem
Ecclesie xpe per te hinc dolor ac quo q; fistus
EGO FLOS CAMPI
Bibliotheca Angelo Montana

BIBLIOGRAPHY

Bernard of Clairvaux, *On the Song of Songs*, ed. K. Walsh and I. Edmonds; *Bernard of Clairvaux: Selected Works*, trans. G. R. Evans; *St Bernard of Clairvaux, His Life as Recorded in the Vita prima Bernardi, by William of St Thierry*, trans. G. Webb and A. Walker; E. Gilson, *The Mystical Theology of St Bernard;* J. Leclercq, *Recueils d'études sur S. Bernard;* E. A. Matter, *The Voice of My Beloved. The Song of Songs in Western Medieval Christianity.*

five

Richard of St Victor, *Liber exceptionum*

Paris, Bibliothèque nationale de France, MS Arsenal 266A, fol. 50^{r}
St Victor, Paris; late twelfth century

The *Liber exceptionum* ('book of notes'; often wrongly *excerptionum*, 'book of excerpts'), is an illuminating example both of a later twelfth-century classroom book and, in its subsequent circulation, of the medieval laws of supply and demand, as they applied to knowledge. In Châtillon's phrase, the *Liber* is an encyclopedia made both 'to inform and to edify'. Although this is a mark of all medieval writing, it is seen perhaps most clearly in encyclopedic works like this, where modern eyes would not see the need for morality. The *Liber* has two parts. The first (in ten books) deals with questions of philosophy ('What is the condition of rational creatures?' 'On the three types of good' etc.), geography, and history (mingling sacred and secular, for example, in lists of Roman emperors and kings of Israel). Part two is quite different. The first nine books form an allegorical commentary on selected portions of the Old Testament; book ten is made up of sermons; books eleven to fourteen conclude with interpretations of Gospel passages.

The *Liber* lives up to its name. It is not a smooth, complete exposition or exegesis of any of its topics. Neither is it a *catena* of scriptural or patristic extracts (no. 13). Rather, it is a series of short notes and lists, as though to jog the memory, quickly skimming the surface of all it touches. When there are patristic quotations these are rarely acknowledged, and have been shown mostly to have been lifted from the works of Hugh of St Victor—one of Hugh's great strengths was to act as a painless compendium of the Fathers. Partly because of this, and partly because it follows the schema of desirable knowledge laid out in the *Didascalicon*, Richard's work was often attributed to Hugh.

The 'notebook' quality is particularly evident in the section of the *Liber* which circulated separately, and had a great vogue in the schools. Books 1–9 and 11–14 of part two of the work led an independent existence as the *Allegories of the Old and New Testaments*, forming a useful reference book on the spiritual senses of Scripture. Since they provide a kind of 'spiritual'

PARCHMENT: i + 268 fols.; page 215 x 155 mm; text 2 cols., each 180 x 50 mm; 40–42 lines; one scribe, carefully correcting his own text. Ten MSS or fragments, bound together at least since Claude de Grandrue's catalogue of 1514. Binding: white leather on wooden boards. Titles in red; early Arabic folio numbers. Red, green or blue initials.

CONTENTS: fol. i^v contents-list of whole MS by Claude de Grandrue.

A: fols. 1^r–140^v Richard of St Victor, *Liber exceptionum.*

B: fols. 142^r–200^v Richard of St Victor, *Liber exceptionum*, pt 2, *Allegories.*

C-K: fols. 201^r–68^v eight fragmentary texts, mostly 13th c., including parts of Isidore, *Sentences* and *Soliloquies*, patristic excerpts, sermons and Marian material.

Both copies of Richard's work are here attributed, in 13th-c. hands, to Hugh of St Victor.

counterpart to the literal exegesis of the Bible given in Peter Comestor's *Historia Scholastica* (no. 3), the *Allegories* are also found under his name, and the two works are regularly found side-by-side. But Richard's authorship of the *Liber* fits with his absorbed interest in the spiritual senses of Scripture; he is best known today as a writer of mystical, contemplative treatises like the *Twelve Patriarchs* and the *Mystical Ark* (sometimes called the *Benjamin major* and *Benjamin minor*), which meditate on the human relationship with God.

This MS comes from the St Victor library and is thought to be closely related to Richard's original text. The *Liber* has an extensive, original set of tables of contents, covering both the books in each part of the work, and the chapters in each book. Dating Richard's works is largely guesswork, but the *Liber* was probably written between 1153 and 1162, when he became prior of St Victor.

This page shows part of the *Allegories* (*Liber*, pt. 2, bk. 3, cc. 8–9). The erasures and corrections of the scribe are clear. Chapter 8, *De furto et mendacio* [On theft and lying] is a *catena* of three common patristic definitions of theft, lying and perjury, drawn not from the originals but from Hugh's *De sacramentis.* Chapter 9, *De constructione tabernaculi* [On the construction of the tabernacle] is a set of straightforward notes giving allegorical interpretations (mid-left col.): 'Tabernaculum significat Ecclesiam. Tabule designant animas, que bene de lignis sethim esse dicuntur, quia anime et immortales sunt per naturam, et incorruptiles flunt per gratiam.' [The tabernacle signifies the Church. The tables signify souls, which are well described as being made of acacia wood because they are immortal by nature and become incorruptible through grace.]

De furto et mendacio.

Non furtum facies. Furtum accipitur in hoc loco pro qualibet illicita usurpatione rei aliene, sive occulta sive manifesta. Qui enim furtum prohibuit rapinam non concessit. Est maius peccatum sit ut testantur sancti aperte et violenter rapere quam occulte subtrahere quia maius odium et iram excitat. Sub furto et comprehenditur usura. Mendacium est falsa significatio cum voluntate fallendi. Quod vel presentialiter adest. Vel postea advenit. Nam si quis alii promittet se aliquid daturum habens voluntatem dandi cum promittet, postea vero mutata voluntate dare noluit mendacium non esset. Non quia in promissione eius duplex fuit. Sed quia promittens eius postea duplicavit. Periurium est mendacium sacrosancta attestatione inducta confirmatum.

De constructione tabernaculi.

Tabernaculum significat ecclesiam. Tabule designat animas. Que bene de lignis sethim esse dicuntur. quia anime et inmortales sunt per naturam et incorruptibiles fiunt per gratiam. Bases argentee fidem significant super quam sancta ecclesia consistit fundata. Que bases ideo non inconvenienter plures sunt. quia unicuique distribuit deus suam mensuram fidei. Alius habet fidem cognitione et affectione magnam. Alius cognitione et affectu parvam. Alius cognitione magnam et affectu parvam. Alius cognitione parvam et affectu magnam. Due bases singulis tabulis supponebantur. quia fides in duobus constat cognitione et affectu. Vel quia credimus deum esse creatorem universorum et redemptorem electorum. In constructione huius tabernaculi offerre debemus aurum, argentum, es, iacintum et cetera. Aurum pro sui fulgorem sapientiam exprimit. que in cordibus fidelium renitescit. Argentum quod dulcem et clarum habet tinnitum eloquentiam figurat. Es quia percussum magnum reddit sonum. designat predicationem per orbem terrarum longe lateque sonantem. Iacintus quia aerium sive celestem pretendit colorem celestium honorum significat spem sive celestem conversationem. Purpura corporis significat passionem ad quam pro Christo parati esse debemus. Coccus quia flammam imitatur caritatem exprimit que in cordibus sanctorum flagrascit. que bis coctus bistincti dicitur. quia per duplicem dilectionem dei videlicet et proximi coloratur. Bissus quia candore castitatem designat. Pelles que rubente significant martires. Pelles iacintine viros celestem vitam agentes. Ligna sethim viros in fide firmos. Oleum quia ceteros liquores excellit misericordiam designat. que alios virtutes transcendit. Aromata et timiamata bone fame redolentia figurant. Unguentum dulcedinem et pinguedinem sive suavitatem pretendit internam. Lapides preciosi propter sui fulgorem miraculorum significant operationem longe lateque coruscantem. Atrium significat rudimenta incoantium. Columpne fortes quosque et perfectos exprimunt viros. Decem cortine illos figurant que decalogum legis complent. Undecim saga illos designant qui per transgressionem legis asperam agunt penitentiam. Undenarius namque quia denarium transgreditur significat decalogi transgressionem. Et saga que sunt aspera penitentie designant asperitatem. Ansule quibus cortine copulabantur virtutes sunt sanctorum quibus ipsi sibi coniunguntur. Circuli aurei preciosum fulgorem future retributionis insinuant. Preciosum quod

BIBLIOGRAPHY

Richard of St Victor. Liber exceptionum, ed. J. Châtillon; *Richard of St Victor. The Twelve Patriarchs, The Mystical Ark, Book Three of the Trinity*, trans. G. Zinn; *Richard of St Victor. Selected Writings on Contemplation*, trans. C. Kirchberger; J. Châtillon, 'L'heritage littéraire de Richard de Saint-Victor'; P. S. Moore, 'The Authorship of the *Allegoriae super vetus et novum testamentum*'.

six

Pocket Bible with Jerome, *The Interpretation of Hebrew Names*

Baltimore, Walters Art Gallery, MS 23 (W. 48), fols. 1r & 481v
Paris; mid-thirteenth century

Although in school situations a copy of the Bible with the *Ordinary Gloss* was likely to be the most-used version (no. 1), the demand for plain texts did not at all die out. Bibles were still in use for liturgy and private devotion. Though the text was static, the presentation and accompaniments changed. As the mendicant orders grew in strength, so too the need increased for one-volume ('pandect') pocket-sized editions that could travel along with their users. Preachers' Bibles became small, fat copies, written on very fine 'split skin' or 'onion skin' parchment. The script is usually minute and heavily abbreviated (leading to the invention of spectacles), and yet there is generally some decoration, at least in the form of a historiated initial to begin each biblical book, reminding the reader of a key point in the story. These features still largely determine the format of printed Bibles today.

Alongside the biblical text, it became common to find a variety of useful tools in differing permutations. It is rare to find a Bible without Jerome's prologues and introductory letter to Paulinus; there may also be indexes (by topic or word), cross-references, canon tables, chapter lists and, most often, Jerome's *Interpretation of Hebrew Names*. Although some of the personal and place names of the Old Testament Hebrew text were and are thought to be meaningless, many can be literally interpreted, their meanings giving clues to, or reflecting, character or situation. These literal meanings could then be re-interpreted allegorically, adding even greater spiritual significance. Thus, for instance, Bethlehem, the birthplace of Jesus, literally means 'house of bread', which could be allegorized to mean the provider of spiritual food, that is, of Jesus, who provides himself as food for his followers in the bread of the Eucharist. For Hebrew-speakers the meaning of names could be important to understanding. Naomi makes

PARCHMENT: 523 + i (modern) fols.; page 130 x 92 mm; text 2 cols., each 92 x 30 mm; 48 lines; several scribes. Bk. names and chapter nos. in red and blue; *tituli* for psalms. Historiated or decorated initials begin all biblical books and the eight major divisions of the psalter. Elsewhere, blue and pink major initials with flourishing; minor initials alternately blue or pink.

From 'Sainte-Marie de Oliva' (probably the Cistercian abbey in Clairmont, France), fol. 523ʳ.

CONTENTS: fols. 1ʳ–481ᵛ Bible with 64 prologues; 481ᵛ–523ʳ Jerome, *The Interpretation of Hebrew Names*, beginning 'Aaz apprehendens'.

a pun on her name in the Book of Ruth: 'Call me not Naomi [beautiful], but call me Mara [bitterness], for the Lord has dealt bitterly with me'.

The ability to make the original Hebrew connections was lost on most Christians. So in order to convey the full meaning of the text, Jerome (*c.* 342–420), the outstanding textual scholar of his time, adds to his Latin translation of this passage two short interpolations or glosses, 'Naomi (that is, beautiful) . . .', and 'Mara (that is, bitterness) . . .'. But this was not an ideal solution. Finally, he solved the problem by writing his book of the *Interpretation of Hebrew Names*, which provided short explanations of proper names throughout the Bible. During the thirteenth century, the work became increasingly popular as masters became more interested in reaching back to the original texts and their literal meanings. They wanted to begin at the beginning, and that meant knowing what the original words had conveyed. Further, a growing numbers of preachers found that the interpretation of a name might well form a simple starting point for a sermon—in just the manner of the Bethlehem example, above.

The proper nouns of *Hebrew Names* could be arranged in two principal ways, either alphabetically, or by book of the Bible. Here (right-hand picture) they are alphabetical, giving the work its famous *incipit* 'Aaz apprehendens'. The combination of translation, prologues and *Hebrew Names* meant that Jerome virtually *was* the thirteenth-century Bible, and here (left-hand picture), as in hundreds of other manuscripts, he is shown in the *incipit* of the prologue, 'Frater Ambrosius', writing the book. Just as portraits of the four evangelists preceded their respective gospel books, so Jerome preceded the Old Testament which had become so much his own.

BIBLIOGRAPHY

Jerome, *Liber de nominibus hebraicis;* D. Brown, *Vir Trilinguis. A Study of the Biblical Exegesis of St Jerome;* M. Gibson, *The Bible in the Latin West;* J. N. D. Kelly, *Jerome, His Life, Writings and Controversies;* L. Light, *The Bible in the Twelfth Century: An Exhibition of Manuscripts at the Houghton Library; eadem,* 'Versions et révisions du texte biblique'.

seven

The Verbal Concordance to the Scriptures

Oxford, Bodleian Library, MS Canon. Pat. Lat. 7, fols. 48^{v}–49^{r}
Probably Paris; second half of the thirteenth century

Perhaps it was not until the peripatetic preaching practices of the newly formed orders of friars (especially the Franciscans and the Dominicans—the Order of Preachers) that a need quickly to find scriptural passages on a given word or topic was felt. Not tied to the weekly pericopes of the lectionary used in parish churches, the friars tailored their sermons much more closely to audience and circumstances. They saw the Bible as a mine of gold nuggets that, extracted and polished, could shine with the light of theological truth, dazzling onlookers. Their more spontaneous methods required new tools; they needed to be able to manipulate the biblical text on demand.

It was the Dominicans from the convent of St Jacques in Paris who rose to the challenge. First they needed a standard Bible (for chapter divisions and numbering were not yet universally agreed upon [see Smalley, *SBMA*, pp. 222–24]); then they developed tools to find their way around it. Alphabetization as such was not new: its usefulness for ordering words had not been lost on the Greeks themselves. But it was not widely applied until these thirteenth-century innovations, and especially in the verbal concordances, among the first of the reader aids produced in Paris.

A concordance lists, in alphabetical order and with references for finding them, all words used in a text. Again, the concept was not new, but the attempt to be comprehensive, coupled with the useful layout, was. The concordance shown here—the so-called St Jacques' concordance—was the first of the three types of concordance developed in the thirteenth century. It lists about 10,000 words, giving biblical references by book, chapter, and position in the text. For this, the Dominicans invented a system of dividing a chapter into seven equal sections, denoted by the letters A to G. Sometimes pages were physically marked with these letters; more often the divisions were left to the mind's eye. Until a standard system of division into verses, as well as chapters (not until the sixteenth century), this was the best biblical reference system

PARCHMENT (very thin, 'onion skin' quality): ii (paper) + 325 (19 trebled, 69 and 259 doubled; 158/59 and 248/49 the same leaf) + ii (paper) fols.; page 130 x 90 mm; text 5 cols., each 105 x 11–12 mm; 55–60 lines; ruled in lead-point; one minute hand, heavily abbreviated. Running heads in red and blue; lemmata underlined in red; red paraph signs, fols. 1^{r}–3^{r}; red and blue paraph signs, fols. 3^{v}–35^{v}. Space left for decorated initials, never added.

Belonged to Domenico Grimani (1461–1523), cardinal of St Mark's, Venice (arms added on fol. 1^{r}).

CONTENTS: fols. 1^{r}–255^{v} concordance of biblical words, arranged alphabetically; 257^{r}–320^{v} biblical concordance arranged by subject matter.

A truly pocket-sized handy reference book.

in operation. This first type of concordance is often credited to Hugh of St Cher (no. 8), but it is more likely that he was simply the director of a team of Dominican scholars creating new tools and reader technology at St Jacques. The date of the first concordance is uncertain, but they had completed their work by 1247, when William of Rouen made a copy.

Around 1252, a second type of concordance (sometimes called 'the English concordance') was made at St Jacques. The first type of concordance listed only a biblical reference to the words; this second type gave a complete lemma with the word in context. Although more informative than the first, this version took up much more room. Pocket-versions, such as the book shown here, were out of the question. It was not an immediate success. The potential of the first version, however, was instantly grasped. Although it was probably originally made for in-house, Dominican use only, the oldest surviving copies belonged to houses of Benedictines. But very wide circulation only came with the third, hybrid, concordance, made in the later part of the century, again probably by a team at St Jacques.

About thirty manuscripts of the first concordance survive (beg. Aaa. Je. Ic. xiiiid.), almost all from the mid-thirteenth century. Their layout is virtually identical. The opening shown here includes many versions of *Deus* (God). In the third version of the concordance, all the references to God are grouped together, since they can be separated by their lemmata; but here, without lemmata, it was expedient to divide them.

3rd column:
iiii R[egum] v.d.e. = 4 Kings = 2 Samuel
xvii.b.g. Iud[i]t[h].viii.
d. ps[almus].lxxx.d.
[H]ose[a].iii.b.
Deus alius (another God)
tob[it].xiii.b.
deus celi (God of the heavens)
tob[it].i.c.vii.g.
xii.c. Iudit[h].v.b

.De.

de sinistra
de sacerdotib(us).
de sacrificiis
de sanctitate
de sanctificatione
de sanctuario
de sanguine.

.De.

de sermone.
de sermonib(us).
de femoralib(us)
de sepulcris et
de silencio
de silo
de similitudine
de sole
de sompnis
de sorte
de sponsa
de spiritu
de strepitu
de stratu
de superbia
de superficie
de tenebris

.De.

de tabernaculo
de tempore
de templo
de tentatione
de terra
de terremotu

.De.

de terra aquilonis
de terra aufrica
de terra babilonis
de terra chanaan
de terra caldeorum
de terra egypti
de terra longinqua
de terra moab
de terra sichem
de torrente
de tribulatione
de tribu
de turba

.De.

de veritate
de volucre
de vulnere
de vestimento

.De.

deus abraham
deus israel
deus iacob
deus omnipotens

.De.

deus altus
deus celi
deus deorum
deus dominus
deus exercituum
deus ysaac
deus iudex
deus misericors
deus noster

.De.

deus omnipotens
deus omnium
deus patrum
deus pacis
deus rex
deus excelsus
deus salvator
deus sanctus
deus solus
deus vivens
deus verus

.De.

de venatione
de ventis
de veritate
de veste
de vestimento
de via
de vinea
de vino
de virtute
de voluntate
de volumine
de universis
de unda
de usura

vi.f.ix.g. ps[almus].xc.a

Deus deorum	(God of gods)
ps[almus].lxxxiii.d	
dan[iel].ii.f.xi.f	
iiii. R[egum].xix.a	
Deus dominus	(Lord God)
ps[almus].lxvii.f	
Deus excelsus	(highest God)
Iudit[h].xiii.e	
ps[almus].lxxvii.f	

Note that there is not simply one reference per line, and that multiple references to the same book simply carry on, e.g., Daniel chap. 2, f; 11, f.

BIBLIOGRAPHY

R. H. and M. A. Rouse, 'Biblical Distinctions in the Thirteenth Century', 'The Verbal Concordance to the Scriptures', and *Preachers, Florilegia and Sermons: Studies on the* Manipulus florum *of Thomas of Ireland.*

eight

Hugh of St Cher, *Postills on the Whole Bible*

Durham, Cathedral Library, MS A.i.16, fol. 92r
Probably French; written before 1258

If one man sums up what this book is about, it must be Hugh of St Cher. Already a doctor of canon law before studying theology and entering the Order of Preachers in 1225, his career spanned teaching (master of theology and lector at the Dominican *studium* in Paris), administration (prior of the French Dominican province, twice), and high ecclesiastical office (made cardinal in 1244, a frequent aide to the pope, and attended the Council of Lyons in 1245). His academic work centered on the Bible, and the problems of making it more accessible to other preachers. He prepared corrections to the text, worked to produce a usable concordance (no. 7), wrote a commentary on Peter Comestor's *Historia scholastica* (no. 3), and his postills on the whole Bible became the equivalent of the *Ordinary Gloss* (no. 1) for the thirteenth century. He produced not only new writings in the old modes, but new forms of text and new tools for making old texts more readily available to the new preaching orders. He did all this, it seems, not by himself, but at the head of a team of trained Dominicans, who worked under his guidance at their convent of St Jacques in Paris. A lawyer-theologian, trained at the new universities, altering books and knowledge to fit the needs of the new orders in their scholastic setting, Hugh epitomizes the changes chronicled in the rest of this book.

Hugh was not the first scholar since the *Gloss* to produce a commentary on the whole Bible; but he had the distinct advantage over someone like Stephen Langton (d. 1228) of having the publication resources of the Dominicans behind him. St Dominic himself had laid out an organizational structure for his order, which spread quickly across Europe. The Preachers insisted on learning among their friars, and this meant books and houses of study. With a well-trained production team, Dominican masters could be sure of an unparalleled circulation—and not only to houses of their own order: such ready-made utility was not likely to be sniffed at elsewhere.

PARCHMENT: ii (paper) + 218 + i (paper) fols.; page 400 x 280 mm; text 2 cols., each 275 x 85 mm; 60 lines; one scribe. Elaborate running heads and footers; notes whether the exposition is ˙t˙ ('textus' = literal) or ˙g˙ ('glosarum' = allegorical); NOTA signs; marginal headings and notes; tree diagrams in bottom margins. Lemmata underlined in red; rubrication. Catchwords. Major initials are blue and red 'jigsaw puzzle' type with a little flourishing; minor initials in blue or red with alternate color flourishing. Overall, little decoration.

MSS A.i.12 and 16 were given to Durham by prior Bertram of Middleton in 1258 (date in A.i.12).

CONTENTS: fols. 1^v–2^r lectionary list for Epistles and Rev; 2^v 'Liber sancti cuthberti ex dono Bertrami de Midelton. prioris dunelm. Epistole pauli'; 3^r–217^r Hugh of St Cher, *Postills* (Romans to Hebrews).

A marvelously usable book, clearly appreciated by its readers.

Not much is original about the postills, although they are clear, comprehensive, sensible, and popular in style, with occasional jokes and chatty asides; they proved to be immensely influential on later writers. But the word 'postills' (*postillae*) *is* thought to be a new coinage associated with Hugh and his work. Although Beryl Smalley speculated that it developed from *post illa verba* ('after these words'—the lemmata after which came the comment), the phrase is never found in commentaries themselves. It is hard to discern any consistent difference in content between a 'commentary' and a 'postill'; and although, after Hugh, the word slowly became the normal title for a scriptural commentary, it seems to be more of a librarian's description of a type of book than a name used by the commentators themselves.

This MS is part of a set of the postills (5 MSS: A.i.12–16), and was given to Durham in 1258, while Hugh was still alive. This page shows the end of the allegorical exposition of 1 Cor. 13 and the beginning of the literal ('textus') exposition of chapter 14. The new chapter is in roman numerals in the right margin. The decorator's guide letter (S) is clearly visible under the blue initial, as are the rubricator's guide dots under the underlining for each lemma—two dots to begin the line and one to finish.

(Mid-right col.) *Sectamini caritatem.* Quoniam spiritus sanctus non solum in igne apparuit in signum caritatis, sed etiam in linguis ob signum edificationis. commendata caritate mentium docet apostolus concordiam unitatis esse etiam in verbis agens de officiis lingue. Que sunt sex, scilicet, loqui, interpretari, prophetare, orare, benedicare, gratias agere. Hec omnia docet spiritus sanctus unde actus ii et ceperunt loqui variis linguis. . . . [*Pursue love.* For the holy spirit appeared not only in fire, as a sign of love, but also in tongues as a sign of instruction; the apostle teaches that concord of unity, protected by the charity of minds, is effective even in words doing the duties of the tongue. These are sixfold, namely, to speak, to interpret, to prophesy, to pray, to bless and to give thanks. The holy spirit teaches all of these, hence Acts 2: 'and they began to speak in various tongues. . .'].

clio. ii [illegible] euacuatur. So [illegible] in illo p medium.
p speculum [illegible] ima q̄ sū medio [illegible] speculum [illegible]
[illegible] p speculum [illegible] in speculo
[illegible] p speculum [illegible]
[illegible] uider p speculum [illegible] ymagine q̄ ei appar; i spe
clo [illegible] in speculo n̄ cogitat de se s;
cū de illa ymagine [illegible] illam [illegible]
[illegible] ymagine sua [illegible] in speculo re
flectit ad se [illegible] de se cogitat [illegible] se uidet in speculo.
[illegible] per illam ymaginē de se [illegible] sua cogitat [illegible]
destruetur de q̄ scia [illegible] de scia [illegible]

[illegible]

de. i. in egmeneuein.

[S]cietatum [illegible] qui [illegible] in igne apparuit [illegible]
[illegible] edificationes [illegible]
[illegible]
[illegible]
[illegible]
[illegible] loqui linguis [illegible]
[illegible] linguis [illegible]
& ce. musicor̄ instrumēta tybie. cythare. tube. In [illegible]
[illegible] dona maiora [illegible]
[illegible]

[illegible]

BIBLIOGRAPHY

There are unfortunately no modern editions of the postills, but there are several good 16th-c. ones, including Paris 1533–39 and Paris 1545; W. H. Principe, *Hugh of St Cher's Theology of the Hypostatic Union;* B. Smalley, 'Some Thirteenth-century Commentators on the Sapiential Books'.

B

Sources

nine

Augustine, *On Christian Doctrine* (*De doctrina Christiana*)

Chicago, Newberry Library, MS 12.1, fol. 37^{r}
English; mid-twelfth century

It would be hard to overestimate the influence of Augustine of Hippo (354–430). If all philosophy is a footnote to Plato, then all theology is a footnote to Augustine. He himself thought it astounding that his God had worked through a provincial pagan who had become Christian via the unorthodox Manichaean sect, and was bishop of an ancient African town. That we know his view of events—and much of his life—is due to his remarkable autobiography, the *Confessions* (*c.* 400), remarkable for his having written it, in an age unaccustomed to such things, as well as for its intrinsic merit.

Augustine's enormous written legacy, addressing all the issues of early Christianity, and directly confronting the major heresies of his day, gave both skeleton and flesh to subsequent Christian doctrine, and to its study. It is almost ridiculous to single out any one of his works for inclusion here. He is not a writer remembered for only a fraction of his output—he was actively quoted across a huge range of his work: *The City of God*, the *Enchiridion*, *Notes on the Psalms*, *The Trinity*, *The Literal Meaning of Genesis*, writings against Donatists, Pelagians and Manichaeans, and endless sermons and letters on every possible topic. Nothing human was foreign to Augustine; and he wrote about it all. Only straight biblical study, where his contemporary Jerome was much more linguistically skilled and scholarly, did he leave to someone else. Even then, his sermons are largely exegesis and development of readings from Scripture.

None of this was strictly 'academic'. Most of his writing was done while priest and then bishop of Hippo, in response to the questions posed by circumstances and correspondents throughout the Mediterranean. He lived in worrying times. Scarcely had Constantine (d. 337) made Christianity the official religion of the (Roman) Empire than Alaric and his Goths were

PARCHMENT: i (modern) + 120 + i (modern) fols.; page 260 x 190 mm; text 180 x 110 mm; 31 lines; drypoint ruling; one scribe. Titles in red; chapter divisions in *De doctrina* marked with 14th-c. Arabic numerals in margins; catchwords; paraph marks, heads etc. added later. Original table of contents now pasted on back flyleaf. Three caution notes for loans made to William de Borghildbiri at Oxford, dated 1325, 1326, 1327 (fol. 120^{v}). Blue, green, and red patterned initials.

Made in or for St Mary's Benedictine abbey, Reading (fol. 1^{r}); William de Borghildbiri (fol. 120^{v}); bought by Newberry in 1937.

CONTENTS: fols. 1^{r}–34^{r} Augustine, *True Religion;* 34^{r-v} *idem, Retractions,* II.30; 34^{v}–104^{v} *idem, On Christian Doctrine;* 104^{v}–18^{r} Ps.-Augustine, *Against Felicianus;* 118^{r-v} Ps.-Augustine, *Sermon 235.*

storming the gates of Rome (410). Augustine needed to be certain of the ground he was standing on. As an adult convert himself (his saintly mother Monica fretted over his early paganism), he was very much concerned with the propagation of the faith. His first training and career had been in rhetoric; he agonized over whether it was right to use his education in grammar and composition in Christian service, but he could not help himself. *On Christian Doctrine* is his successful attempt to build alongside the classical scheme of learning and culture a new Christian alternative.

His background led Augustine to depreciate the pagan learning later revived in the twelfth-century schools; having delimited it, he judges most of it unsuitable and unnecessary for Christians. His primary criterion for suitability is the usefulness of knowledge for the interpretation of the Bible, for Augustine regards the study of Scripture as the way to perfection for ordinary believers. The purpose of learning is not knowledge *per se*, but the increase of love, since in the end, if we love God, we may do as we please—our will will be what pleases God ('Dilige et quod vis fac', *In epist. Joann., tr. 7.8, PL* 35:2033C).

On Christian Doctrine begins (bk. I.2) with a famous distinction that has resurfaced and reverberated in modern semiotic theory (line 4):

> Omnis doctrina vel rerum est vel signorum. Sed res per signa discuntur. Proprie autem nunc res appellavi quae non ad significandum aliquid adhibentur. . . . Sunt autem alia signa, quorum omnis usus in significando est, sicuti sunt verba. Nemo enim utitur verbis, nisi aliquid significandi gratia. [All knowledge is either of things or of signs. But things are learned about through signs. Properly speaking, however, I have called 'things' only whatever cannot be made to signify something else. . . . There are, however, other signs whose only use is to signify something else, as is the case with words. For no one uses words except to signify something else.]

accreuit. sic ea que ad hoc opus aggrediendum iam dominus prebuit. cum dispensari ceperint: eo ipso suggerente multiplicabuntur. ut in ipso hoc nostro ministerio non solum nullam patiamur inopiam: sed de mirabili abundantia gaudeamus. Omnis doctrina: uel rerum est uel signorum. Sed res per signa discuntur. Proprie autem nunc res appellaui. que non ad significandum aliquid adhibentur: sicuti est lignum. lapis. pecus. atque huiusmodi talia. Sed non illud lignum quod in aquas amaras moysen misisse legimus. ut amaritudine carerent. neque ille lapis quem iacob sibi ad caput posuit: neque illud pecus quod pro filio immolauit abraham. Hec namque ita res sunt: ut aliarum etiam signa sint rerum. Sunt autem alia signa. quorum omnis usus in significando est: sicuti sunt uerba. Nemo enim utitur uerbis: nisi aliquid significandi gratia. Ex quo intelligitur quid appellem signa. res eas uidelicet: que ad significandum aliquid adhibentur. Quam ob rem omne signum. etiam res aliqua est. Quod enim nulla res est: omnino nichil est. Non autem omnis res etiam signum est. Et ideo in hac diuisione rerum atque signorum cum de rebus loquimur ita loquimur: ut etiam si earum alique adhiberi ad significandum possint. non impediant partitionem. qua prius de rebus. postea de signis disseremus. Memoriterque teneamus id nunc in rebus considerandum esse quod sunt: non quod aliud etiam preter se ipsas significant. Res ergo alie sunt quibus fruendum est: alie quibus utendum. alie que fruuntur et utuntur. Ille quibus fruendum est: nos beatos faciunt. Istis quibus utendum est tendentes ad beatitudinem adiuuamur. et quasi adminiculamur: ut ad illas que nos beatos faciunt peruenire atque his inherere possimus. Nos uero qui fruimur et utimur inter utrasque constituti. si eis quibus utendum est frui uoluerimus: impeditur cursus noster. et aliquando etiam deflectitur: ut ab his rebus quibus fruendum est obtinendis. uel retardemur uel etiam reuocemur. inferiorum amore prepediti. Frui enim est: amore inherere alicui rei propter

nota res et signa distincte

nemo utitur uerbis nisi significandi gratia

nota distinctionem fruendi et utendi

BIBLIOGRAPHY

De doctrina christiana, ed. J. Martin; *De doctrina christiana*, ed. G. M. Green; *On Christian Doctrine*, trans. D. W. Robertson; P. Brown, *Augustine of Hippo;* H. Chadwick, *Augustine;* R. A. Markus, *Speculum: History and Society in the Theology of St Augustine;* H. Marrou, *S. Augustin et la fin de la culture antique.*

ten

Gregory the Great, *Moralia in Iob*

Manchester, John Rylands University Library, MS 83, fol. 130^r
Written in 914 at San Pedro de Cardeña, near Burgos: dated colophon, fol. 80^v

Born (*c.* 540) the son of a Roman senator, Gregory liquidated the family wealth, founded seven monasteries, and entered the last, in Constantinople, himself. He hoped to live a life of seclusion, but was forced by the pope to return to Rome, to labor within the papal bureaucracy, for he had a justified reputation as a good organizer. In 590 he found himself, unwillingly, pope. Gregory I (the Great) applied his administrative talents to the papal see, actively promoting the Church's claims to temporal, as well as spiritual, power, extending her boundaries (he is famously remembered for the conversion of England and his Latin pun, 'non Angli sed angeli' (not Angles [English] but angels!) and upholding the Western Church's claim to independence from the Eastern Orthodox. But he was not simply a papal prince: he spent a great deal of money in charitable works (he first used the phrase 'servant of the servants of God' to describe the pope), wrote a highly influential treatise on pastoral care, and reformed the Western liturgy, where his name is remembered in 'Gregorian chant'.

The *Moralia* are Gregory's earliest long work. They began life as a series of homilies preached to Leander of Seville and his brother monks, interpreting the book of Job. In the preface, written five years after he had begun, Gregory describes the process of creation: the first sermons were preached *ex tempore* and noted down by the monks; later sermons were dictated by Gregory before he preached them, although he took care to maintain a colloquial tone. Here he intended to stop; but he was persuaded to revise and edit the whole series. He never quite finished the task, but nevertheless sent the work to scribes for copying, sometime before April 591.

There were no real Christian models for interpreting Job; no previous author had covered the whole book, so Gregory was largely on his own. The monks had specified a *moral* interpretation of the book, which they could apply to their own lives as an aid to ascetic practice and contemplation. Although grounded in Job, Gregory allowed himself to range over the

PARCHMENT: iii (modern) + 360 + iii (modern) fols.; fol. 214 inserted later (mid-10th c.) to fill a lacuna; early leaves much affected by damp; page 410 x 300 mm; text 2 cols., each 315 x 105 mm; 47 lines; three Visigothic scribes. 1: fols. 1^r–213^v, 242^v–361^r = Gomez; 2: fols. 215^r–42^r; 3: 214^{r-v} = archpresbyter Aeximinus. Lemmata from Job written in red; running heads and titles in color as well as ink of text; quire numbers in Roman numerals; many contemporary marginal notes. Many small decorative initials in green, red, yellow and white. Mostly abstract; but those on fols. written by scribe 2 are also anthropo- and zoomorphic.

From the collection of Count Libri (1802–69) and therefore probably originally stolen; eventually bought by Rylands in 1901.

CONTENTS: fols. 1^r–20^v (fragmentary) Gregory, *Moralia in Iob,* beginning imperf. bk. iv.6; 21^r–214^v *Moralia* bks. 7–22; 214^v ?12th-c. drawing of wheel of Fortune; 215^r–361^r *Moralia* bks. 23–35 (ends imperf.).

Aeximinus' script demonstrates the first evidence of a *graphically* presented difference between assibilated and unassibilated 'i' sounds.

A marvelous early Spanish book.

whole of Christian life and doctrine, using Job as a figure of the Church and of Christ. Gregory confined his quoted sources to Scripture, but the work shows a deep knowledge of both the Eastern and Western Christian traditions, with a particular debt to Augustine. The *Moralia* were phenomenally successful, surviving in hundreds of manuscripts from the seventh century onward.

This page shows the end of bk. 15 and the beginning of bk. 16. The quotations from Job are clearly visible in red. The script exhibits many distinctive letter forms and ligatures, e.g., t, a, ti, ec. This excerpt begins bk. 16 (mid left col.):

> Qui contra veritatis verba in allegatione deficiunt, sepe etiam nota replicant ne tacendo victi videantur. Unde elifaz beati Iob sermonibus pressus, ea dicit que nullus ignorat. Ait enim, "Numquid deo comparari potest homo, etiam quum perfectae fuerit scientie?" In conparatione etenim dei, scientia nostra ignorantia est. ex dei namque participatione sapimus, non conparatione.' [Those who oppose the words of truth make a poor show of argument, often repeating themselves in case, by staying silent, they seem to be defeated. Whence Eliphaz, caught out by blessed Job's words, says things which no one does not know. For he says: 'Can a man be compared to God, even when he has perfect knowledge?' (Job 22:2). In comparison to God, indeed, our knowledge is ignorance. For we become wise by participation in God, not by comparison with God.]

ticula et unitate sibi innumerabiles. Quia
et tunc mistice tollitur cum omni saeculari
et nunc amplius diripitur cum corda omnium non invadit. Haec beatus Iob quia
contra iniquorum principem mente disseruit
qui in hac vita extolli permittitur sed in
adventum domini detruditur. Decrepitantes
ostendit quia flagella dominica non et offen-
sione susceperit. quoniam si iniquus quisque in hac
vita permittitur prosperari, necesse est
ut electus dei debeat sub flagello freno re-
tineri. Sequitur unico sicut qua dicens.
Quomodo igitur consolamini me frustra,
cum responsio vestra repugnare ostensa sit
veritati. Amici beati Iob eum
consolari non poterant, in quorum magis sermonibus veritati contrariabantur. Qui namque hunc
hypocritam vel impium dicerent, pro hoc
quod ipsi meritis eius per peccata tribuant culpam
augebant, procul dubio poenam laesi vul-
neribus adfligebant. Num sanctorum merita quia
veritatem diligunt, etiam culpe fallacie torquet ulcere. Quamvis enim grave
mendacii esse crimen aspiciunt, tamen
hoc non solum in se sed etiam in aliis oderunt.

EXPLICIT LIBER PAPE GREGORII XV
INCIPIT LIBER EIUSDEM XVI

Cap. XX

Qui contra veritatem in nulla usque locutione
deficiunt, saepe et tamen nocentius replicant
ne tacendo victi videantur.
Unde Eliphaz beati Iob
sermonibus pressus adicit aut nullus
ignorat. Ait enim: Numquid deo comparari
potest homo, etiam cum perfectae fuerit scientiae?
In comparatione etenim dei scientia nostra
ignorantia est. Ex dei namque participa-
tione superni non conparatione. Quid
ergo mirum quia illud quasi pro doctrina
dicitur, quod sciri poterat etiam si tacetur,
quia adhuc de eo potentiam quasi defendendo
sublinguit? Quid prodest deo si iustus
fueris, aut quid ei confers si immaculata
fuerit via tua? In omne quippe quod
bene agimus nosmet ipsos non illum
dominum iuvamus. Unde et per psalmistam dicitur: Dixi domino deus meus es tu quoniam bonorum
meorum non indiges. Ipse enim vere nobis
dominus qui vere vivit est deus, qui bono non indiget servi viventis, sed bonitatem confert
quam recipiat, ut oblata bonitas non ipsi
sed prius accipientibus et post reddentibus
prosit. Nam et si in iudicio dominus veniens
dicit: Quamdiu fecistis uni de his fratribus
meis minimis mihi fecistis, mirum hoc pie-
tatis loquitur, et suorum conpassione
membrorum et ipse nos per hoc quod caput nostrum
est adiuvat, quod per suo bono opere in suis
membris adiuvatur. Adhuc adiungit
Eliphaz quod nullus ignorat dicens: Numquid ti-
et veniet tecum in iudicium
more arguet te? Quis hoc vel desipiens
senciat quod dominus ex timore nos arguat,
et ex metu contra nos suum iudicium pro-
ponat? Sed quia verbosa mentis intercidunt
procul dubio ad otiosa dicta delabuntur.
In quibus si se minime reprehendunt,
statim ad noxia et contumeliosa prosi-
liunt. Unde Eliphaz qui otiosa in alia
ad contumeliosa protinus verba prorumpit
dicens: Et non propter malitiam tuam
plurimam et infinitas iniquitates tuas.
Ecce vitiorum paenitet corde ad verba venit
otiosa. Ab otiosis etenim verbis per mentem
fallacie ad contumeliam exurit. Isti
quippe sunt cuius culpe crementis ut in
qua cum non reteriniquitatur, nequaquam
ubi ceciderit iaceat, sed semper ad deteriora
descendit. Et unde que sublimi causa
quam valde laxauisse torrum putentur et po-
tenda validatorium non sunt. Sed quia
amicos beati Iob hereticorum speciem diximus
ipsum vero significationem sancte ecclesie generalem
hominum nunc Eliphaz verba quomodo hostium
eorum falsitati congruunt, demonstrantur.
Num sequitur: Abstulisti enim pignus
fratrum tuorum sine causa et nudos spoliasti
vestibus; aquam lasso non dedisti, et esu-
rienti subtraxisti panem. In fortitudine
brachii tui possidebas terram, et potentis-
simus obtinebas eam. In scriptura hoc loco
appellatione pignoris aliquando dona

BIBLIOGRAPHY

S. Gregorii magni. Moralia in Iob libri I–X, ed. M. Adriaen; *Grégoire le Grand. Morales sur Job,* ed. A. de Gaudemaris and R. Gillet; *Morals on the Book of Job,* trans. C. Marriott; R. A. Markus, *Gregory the Great and His World;* B. Shailor, 'The Scriptorium of San Pedro de Cardeña'.

eleven

Ambrose of Milan, *Letters*

Oxford, Bodleian Library, MS Bodl. 866, fol. 153^{r}
S. French; eleventh century

Early 'Fathers' of the Christian Church were educated in the Roman tradition of the liberal arts. These included the arts of letter writing, composition and grammar. Just as Cicero, Seneca or Pliny had written letters for public as well as private circulation (publishing them, in effect), so too the letters of the Latin Fathers circulated as a means of instruction and exhortation. Ambrose (339–397), the son of a Roman civil servant in Trier, trained to be a statesman himself in Rome. While still taking lessons in the Christian religion, he was pressed by the Church in Milan, the imperial capital, to become their bishop. This he did with consummate skill for the next twenty-three years, becoming known throughout the Roman world.

His considerable body of writing was produced in response to the needs of his busy episcopate, and includes exegesis, dogmatic theology (often written to rebut the Arian sect, strong in Milan throughout his ministry), and moral writings such as his famous work on virginity. Unfortunately, fewer than one hundred of his letters survive; but being addressed to emperors (he knew four), bishops, provincial synods, priests, laymen and his sister Marcellina, they do reflect the range of his life. Many of the letters deal with the interpretation of Scripture, but he also writes 'news' to his sister, moral instruction and official requests or complaints.

PARCHMENT: iii + 166 fols.; page 260 x 170 mm; text 200 x 110 mm; frame-ruled in drypoint; 35 lines; one scribe for the Letters. Three volumes (fols. 1^{r}–48^{v}; 49^{r}–153^{v}; 154^{r}–165^{v}) bound together since the late 12th c. (table of contents written by Bernard Hier, d. 1225, librarian of the abbey of St Martial, Limoges, fol. iii^{v}). The Letters are in vol. 2. Binding: 12th-c. white leather on wooden boards. Titles in red (exceptionally, fol. 121^{v}, in blue). Vol. 2 has some quire nos. (Roman numerals) at bottom center, beginning at quire 6 (fol. 97^{v}), which are correct according to the old foliation of the volume, although two read 'xi'. Occasional NOTA signs, pointing hands, and scattered later notes by John Lipomano and John Tiptoft. Red initial with acanthus leaf decoration (fol. 50^{r}); spaces left in *De officiis* for capitals, not executed. The sermons, letters and epitaph begin with plain red initials, some with slight decoration. From fol. 124^{r} there are rubricator's instructions in the margins, not always executed.

By the late 12th c. it belonged to the abbey of St Martial, Limoges (fol. iii^{r}); acquired by John Lipomano (Venetian; student in Oxford in 1425; owner's note, fol. ii^{r}), who brought it to England; probably bought by John Tiptoft, earl of Worcester, while studying in Oxford, 1440–44; presented to the Bodleian by the dean and canons of Windsor, 1612.

CONTENTS: fol. iii^{v} late 12th-c. table of contents for all three volumes.

A: fols. 1^{r}–45^{v} Augustine, *On the Sermon on the Mount;* 45^{v}–48^{r} Jerome, sermon on the Assumption (imperf.).

B: fols. 50^{r}–119^{r} Ambrose, *De officiis;* 119^{r}–42^{v} three short treatises attrib. to Ambrose; 143^{r}–53^{v} Ambrose, *Letters,* CSEL 82, nos. 1–7.

C: fols. 154^{r}–65^{v} Hildebert, poem on the Mass [*PL* 171:1177–1196], followed by three short poems also attrib. to him.

This page shows the end (note the *vale* near the top of the page) of letter six, to Irenaeus, and the beginning of letter seven, to Simplicianus. Simplicianus was a priest who had instructed him as a Christian *catechumen* (or learner) and stayed with him when he was made bishop. Simplicianus was clearly an extraordinary man, responsible for the conversion of Augustine and Marius Victorinus, as well as Ambrose. He was made bishop of Milan after Ambrose's death. Four letters to him from Ambrose survive. This one is a response to his questions about the interpretation of 1 Cor. 7:23. Like most of Ambrose's exegesis, it is heavily allegorical.

In the right-hand margin are two sets of rubricator's instructions (a*m*b*rosius* si*m*plicano sal*utem*: Ambrose to Simplicianus, Greetings!), which have not been followed for this letter, since there is no heading in the text, although space has been left. At other letters, the heading has been added in red, like the initial *P*(*roximo*) here. The text next to the pointing hand speaks of the 'fatherly love' existing between Ambrose and Simplicanus. At the bottom of the page, a reader has bracketed text he thought important:

> Sapiens enim non metu frangitur, non potestate mutatur, non atollitur prosperis, non tristibus mergitur. Ubi enim sapientia, ibi virtus animi, ibi constantia et fortitudo. Sapiens ergo idem est animo. [For a wise man is not crushed by fear, nor changed by power, nor

suis etiã ipse rex ægiptiorũ in potestate dat' cui cõ-
paratione moyses d's estimatus ē. imperans regnis
subiciens sibi potestates. Unde ei legim' dictũ. Faciã
te in dm̃ regi pharaoni. Vale. & nos ut facis quasi filius dilige. Contuli.

PRoxime cũ ueteris amoris usu familiaris int nos ser-
mo cederet. delectari te insinuasti m. cũ aliqd de
pauli apli scriptis corã poplo ad disputandũ assumere.
qd ei' pfundũ in cõsiliis uix cõphendat' sublime in senten
tiis. Audientẽ erigat. disputantẽ accendat. tũ q̃ impleris
que ita se ipse suis exponat sermonib; ut his q tractat
nichil inueniat qd adiciat suũ. Ac si uelit aliquid dicere
gramatici magis quã disputatoris fungatur munere.
Ideo tam̃ qm̃ & ueteris affectũ amicicie. & qd plus ē patne
grẽ amorẽ recognosco. Nã uetustas habet aliquid cũ pluri-
mis cõsociabile ē. patrius amor nõ habet. Tũ q̃ nõ ieiunem
me fecisse ii qd postulas arbitratus es. Parebo uoluntati
tue admonitus pserti & puocat' exẽplo meo qd m̃ nõ diffi-
cillimũ. q̃ nõ magnũ aliquẽ sed me ipsũ imitabor. cũ in
meos nõ magnos aliquos usus reuertor. Et de cõsiliis
qdẽ cũ beate uite imago atq; effigies nrõ sermone exp-
meret. putam' eã factã cõplexione ut pluribus forsitan
alias tibi certe amanti nri nõ inpbem. Licet diffibili-
us sit tuo iudicio quã plurimũ non displicere. sed iudi-
cii pondus affectu ablevas eoq; m̃ blandior. hec aut̃ epla
qm̃ te absentẽ offendit de sententiis pauli ē apli. q nos a seruitute in libertatẽ uocat dicens. p̃cio empti estis. nolite
fieri serui hominũ. Ostendens libtatẽ nrãm in xp̃o ēē.
sapientie. Que sententia magna a filosophis fluctuata
atq; iactata ē disputacionis molimine dicentib;. Quod omnis
sapiens lib omis aut̃ insipiens seruiat. Sed multo hoc
p'us dd dix. q ait. Stultus sic luna mutat. Sapiens eni
nõ metu frangit. nõ potestate mutat. nõ atollit psppis.
nõ tristib; mergit. Ubi eni sapientia ibi uirt' animi.
ibi cõstantia & fortitudo. Sapiens g idẽ ẽ animo non

elated by good fortune, nor overwhelmed by sadness. For where there is wisdom there is strength of spirit, there is perseverance and fortitude. The wise man, then, is constant in spirit.]

BIBLIOGRAPHY

Sancti Ambrosii Opera, part 10: *Epistulae,* ed. O. Faller and M. Zelzer; *St Ambrose. Letters,* trans. M. Beyenka; *Duke Humfrey's Library and the Divinity School 1488–1988,* exhibition catalogue, no. 64; N. B. McLynn, *Ambrose of Milan.*

twelve

Isidore of Seville, *Etymologies*

London, British Library, MS Harley 2686, fol. 68v
Probably French; late ninth century

The word 'encyclopedia' derives from the Greek for 'circle of knowledge', and some scholars consider the comprehensive works of Aristotle to be the first example of the genre; but long before full knowledge of Aristotle had reached the medieval West, Isidore's *Etymologies* had carved out a central place in the transmission of knowledge. Isidore (*c.* 560–636) was a Spanish monk and archbishop of Seville, known as the most learned man of his age. His massive literary output included biblical exegesis, theology, works of history and treatises on the liberal arts. The *Etymologies* was his attempt to produce a compendium of all the knowledge of the time, and the work for which he was best known. It was left unfinished at his death and was completed later, possibly by Bishop Braulio of Saragossa.

The *Etymologies* is divided into twenty books covering every possible topic, from God, philosophers and poets, to minerals, buildings and food. Each book treats its topic by considering the etymology of certain key words. It aims not to be novel or ground-breaking, but to preserve the knowledge of the ancients in the uncertain times of the seventh century. To this end, Isidore was prepared to use whatever learning came to hand; he does not simply copy his sources, but twists them to fit his comprehensive purpose. Indeed, in his desire to cover all topics, some of his information is more than a little suspect. Nevertheless, the false shared in the popularity of the true, since both were combined in that form preferred by students throughout history—the one-volume collected work. Even when spurious, the Greek etymologies and the definitions derived from them had the virtue of pedigree (they had been wrong for a long time!), as well as providing a jumping-off point for any subsequent discussion. The Greek words used in the text (although often transliterated or badly garbled) provided a satisfactory aura of mystery and learning which lasted until the revival of linguistic studies in the twelfth century.

PARCHMENT: iii (paper) + 225 + iii (paper) fols.; leaves missing after fols. 12, 223, 224; page 330 x 230 mm; text 2 cols., each 265 x 85 mm; frame-ruled in drypoint; 36 lines; several, mostly small and even, hands (fol. 183^r names an 'Adalgarius, subdeacon'). Red chapter headings; chapter nos. (Roman numerals) in margins; lists of chapters before each book. Carefully (and necessarily) corrected. Greek either transliterated or garbled. Three good, full-page diagrams, fols. 102^v–3^v. Initial with interlace and birds' heads (fol. 5^r) in ochre, green and ?red; elsewhere, capitals in ink of text infilled or outlined in ochre or emerald green.

Bought for Edward Harley, earl of Oxford, by his librarian, Humfrey Wanley, in 1724.

CONTENTS: fols. 1^r–4^r six letters between Braulio, bishop of Saragossa, and Isidore, the last of which is sometimes called the preface to the *Etymologies;* 4^r 10th-c. verse about the Cross; 5^r–225^v Isidore, *Etymologies,* missing parts of bks. 1 and 20; 225^v short epitaph composed by Pope Damasus I for himself (here apparently incorporated into the *Etymologies*), followed by an incomplete epitaph for St Monica.

This comprehensive collection of revered knowledge, presented in a handy format, made the *Etymologies* enormously popular in the Middle Ages, both earlier, when theologians had little else to consult, and later, when their interests widened to encompass the natural world. Subsequent encyclopedias, such as Hrabanus Maurus' ninth-century *De universo,* were often little more than copies. The greatest thirteenth-century encyclopedia, Vincent of Beauvais' *Speculum maius,* relied heavily on extracts from Isidore supplied by its patron, Louis IX. The more than 1,000 surviving manuscripts of the *Etymologies* divide into three distinct families of texts, known as the Frankish (complete), the Italian (contracted), and the Spanish (interpolated) versions.

Our manuscript is from the Frankish family. The right-hand column of the page shows the beginning of book 7, about God (*De Deo*), starting with a list of the fourteen chapters it contains. It goes on:

> Beatissimus Hieronimus [altered from beatus hilarius], vir eruditissimus et multarum linguarum [three words added on line above] peritus, ebreorum nominum interpretatur [Latin here usually reads interpretationem] primus in lat[inam] lingua[m] convertit. Ex quibus pro brevitate praetermissis multis quedam huic operi adiectis interpretationibus interponenda studui. Vocabulorum enim expositio satis ind[icat] quid vellint [usually reads velit] intellegi. [The most blessed Jerome, a most learned man expert in many languages, interpreted the Hebrew proper names which he was the first to translate into Latin. I have diligently inserted in this work many interpretations which were fit to be included but were omitted for the sake of brevity. For the exposition of words discloses enough to be understood what they might be concealing (*or* discloses well enough what he might wish to be understood).]

Note the use of ampersand (&) in the middle of a word as an abbreviation for *et.*

Reconciliatio uero ē. qui p̄ conplementū paenitentię adhibetur. Nam sicut conciliamur dō quando primū a gentilitate conuertimur. Ita reconciliamur quando p̄ peccatū paenitendo regredimur.

Exhomologesis grec̄ nomine dicitur quod latini confessio int̄pretatur. cuius nominis duplex significatio aut enim in laudem intellegitur confessio sicut ē confitebor tibi dn̄e pat̄ caeli & terrę Aut dū quisque confitetur sua peccata ab eo indulgentia cuius indifficiens ē. misericordia. Ex hoc igitur nomine grec̄ exprimitur & frequentatur exhomologesis. qua delictū nr̄m dn̄o confitemur. non quidem ut ignoro cuius cognitioni nihil occultū sed confessio ē rei &iam eiusque ignoratur p̄fessa cognitio ut tale enim sibi acta. e[illegible]ndū quisquā esse existimauerat rapere adulterari furaris. sed ubi hoc &ern̄e damnationis obnoxia ē cognouit cognitis. his confitetur errorem. Confessio aut̄ erroris p̄fessio ē disinendi. Dissinendum ergo ē apeccatis. dū confessio ē. Confessio aut̄ antecaedit. remissio seq̄r. Caeterū extra ueniā ē qui pec & cognouit non cognitū confitetur. Itaque exhomolo p̄sternendi & humilificandi hominis disciplina ē. habitu & uictu sacco & cinere incubare. corpus sordib; obscurare. animā moerorib; dicere. Illa quę peccant tristi tractione motare.

Laetanię aut̄ grec̄ nomine dicunt̄ q̄ lat̄ dicuntur rogationes. Int̄ laetanias uero & exhomologesin hoc dē fert. quod exhomologesin p̄ sola confessione peccatorū agitur. Laetanię uero q̄ inducant̄ p̄pter rogandū dm̄ & inpetrendū in aliquo misericordiā ei. sed nunc iam utrūq; nomen sub una designe habetur. non distat ulgo utrū laetanię an̄ exhomologesin indicantur. Supplicationes aut̄ nom̄ quodāmodo nunc ex gentilitate retinetur. Nam feriae aut legitime erant apud eos aut indictę. Indictę aut̄ q̄ pauptas antiqua romanorū ex conlatione sacrificabant. aut terte de bonis damnatorū unde sub plitia dicunt̄ subplicationes quę fiebant de bonis pauperū suplitia. Sacre enim res de reb; execratorū fiebant

EXPLICIT VI INCIPIT VII LIB

I DEDO [de multarū linguarū]

Beatissimus hieronimus uir eruditissimus peritus ebreorū nominū int̄pretatur primū in lat ling conuer[illegible] ex quib; pro breuitate p̄termissis [illegible]tis quędam huic operi adiectis [illegible] pretationib; int̄ ponenda studui Uocabulorū enim expositio [illegible] quid uellint intellegi. habi[illegible]

BIBLIOGRAPHY

Isidori Hispalensis episcopi. Etymologiarum sive originum, ed. W. M. Lindsay; G. B. Ford, *The Letters of Isidore of Seville;* J. Fontaine, *Isidore de Séville et la culture classique dans l'Espagne wisigothique;* R. L. Collison, *Encyclopaedias: Their History throughout the Ages.*

thirteen

Florilegium: Defensor of Liège, *Liber scintillarum*

London, British Library, MS Royal 7 C. IV, fol. 50^r^
English; early eleventh century

It was part of the success of the early Church Fathers that they considered so many aspects of Christian thought and life in comprehensive detail. From the nature of God to the right manner of eating and drinking, nothing was too great or too small; everything had its place in the Christian worldview. For the scholar dedicated to learning, and with the ability to understand Latin (the universal language of the Church and of the educated), the works of the Fathers were a jewel-house of knowledge. But for the less able, or those with less time to spend, the riches were available as ready-made necklaces, with chains (*catenae*) of brilliants hewn from the treasures, and strung together in a variety of forms. Some are simple gatherings of favorite or useful sayings; others are excerpts from a particular author; the most sophisticated are proto-*Sentences* books (no. 18), collecting together brief quotations under particular headings. They are generally known as *florilegia:* bunches of flowers. Many of these collections exist in unique copies or at most in a few examples. A few had greater popularity and circulation: the *Liber scintillarum* (a *scintilla* is a spark or sparkling thing, and the image created in the title is of bright gems or flashing points of light) was probably the most influential of its type, still extant in over 360 MSS.

Such a compilation requires wide reading and a good command of sources, and so it is not surprising that the *Liber* has been attributed to Isidore, Cassiodorus, and Bede. Working from a MS from Monte Cassino, however, the great seventeenth-century Benedictine scholar Jean Mabillon discovered a prologue ascribing the text to an eighth-century monk named Defensor, from the monastery of St Martin, Ligugé, in Poitou, who made the work at the request of his abbot, Ursin, later bishop of Autun: 'I have avidly collected sparkling quotations as though they were pearls or gems.'

PARCHMENT: iv (paper) + 107 + iv (paper) fols.; page 315 x 195 mm (but many pages cut down to 270 x 145 mm); text 235 x 120 mm; 26 lines; drypoint ruling; one beautiful hand. The bifolia have been bound in the wrong order; about seven are missing. For correct order see EETS edition, below. Plain red or green capitals; red title, chapter nos. in Roman numerals and chapter headings; sources (e.g., *Hieronimus dixit*) named in red.

Belonged to Christ Church Canterbury (fol. 1r); Br. T. Asceford (fol. 106r); John Apsley of Thakeham, Sussex (fol. 19r; d. 1587); John, Lord Lumley (fol. 1r; d. 1609); thence to Royal collection.

CONTENTS: fols. 1r–100v Florilegium, *Liber scintillarum* (*inc.* 'Deus dicit in evangelio') with Anglo-Saxon interlinear translation; 100v Isidore of Seville, *Sentences,* excerpts from bk. 2 (*PL* 83:606); 100v–6r anonymous notes, *inc.* 'Hic pauca incipiunt de vitiis et peccatis'.

A book whose utility is exceeded only by its beauty.

Also known by its first words, *De caritate. Dominus dicit in evangelio* (About charity. The Lord says in the Gospel), the *Liber* groups its texts under eighty-one headings of remarkable variety. As well as such expected theological topics as charity, patience, humility and pride, we find practical issues like tithes, drunkenness and oaths, and a few oddities such as 'about doctors and rulers' or 'on reading'. There is no clearly discernible order to the subjects covered. The authorities quoted cover seventeen sources (Greek and Latin), including Basil, Ephraim, Eusebius and Cyprian, as well as the more usual Augustine, Josephus, Caesarius and Jerome. The first quotations for any topic, however, are from a Gospel: each heading starts *Dominus dicit in evangelio* (The Lord says in the Gospel). All other quotations are given in the past tense (*dixit*): only the Gospel is still a living word. After the Gospel come other biblical passages, with particular emphasis on the Wisdom books and Pauline epistles, and these are followed by the other writers in roughly chronological order.

The immense usefulness of such a book, when originals were scarce or expensive, and the lack of reference tools or even chapter headings and text divisions made searching for topics an arduous process, is particularly highlighted by the presence in this MS of a contemporary Anglo-Saxon interlinear translation. Thus the treasures of knowledge were made linguistically as well as physically accessible to many more readers.

This page shows section twenty-nine (its Roman numeral is at the bottom of the previous page), on tithes (*De decimis*). Notice the accents that the scribe has placed over some of the Latin words, presumably to aid pronunciation; abbreviations for 'and', although different, are used in both the Latin (&) and Anglo-Saxon (7); and alternative Latin usages are visible between the lines, e.g., *i. lucrum ł conpositionem:* 'id est lucrum vel conpositionem' (line 19).

betēodunge.

De decimis

drihten segð on godspelle
Dns dicit in euangelio.

ealle teoþunge eowre
Omnem decimationem uestram
dælað he þurh witegan spræcð
distribuite ; Ipse per prophetam loqui
in bringað ealle teoþunge on bern
tur. inferte omnem decimationem in hor
min þæt sy mete on huse minum
reum meum. ut sit cibus in domu mea
7 afandiað me on þam segð drihten
& probate me in his dicit dns ; Paulus
se apostol sæde of bearnum mæsse preost had
apls dix. De filiis leui. sacerdotiu
onfonde bebod hi habbað teoþunga
accipientes mandatum habent decimas
niman fram folce æfter lage þæt is fram
sumere a populo secundum legem id est a fra
gebroþrum hir bliðne soðlice syllend lufað
trib; suis ; hilarem enim datorem diligit
god sæde sume dælað
ds ; Salomon dix. Alii diuidut
agene 7 hi welegran hi gewyrþað sume gripað
propria. & ditiores fiunt. alii rapiunt
na i. alioꝝ hyra 7 symle on wædle hi synd
non sua. & semp in egestate sunt ; Hie
sunu sæde
sus filius Sirach dixit.
on ælcere sylene bliðne do ansyne þine
In omni dato hilarem fac uultum tuum.
7 on gefægenunge ge halga teoþunga þine
& in exultatione scifica decimas tuas ;
syle þam hehstan æfter sylene his 7 on godum
Da altissimo secundum datu eius. & in bo
eage to fyndele i. lu... compositione do handa
no oculo adinuentione fac manuum
þinra forþi þe drihten leaniende ys 7 seofonsiþan
tuaru. qm dns retribuens est. & septies
swa fela he agylt þe
tantum redd& tibi ; Augustinus
sæde teoþunga soðlice gafelu synd þearf
dix. Decime enim tributa sunt egen
endra sawla þæt gif þu teoþunge sylst
tium animarum. quod si decima dede
na þæt an genihtsumnysse wæstma
ris. non solum abundantiam fructuum
onfehst ac eac swylce hæle lichamena
recipies. sed & iam sanitatem corporum
þu begyst na behearf drihten god na mede
consequeris ; Non eg& dns ds. non pre

BIBLIOGRAPHY

Defensor's Liber Scintillarum *with an Interlinear Anglo-Saxon version,* ed. E. W. Rhodes (from this MS), EETS; *Defensor Locogiacensis monachi. Liber scintillarum,* ed. H. M. Rochais; H. M. Rochais, 'Contribution à l'histoire des florilèges ascétiques du haut moyen âge latin: le "Liber scintillarum"'; R. H. and M. A. Rouse, *Preachers, Florilegia and Sermons: Studies in the Manipulus florum of Thomas of Ireland.*

fourteen

Compendium of Theology on the Eucharist

London, British Library, MS Royal 7 C. VIII, fol. 37v
Probably English; late twelfth century

A great number of volumes from the Middle Ages contain more than one work. (Indeed, from the mid-thirteenth century, at least at professional Paris stationers, it was possible to choose and buy a series of works 'off-the-peg' and have them bound together in one volume.) At first sight, the selections may appear haphazard, but more careful scrutiny will often reveal a method in the apparent madness, and indeed, the juxtaposition of works can tell us much about medieval ideas of order and taxonomy. No great leap of imagination is needed here, however, for this compendium contains a series of works on the arguments over transubstantiation, including the seminal treatise (shown here) by Lanfranc of Bec *On the Body and Blood of Christ.*

What exactly happens to the elements (bread and wine) at the Eucharist (Mass or Holy Communion) is one of the crucial questions of Christian theology, even now dividing believers into radically different camps. Is the eucharistic meal simply a memorial of the Last Supper, or is Christ 'really present' in the everyday food, in more than a mystical sense? Two ninth-century theologians, both monks of the abbey of Corbie in northwest France, summed up the opposing viewpoints. Paschasius Radbertus, in *The Body and Blood of Christ* (fols. 1r–24r), argued that Christ's body was substantially present in the Eucharist, the transformed body of Christ acting to transform human nature when it is physically eaten; Ratramnus believed that the body and blood are real only in sign or figure, and that it is the faith that this engenders, rather than the act of eating, that transforms.

These two positions formed the basis of eucharistic controversy for many generations. Berengar (d. 1088), teacher at the school at Tours, was involved in a thirty-year dispute on the true interpretation of the act. He followed Ratramnus' line, arguing that Christ was really present only in a spiritual sense. His views were finally condemned by Gregory VII in 1079, but before that, his writings provoked a number of treatises attacking his position. The most

PARCHMENT: i (paper) + 106 + ii (paper) fols.; some folios given modern supports, for conservation; page 315 x 210 mm; text 2 cols., each 220 x 60 mm; 34 lines; drypoint ruling; one, clear hand. Space left for titles and chapter headings, rarely supplied. Lanfranc, Guitmund and Arnulf begin with three-color initials of red, green and pale blue; minor initials in plain red or green, or very simple two-color combinations. Marked up by later readers.

Purchased for the Royal collection from John Theyer (1597–1673).

CONTENTS: fols. 1^r–24^r Paschasius Radbertus, *De corpore et sanguine Domini* (imperf. at beginning); 24^r–28^r patristic extracts on the Eucharist, including part of Hilary of Poitiers, *De trinitate* and a sermon of Augustine; 28^r–37^r Paschasius Radbertus, *Letter to Fredugard on the Eucharist;* 37^{r-v} Anon. extract on the Eucharist, *inc.* 'Fuit nanque [sic] Iudas cum ceteris'; 37^v–58^r Lanfranc, *De corpore et sanguine Domini;* 58^v–100^r Guitmund of Aversa, *De corporis et sanguinis Domini veritate;* 100^r–6^v Arnulf of Rochester, *Letter to Lambert of St Bertin on the Eucharist.*

brilliant member of the opposition was Lanfranc (*c.* 1010–1089), theologian and abbot of Bec in Normandy, and later (1070) archbishop of Canterbury. His treatise *On the Body and Blood of Christ* was the best-known work refuting Berengar, who was moved to reply in his *The Sacred Feast.* Both admitted to the presence of Christ in the Eucharist, but they differed on the necessity and type of any change in the elements, Berengar insisting that no material alteration was needed, Lanfranc arguing that an outward identity concealed an inner transformation. Their differences were exacerbated by method: Berengar proceeds via grammatical points; Lanfranc is more interested in moving forward by dialectical argument.

Space is too limited to discuss the eucharistic issue properly here; no philosophically acceptable formulation of what happens to the elements was arrived at until Aristotle's metaphysical language of essence and substance had been integrated into theology in the later thirteenth century, although these theologians paved the way for that integration by using logic and dialectic to explain Christian doctrine.

This page shows the beginning of Lanfranc's treatise. Left col., display script: 'Lanfrancus misericordia dei catholicus, Berengerio catholicae ecclesiae adversario' [Lanfranc, by the mercy of God a catholic, to Berengar, adversary of the catholic church]. From these first words, Lanfranc emphasizes the seriousness of the issue by the extremity of the accusations he makes against Berengar. Note, too, the common type of error at lines 20–21 (right col.) where, by breaking the word to fit the line, the scribe absentmindedly doubles a syllable, giving *exposititionibus.*

sed omni tempore sentit effectum
ad generationem operante natura. ita et uox illa semel quidem
dicta est sed per omnes mensas ecclesie
usque ad hodiernum et usque ad eius
aduentum prestat sacrificio firmi-
tatem. Nullus igitur fictus accedat.
nullus fucato animo tantis
audeat appropriare mysteriis.
ne condempnetur. et sententiam
mereatur et quod iudas sustinuit
patiatur. Nam in illum post com-
munionem mense diabolus in-
trauit. non solum quia contempse-
rat dominicum corpus. sed quia impu-
dentia iude. et malignitas
mentis. et aduersarius hec
fecit. ut discas quod indigna
et fucata mente misteriorum
secreta celebrantibus a diabolo
preparantur insidie. et magis
ac magis ad se inuitantur qui
nequaquam animo communicare fe-
stinant.

INCIPIT LIBER LANFRANCI VENE-
RABILIS ARCHIEPISCOPI CANTVA-
RIENSIS ECCLESIE DE CORPORE ET SAN-
GVINE DOMINI CONTRA BERINGA-
RIVM.

LANFRANCVS
misericordia dei ca-
tholicus BERINGERIO catho-
lice ecclesie aduersario. Si diuina
pietas cordi tuo inspirare dig-
naretur. quatinus respectu eius
atque anime tue mecum loqui uel-
les. locumque opportunum in quo
id competenter posset fieri sa-
lubri deliberatione eligeres.
multum fortasse uel procul dubio
autem plurimum iis consuleres
quos decipis. deceptos uero ac mor-
te preuentos in penas eternas
transmittis. Et enim cooperante
spiritu qui ubi uult spirat. et quem
uult aspirat. eueniret e duobus alterutrum. uidelicet ut
aut tu ipse deposito superbie
fastu quo plenus contra orbem
terrarum sentire cepisti. aucto-
ritati totius sancte ecclesie rectisque
sanctarum scripturarum expositi-
onibus adquiesceres. et sic te
ac sequaces tuos de tenebris erroris ac profundo iniquitatis
erueres. aut te in tua pertinatia
persistente. ipsi auditis rationi-
bus miserante deo resipiscerent.
et ad ueram fidem quam sancta ecclesia predicare non cessat. consilio
meliore redirent. Sed quia
elegisti peruersitatem quam semel imbi-
bisti. clandestinis disputationi-
bus apud imperitos tueri. palam
autem atque in audientia sancti con-
cilii orthodoxam fidem non amore

BIBLIOGRAPHY

Paschasius Radbertus. De corpore et sanguine Domini cum appendice epistola ad Fredugardum, ed. B. Paul; Lanfranc, *De corpore et sanguine Domini;* G. Macy, *Theologies of the Eucharist in the Early Scholastic Period;* R. W. Southern, 'Lanfranc of Bec and Berengar of Tours'; H. de Lubac, *L'Eucharistie et l'Église au Moyen Age.*

fifteen

Andrew of St Victor, *On the Vision of Ezechiel*

Oxford, Bodleian Library, MS e Mus. 62, fol. 110[r]
English; second half of the thirteenth century

Whether Andrew of St Victor turned to the literal sense of Scripture from natural inclination or from a desire to avoid ground already well trodden by his master Hugh (no. 17), we cannot know. He may have been moved by his admiration for Jerome, whose exegesis is the basis of much of Andrew's work. Whatever the reason, his 'unswerving dedication to the explication of the letter of Scripture' (Signer) is clear; and it was this desire to understand all he could of the meaning of the Hebrew text that led him to seek out contemporary Jewish scholars and mine their knowledge of rabbinical tradition. Possibly he learnt a little Hebrew as well; but it is more likely that the Jews translated and explained syntactical problems to him in French.

Today it is not Andrew's own essays in textual criticism (for example, the transcription below) that interest scholars, as much as his recording of contemporary Jewish exegesis. None of the Jewish opinions Andrew reports is at all unusual. Most could have been drawn from the Talmud, or from the popular commentaries by Rashi (Rabbi Shlomo ben Isaac, d. 1105) or Joseph ben Simon Kara (d. 1130–40).

Andrew's approach may endear him to us, but it left him open to criticism by his peers, such as his fellow-Victorine, Richard. However, although he is generally sympathetic toward the Jewish understanding of Scripture, Andrew never forgets that he is a Christian scholar: he is studying the literal text not for its own sake, but for the Christian teaching it can impart.

The glossing of biblical books ran in fashions, and Ezechiel was never especially popular. Although both Andrew and Richard of St Victor commented on Ezechiel's visions, Andrew's was the first full-scale commentary since Jerome, whose text he incorporates into his own. Four manuscripts of the commentary survive, although this one contains only visions 1–2 and 40–43. It describes Andrew as from Wigmore (he was abbot of the abbey in Herefordshire), the sole manuscript of his works to do so.

PARCHMENT: ii (paper) + 137 + ii (paper) fols.; page 320 x 215 mm; text 2 cols., each 215 x 70 mm; 36 lines; ruled in lead-point; one practiced scribe. Running heads in ink of text; red titles; lemmata underlined in red; NOTA signs; references and marginal subject headings in red; quire signatures in Roman numerals; catchwords. One pale blue and red initial with infilling and flourishing; two red capitals with slight pale blue flourishing and infilling.

Belonged to the Cistercians of St Mary's, Kingswood, Gloucs. (fol. 1^{v}); given to the Bodleian by Sir Thomas Herbert in 1666.

CONTENTS: fol. 1^{v} contemporary *ex libris* and contents list; 2^{r}–46^{v} Richard of St Victor, *On the Trinity;* 46^{v}–66^{r} idem, *On the Ending of Evil and the Promotion of Good;* 66^{r}–75^{r} idem, *The Three Principles of Procession;* 75^{r}–106^{r} idem, *On the Vision of Ezechiel,* with remarkable colored drawings; 106^{r}–9^{v} Description of the Temple; 110^{r}–23^{r} Andrew of St Victor, *On the Vision of Ezechiel;* 123^{r}–37^{v} eight spiritual treatises, including Clement of Llanthony, *The Seraphim's Wings.*

Here we see the first page of the commentary, with both a running head, 'Andreas de i^{a} [prima] visione ezechielis' [Andrew on the first vision of Ezechiel] and a title, 'De visione ezechielis prima; abbas andreas ad litteram' [On the first vision of Ezechiel; abbot Andrew on the literal sense]. There is an extended red NOTA in the right margin; ·r·, meaning *respice* ('look at this' or 'consider') appears twice in the left margin and once in the top right margin. This unusual marking appears elsewhere in this manuscript as *·r· textum.* The left column has a mistake (duplicated words) crossed through in red. Note also the ÷ abbreviation for *est,* and diacritical marks over double *i* and *o* to distinguish the letters.

The text begins:

Et factum est. In propheticis satis usitatum est scripturis capitalibus sententiis orationem huiuscemodi premittere. In hebreo. Et fuit. Sensus autem hic est. Fuit vel contigit hoc quod dicturus sum. Copulativam que preponitur coniunctionem [.scilicet. .et.] non significationis cui nichil cooperatur necessitas, sed hebraice locutionis proprietas apponi coegit.

[And it came to pass. It is usual enough in prophetic writings at the beginnings of sentences to start the clause in this way. The Hebrew says, And it was. But the sense here is: This which I shall speak of was or happened. 'And' is placed before it as a connecting conjunction (that is, and) not for the meaning (to which nothing necessary is added), but because in the Hebrew the proper expression requires it to be put at the front.]

De visione ezechielis prima. abbas andreas ad litteram.

Et factum est. In prophetis satis usitatum est scripturis capitalibus sententiis orationem huiuscemodi premittere. In hebreo. Et fuit. Sensus autem hic est. Fuit vel contigit hoc quod dicturus sum. Copulativam que preponitur coniunctionem non significationis cui nichil cooperatur necessitas: sed hebraice locutionis proprietas apponi coegit. Multis enim in locis. ~~id est in locis~~ apud hebreos ista precipue coniunctio quantum ad sensum superflue apponitur. In .xxx.^mo^ anno. in .iiii. in .v. mensis. etc. Tempus quando. et locus ubi visiones dei vidit. et status ipsius prophete paucis describitur: ut melius his que dicuntur credatur. Eadem de causa de genus ipsius dignitate in sequentibus adiungitur. Cum essem in medio captivorum iuxta fluvium chobar. Cum inter concaptivos essem iuxta flumen quoddam tale nomen sortitum. Iuxta fluvios et inter (a babiloniis) iussa fuit sede captivitas. ut et ad potum. et faciendo operi copiose suppeteret, et clandestinam molientium fuge fugam inhiberet. Ieremias quoque suo secum numerans in psalmis populo. huic rei contestatur captivitatem inter babilonios consedisse fluvios dicens. Super flumina babilonis illic sedimus et flevimus. Hebraicum quod est: cum essem infra captivitatem non inter quos sed in quo tempore et statu captivitatis videlicet fuerit cum iuxta fluvium chobar positus visiones dei vidit. sic legitur.

Donus qui est sicut in psalmis legitur elevatio. oppressio oportuna in angustia. non in diebus prosperitatis sue. sed infra captivitatem. id est infra captivitatis tempus. nec iuxta iordanem et siloam provinciales aquas. sed iuxta chobar: peregrinum et caldaicum flumen. suum ministerium consilii prophete revelavit. Aperti sunt celi et vidi visiones dei. Consequens est ut cui aperiuntur celi: visiones dei que super celum sunt videat. Et licet divine maiestatis cuncta subiecta sint oculis. et cuncta cernentem dominum nichil latere possit: ea tamen precipue que super celos sunt videre dicitur. sic quoniam quamvis ubique sit: in celis tamen specialiter esse commemoratur. Apertis itaque celis dei visiones se dicit vidisse: quia ea vidit que super celos sunt. angelicas videlicet virtutes. quas deus non homo: in sua ipsorum forma et natura vidit. Et quoniam ea vidit que nullius aciei perspicacitas penetrare valet. celorum interpositione a nullo terrestri animante videri possunt: celos asserit apertos fuisse. Cum spiritualia sint que visa sunt. nec ea corporis usquam luminibus videri possint: totam illam visionem spiritualem fuisse perspicuum est. Spiritualem autem visionem iuxta hanc sententiam non secundum eam significationem appellamus qua spiritus a mente discernitur. ut in apostolo. orabo spiritu. orabo et mente. sed ex ea significatione qua dicitur: renovamini spiritu mentis vestre. Mens namque spiritus dicitur iuxta quod legitur: Spiritualis omnia iudicat. Mente itaque et intellectu visiones predictas prophetam vidisse non absurde dici potest. Vel si forte citra celum ea que predicta sunt in forma animalium et rotarum corporeis

BIBLIOGRAPHY

Andreae de Sancto Victore. Opera, vol. 6: *Expositionem in Ezechielem,* ed. M. A. Signer; Smalley, *SBMA,* ch. 4; G. Dahan, *Les intellectuels chrétiens et les juifs au moyen âge;* H. Hailperin, *Rashi and the Christian Scholars.*

sixteen

Ivo of Chartres, *Panormia*

London, British Library, MS Royal 10 A. VIII, fol. 44v
?English; thirteenth century

Subject specialization and the growing importance of academic credentials were two of the byproducts of the medieval university system. Medical doctors, lawyers and theologians all developed their own professional qualifications and entrance tests; membership of any of the groups was jealously guarded, so that, for instance, a doctor like Arnold of Villanova (*c.* 1240–1312) was regarded with suspicion when he wrote on theology. But it had not always been so. Given impetus by the legal emphasis of Gregory VII's attempts at church reform, the study of law, especially canon law, seemed theology's natural partner; many schoolmen, such as John of La Rochelle (d. 1245) display an extensive legal knowledge alongside their theology. It was the need for trained lawyers that fueled the growth of the schools at Bologna, the proto-university.

Canon law (that which governs the Church and its courts, as opposed to the civil law of the state: the two were considered separate disciplines) is made up of *dicta* and precepts drawn from Scripture, writings of the Fathers, Roman law codes, papal decrees and letters, and ecclesiastical traditions. By the eleventh century, the body of this law had grown untidy and inconsistent, and a number of attempts were made to collect and order it, such as the *Decretum* of Bishop Burchard of Worms (completed *c.* 1012), the anonymous *Collection in 74 Titles* (finished by 1067), and the collections of Anselm of Lucca (*c.* 1083) and Cardinal Deusdedit (*c.* 1087), all culminating in the magisterial *Decretum* (or *Concordance of Discordant Canons*) of Gratian, produced at Bologna in about 1140.

Greatest of the eleventh-century collections was Ivo's *Panormia* (*c.* 1094). Like many early canonists, Ivo was a theologian as well as a jurist. Ivo studied at Bec under Lanfranc (no. 14), and at Laon, producing an important collection of theological *Sentences*. A member of the new semi-monastic order of Augustinian canons, he was made prior of their house in Beauvais in 1079, and then bishop of Chartres in 1090. His fullest collection of canons is the massive *Decretum*, and he probably also compiled the *Tripartita* collection; but it was the smaller, pithier *Panormia* ('all the rules') that held the stage until Gratian. Although containing 1,038

PARCHMENT: ii + 151 fols.; very badly damaged in the 1731 British Museum fire, each leaf is now separately attached to a modern support; page *c.* 220 x 150 mm; text 2 cols., each 180 x 50 mm; 37 lines; ruled in lead-point; written above top line; one practiced scribe. Red titles for each canon and quotation heading. Simple red or green initials.

Purchased for the Royal collection from John Theyer (1597–1673).

CONTENTS: fol. ii^{r} a form of confession; 1^{r}–5^{v} misc. theological notes, including Gaufridus, *De corpore et sanguine domini;* 6^{r}–112^{v} Ivo of Chartres, *Panormia,* with preface and capitula list; 113^{r} 17th-c. note on Ivo and his works; 114^{r}–148^{v} Ivo of Chartres, *Sermons* (beginning imperfect); 148^{v}–49^{r} Constitutions of the Council of Westminster, 1127; 149^{v}–50^{v} apocryphal letter of Pontius Pilate to emperor Claudius; 150^{v}–51^{r} misc. notes.

canons, divided into eight books, a large part of the *Panormia*'s success was its comparative brevity, achieved by a strong sense of order combined with a gift for precise legal formulation. In addition, Ivo's preface outlined a new method for resolving discordances between canons, which influenced Gratian. Across disciplines, the *Sic et non* of Peter Abelard (d. 1142) was to use much the same procedure.

Ivo's writings did not stop at law. This MS also contains a collection of his sermons, which are notable for speaking directly to everyday life. In theology, as in law, he was a trailblazer, emphasizing the importance of human experience. His scale was very much down-to-earth. Practical theology and canon law must mix: for instance, it was the canonists' writings on marriage that increased Church interest in matrimony, which the theologians eventually included among the sacraments.

This page is from the section on clergy, and gives a flavor of what counted as 'legal' in this kind of collection. It has *dicta* from popes (e.g., Gel[asius]) and councils (e.g., Toletano), as well as, in this selection, Augustine (left: line 8):

> Duae (*recte* Quae) ipsis sacerdotibus necessaria sunt ad discendum, id est, liber sacramentorum, lectionarius, baptisterium, compotus, kanon, penitencialis, psalterium, omelie per circulum, anni dominicis diebus et singulis festivitatibus aptae. Ex quibus omnibus si unum defuerit sacerdotis nomen in eo vix constabit; quia valde periculose sunt mine evangelicae quibus dicitur: si cecus ceco ducatum praebeat, ambo in foveam cadunt. [These things are necessary for priests to be familiar with, that is, the sacramentary, the lectionary, the liturgy of baptism, the computus, the canon of the mass, the penitential, the psalter, and sermons suited to the Sundays of the whole year and particular feast days. If he is deficient in any one of these, he is not fit to be called priest; because the Gospel threats are very dangerous, saying: if the blind leads the blind, then they'll both fall in the ditch!]

libellum officialem a sacerdote suo accipiant.
ut ad ecclesias sibi deputatas instructi succe
dant. ne per ignorantiam etiam ipsis divinis sa
cramentis offendant. Ut quando ad letanias vel
ad concilium veniunt. rationem episcopo suo reddant
qualiter susceptum officium celebrent vel baptizent.

Que debeant necessario scire presbiteri. Ex
dictis sancti Augustini.

Que ipsis sacerdotibus necessaria sunt ad discendum.
id est liber sacramentorum. lectionarius. baptisterium.
compotus. kanon penitencialis. psalterium.
omelie per circulum anni dominicis diebus
et singulis festivitatibus apte. Ex quibus om
nibus si unum defuerit sacerdotis nomen in eo
vix constabit. quia valde periculose sunt
mine evangelice quibus dicitur. Si cecus ceco du
catum prebeat ambo in foveam cadunt.

Quibus temporibus ordinandi sunt
presbiteri. diaconi. Ex decreto Gel. pp. cap. xiii.

Ordinationes etiam presbiterorum et
diaconorum nisi certis temporibus et
diebus exerceri non debent. id est quarti mensis ieiu
nio. septimi et decimi. Sed etiam quadrage
simalis initii. ac mediane quadragesime
die sabbati ieiunia circa vesperam noverint
celebranda. nec cuiuslibet utilitatis seu
presbiterum seu diaconum his preferre qui ante ip
sos fuerint ordinati.

Quod certis locis
ordinandi sunt presbiteri. Ex concilio Melden.

Si qui ordinari petunt. si. cap. vi.
nullatenus ordinentur. nisi in loco
certo et religioso vel etiam in civitate
saltem uno anno immorentur. ut devita
et conversatione atque doctrina illorum certi
tudo possit agnosci. Ex concilio Calcedo

Conc. Cartha. Can. 6.

Nullum absolute ordinari ensi. cap. vi.
dinari debere presbiterum. aut diaco
num. nec quemlibet in gradu ecclesiastico. nisi
specialiter ecclesie civitatis. aut possessio
nis. aut martirum. aut monasterii cui or
dinandus est pronuntietur. Qui vero absolute
ordinantur. decrevit sancta synodus irritam
haberi huiusmodi manus impositionem.
et nusquam posse ministrare ad ordinan
tis iniuriam.

Quod ante xxx annos non
ordinetur presbiter. Ex concilio Laodicensi.

Episcopum vel presbiterum ante xxx annos. id est
antequam ad viri perfecti etatem per
veniat nullus metropolitanorum ordina
re presumat. ne per etatem si aliquando
evenit. aliquo errore detineantur.

Quia
auctoritate presbiteri sunt ordinandi in
hac etate. Ex decreto Fabiani pp. cun
ctis missis.

Si quis xxx etatis sue non impleverit
annos. nullo modo presbiter ordinetur. etiam
si valde sit dignus. quia et ipse dominus xxx
annorum baptizatus est. et sic cepit docere.
Non oportet ergo eum qui ordinandus est usque
ad hanc etatem legitimam expectari.

Quod ante

Conc. 3.
Can. 4

xxv annos non ordinetur diaconus. Ex concilio

Placuit ut ante. Cartag. cap. xvi.
xxv annos etatis nec diaconi ordi
nentur. nec virgines consecrentur. et ut
lector populum non salutet.

Quia auctori
tate diaconi ordinandi sunt in supra
dicta etate. Ex concilio Toletano v. ca. xx.

In veteri lege ab anno xxv levite in taber
naculo servire precipiuntur. cuius auctorita
tem in canonibus sancti patres secuti sunt.
Nos et divine legis et conciliorum precepti inme
memores infantes et pueros levitas
facimus ante legitimam etatem et ante ex
perientiam vite. Ideoque ne ulterius fiat

Concil. Toletanu 4. Can. 19. quod yn

BIBLIOGRAPHY

Ivo of Chartres, *Panormia;* J. A. Brundage, *Medieval Canon Law;* M. Grandjean, *Laïcs dans l'Église;* P. Fournier and G. Le Bras, *Histoire des collections canoniques;* S. Kuttner, *History of Ideas and Doctrine of Canon Law in the Middle Ages;* R. W. Southern, *Scholastic Humanism and the Unification of Europe. 1: Foundations.*

C

Sentences *to* Summae

seventeen

Hugh of St Victor, *De sacramentis Christianae fidei*

Oxford, Bodleian Library, MS Bodl. 773, fol. 62r
English; mid- to late twelfth century

We know very little about the man who was one of the finest scholars, and who headed perhaps the most interesting school, of the twelfth century. Hugh was probably a Saxon, from a noble family from Blankenburg. He entered the abbey of Augustinian canons at St Victor, Paris, in his late teens, *c.* 1115–18, perhaps having first been educated and taken orders at Halberstadt. Founded in 1113 by William of Champeaux, a renowned master who was a teacher of Peter Abelard, St Victor necessarily had a somewhat scholarly air. Head of the abbey school from 1133, Hugh was its most famous master. St Victor was small, but immensely influential, holding a crucial bridge position between the learning of the monasteries and that of the new Parisian secular schools; its policy of inclusiveness toward learning is well expressed in Hugh's saying, 'Learn everything; you will see afterwards that nothing is superfluous' (*Didascalicon*, bk. 6, c. 3). That he followed his own advice is shown in the range of his writings, covering grammar, geometry, history, theological and devotional spiritual treatises, biblical commentary and hermeneutics. The *De sacramentis* has been called 'the first complete theological treatise of the medieval schools' (Deferrari, p. xx).

Divided into two books, the *De sacramentis* is a map of Hugh's spiritual world. Starting with the six days of creation, Book one moves through the Trinity, the will, angels, creation, the fall and redemption, the institution of the sacraments, faith and law. Book two moves from the Incarnation of the Word to the end of time, covering the holy spirit and his power, the individual sacraments, and ecclesiastical order. Hugh has a gift for making difficult topics seem straightforward and clear.

PARCHMENT: iii (paper) + 178 + iii (paper) fols.; page 303 x 208 mm; text 2 cols., each 204 x 70 mm; 35 lines; ruled in lead-point; neat hand, two scribes. Red titles to articles and chapters; chapter nos. as Roman numerals in margin. Carefully corrected. Occasional NOTA signs and reader's notes, especially bk. 2, art. 1, *On the Incarnation*, e.g., fol. 79ʳ. Major initials to begin each article in red, green or ochre (and occasionally pale blue), with flourishing and infilling in the other two. Plain chapter initials in the same colors, sometimes decorated with large dots or minimal flourishing and infilling.

Once chained; given by the Dean and canons of Windsor in 1612.

CONTENTS: fols. 1r–177ᵛ Hugh of St Victor, *De sacramentis,* in 2 books, each with prologue and list of chapters.

A fine, clear, eminently useful volume.

Here we see the end of the article on the institution of sacraments and the beginning of that on faith (left: line 8):

> De tribus quae necessaria sunt ad salutem. Tria sane sunt quae ab initio sive ante adventum Christi [note use of chrismon sign *xp*] sive post ad salutem optinendam necessaria fuerunt id est fides et sacramenta fidei et bona opera. Que tria ita choerent (corr. from choercent) ut salutis effectum habere non possint si simul non fuerint. [The three things which are necessary for salvation. There are, then, three things which were necessary for salvation from the beginning or before and after the coming of Christ, that is, faith, and the sacraments of faith, and good works. These three things harmonizc, so that they cannot have a salutary effect if they are not present together.]

In line with their genius for codification and order, twelfth-century scholars worked to reconsider and fine-tune the notion of *sacrament.* Although sacraments held a central place in the Christian faith from its beginnings, how exactly they were to be defined and what was to be counted among them was the subject of considerable debate. Peter Lombard's *Sentences* (Bk. 4, d. 1, art. 2) enumerated the seven which have come to be regarded as definitive (baptism, confirmation, the Eucharist, penance, marriage, ordination, extreme unction), and his list was given formal confirmation by the Councils of Florence (1439) and Trent (1545–63). Writing twenty years before Peter Lombard, Hugh of St Victor seems to be the first theologian to make the distinction between sacrament and the sacramental, though he allowed the former category to encompass a broader definition than Peter would accept. He is fully aware of the diversity of opinion on the issue, but prefers the wider formulation in order to include the mysteries of created nature.

sanctificandis et instituendis necessaria sunt quedam in preparantes et sanctificantes: ut circa personas in sacris ordinibus perficiendis. ut in hiis que ad habitum sacrorum ordinum pertinent intitulandis et ceteris huiusmodi. Prima igitur ad salutem: secunda ad exercitacionem: tertia ad preparationem constituta sunt. Hiis igitur prout ratio postulare videbatur pertractatis: ad ea que restant explicanda transimus. De tribus.

·VIII· Tria sane que necessaria sunt ad salutem. sunt que ab initio sive ante adventum Christi sive post, ad salutem optinendam necessaria fuerunt. i. fides et sacramenta fidei et bona opera. Que ita inter se coherent ut salutis effectum habere non possint: si simul non fuerint. Fides enim sine operibus mortua est: teste scriptura. Et rursum. Ubi fides non est: bonum opus esse non potest. Item qui fidem operantem habent si sacramenta dei suscipere renuunt. salvari non possunt: quia dilectionem dei non habent. cuius precepta in sacramentis eius contempnunt. Verumtamen ubi fides cum dilectione est. sic non minuitur meritum: ut si opus quod in voluntate proposito devotionis est: exterius non perficitur: sic salutis effectus non impeditur: ut si sacramentum quod in vera voluntate est et desiderio: articulo necessitatis excluditur. Ubi autem ista simul haberi possunt. sine periculo salutis nullatenus abesse possunt. quia nec fides meritum habet. si operari potest operari negligit. nec opus bonum est aliquid si sine fide sit. Et rursum. Fides operans hominem sanctificare non sufficit: si eam que in sacramentis dei constat sanctificationem suscipere contempnit. Tria igitur simul sunt. fides. sacramentum. et opus. In fide christiana fortitudo tribuitur. In sacramentis arma. In operibus vero bonis tela contra diabolum pugnaturo. Incipit .x. pars de fide. De fide .vii. sunt inquirenda.

I

De fide. Capitulum primum.

De fide tractare volentibus .vii. inquirenda proponimus. quid sit fides. in quo constat fides. de incremento fidei: de hiis que pertinent ad fidem. Si ab initio secundum mutationem temporum mutata sit fides credentium. Quid sit quo minus nichil umquam vera fides habere potuit. De sacramento fidei et virtute ipsius. Singula ordine suo prosequimur. Quid sit fides.

·II· Fides est ut ait apostolus substantia rerum sperandarum. argumentum non apparentium. Si per fidem ea que creduntur fide significata intelligimus. sic per visionem non numquam non eam qua videmus sed quam videmus accipimus. convenienter fides substantia rerum sperandarum dicitur. quia fide ea que vere subsistunt bona sperantibus et expectantibus illa vera creduntur. Secundum quam acceptionem non irrationabiliter et argumentum non apparentium dicitur. quia que ratione humana non comprehendimus: sola fide nobis credibilia esse et vera persuademur. Quod si hanc diffinitionem alio modo exponimus. possumus dicere quia fides non in eo quod sit: sed quid faciat diffinitur. Ut sit sensus. Fides est substantia. i. subsistencia rerum sperandarum. i. futurorum bonorum que ventura sperantur a nobis. et que sola digna sunt spe et expectacione nostra: quoniam in ipsis constat bonum nostrum. Est igitur fides substantia rerum sperandarum. quia bona invisibilia que per actum nondum presentia sunt: iam per fidem in cordibus nostris subsistunt: et ipsa fides eorum in nobis est subsistencia eorum. Cum enim res quelibet apud nos subsistant vel per actum quando videlicet presentes sensu comprehenduntur: vel per intellectum quando absentes vel et non existentes in similitudine sua et in imaginatione

BIBLIOGRAPHY

Hugh of St Victor. On the Sacraments of the Christian Faith, ed. R. J. Deferrari; J. Taylor, *The Didascalicon of Hugh of St Victor;* R. Baron, *Science et sagesse chez Hugues de St.-Victor.*

eighteen

Peter Lombard, *Four Books of Sentences*

Baltimore, Walters Art Gallery, MS Cat. 7 (W. 809), fol. 70r
Probably Paris; *c.* 1180

For centuries, Peter Lombard's *Sentences* was *the* textbook of catholic academic theology. So great was its stranglehold on advanced study, that commentaries on the work were still being written in the seventeenth century, five hundred years after its composition *c.* 1153–55. Yet the book itself was straightforward and unassuming, and its success testifies to the power of organization and timing rather than startling originality. The Lombard gauged the needs of his current audience, and the direction of teaching in the schools, to perfection. Indeed, his book in part drove the direction of teaching for generations.

Radical thinking and novelty were not counted as virtues by medieval theologians. Truth was the accumulation of ancient revelation, with modern supplements, not some rootless paradigm shift into innovation. Consequently, the form of Peter's book was not new. *Florilegia* (no. 13) are forerunners of the genre. Books of *sentences* (*sententiae* = opinions) by that name date back at least to Prosper of Aquitaine's *Liber sententiarum ex Augustino* (mid-fifth century) which, as its name suggests, was a collection of Augustine's opinions, in no clear order. Other collections of one or more Fathers could be grouped in the order of the books of the Bible, like Paterius' *Liber de expositione . . . Gregorii.* A third kind, from which the Lombard's *Sentences* derive, gathered its extracts under doctrinal headings—God, the Trinity, Creation, etc. Initially simply clusters of opinions, from the mid-twelfth century onward, in works like Anselm of Laon's *Sententiae divinae paginae,* they juxtaposed conflicting opinions and developed their own lines of approach.

The four books of Lombard's *Sentences* address the Trinity, Creation, the Incarnation, and the Sacraments and Eschaton, proceeding in a logical order through the various topics. Peter uses the *sic et non* method, asking a question, giving the opinions for and then against it, then (usually) offering a balanced solution. He uses few of his own words; accredited or not, most of what appears on the page is taken from the Fathers and occasional selected 'moderns'. He

PARCHMENT: i (modern) + 219 + i (modern) fols.; page 370 x 250 mm; text 2 cols., each 215 x 65 mm; 43 lines; ruled in lead-point; written above the top line; probably two scribes. Headings and titles in red; textual divisions added in red or blue; red and blue paraph signs. Identity and extant of quotations from authorities (e.g., Augustine, Hilary) marked in red in margins, with corresponding reference marks in the text. Portrait of Peter Lombard as bishop, writing (fol. 1^r); major foliated initials to begin each book; red or blue minor initials with blue or red flourishing. Guide letters for painter of initials still visible in outer margin.

Bought from Quaritch in 1985.

CONTENTS: fols. 1^r–219^v Peter Lombard, *Four Books of Sentences,* including prefaces and chapter lists, missing last fol.

Immensely useful layout for scholarly reference.

uses vast amounts of Augustine, quoting him whenever possible, and skewing the questions he addressed to those which Augustine had discussed. The *Sentences'* subsequent popularity contributed a large part of the massive influence of Augustine in the schools.

Although basically a conservative theologian, Peter did venture opinions on some of the difficult issues of the day. His 'ruling' on some of these, such as the number and order of the sacraments, became orthodox doctrine; others were not so well founded, and a list of those matters in which Master Peter was not to be followed circulated in the schools. When commentary on the book was taken up by Alexander of Hales and incorporated into the statutes at Paris as a necessary part of a theology doctorate, its fortune was made. One might not always agree with the Lombard, but it was not possible to ignore him. This effortless dominance brought vituperation from Roger Bacon, who saw that students preferred easily digested morsels of *Sentences* to rather more grisly lumps of Bible.

Peter (master *c.* 1135; bishop of Paris 1159; d. 1160) was not a one-work author. His glosses on the Psalms and Pauline epistles were incorporated into the standard Bible gloss (no. 1), as the Great Gloss (*Magna glosatura*). Aside from their content, the layout of his works puts them at the forefront of book technology in the twelfth century.

On this page we can see the reference system evolved for careful scholars. The names of authorities ('Beda', 'Strabus') are marked in the margins in red (elsewhere, the limits of quotations from them are clearly marked in the text with dots). Summaries of the arguments are given, in red, on the right. Here, at the beginning of book 2, we can also see (in the two left-hand cols.) the end of the list of questions it will address.

De differentia voluntatis et intentionis et finis.
Quare voluntas dicitur peccatum cum sit de naturalibus? quorum nullum aliud peccatum sit.
Quare actus voluntatis sit peccatum. si actus aliarum potentiarum non sunt peccata.
Ex quo sensu dicitur: naturaliter omnis homo velle bonum.
An ex fine omnis actus pensari debeat in genere et affectu. ut sint omnis sunt boni vel mali.
An omnis intentio. vel actio infidelium sit mala.
Quibus modis dicatur bonum.
Quomodo intelligendum illud peccatum adeo esse voluntarium.
Et illud nusquam nisi in voluntate peccatum est. et item non nisi voluntate peccatur.
Quod mala voluntas est voluntarium peccatum.
An voluntas et actio mala in eodem et eadem idem sunt unum peccatum. ut plato.
Si peccatum ab antiquo omissum in eo sit. quo usque peniteat.
Quibus accipitur modis reatus.
De modis peccatorum quo differant delictum. et peccatum.
De septem principalibus vitiis.
De superbia.
Quomodo dicatur superbia. radix omnium malorum. et cupiditas. cum superbia non sit cupiditas.
De peccato in spiritum sanctum.
De potentia peccandi. an sit homini. vel diabolo a deo.
An aliquando resistendum sit potestati.

r e s
r i t z

Creationem rerum insinuans scriptura: deum esse creatorem: initiumque temporis: atque omnium visibilium: vel invisibilium creaturarum: in primordio sui ostendit dicens. In principio creavit deus celum et terram. His etenim verbis: moyses spiritu dei afflatus: in uno principio: a deo creatore: mundum factum refert. Eludens errorem quorumdam: plura: sine principio fuisse principia: opinantium. Plato namque: tria initia existimavit. deum scilicet. et exemplar: et materiam. et ipsa increata: sine principio. et deum quasi artificem: non creatorem. Creator enim: qui de aliquo nichil: facit. Et creare proprie est: de nichilo aliquid facere. Facere vero non tantum de nichilo aliquid operari: sed etiam de materia. Unde et homo: vel angelus dicitur aliqua facere: sed non creare. Vocaturque factor: sive artifex: sed non creator. Hoc enim nomen: soli deo proprie convenit. qui et de nichilo quedam. et de aliquo: aliqua facit. Ipse est ergo creator: et opifex: et factor. Sed creationis nomen: sibi proprie retinuit. Alia vero: et creaturis: communicavit. In scriptura tamen: sepe creator accipitur: tamquam factor. et creare: sicut facere: sine distinctione significationis.

Verumtamen sciendum est: hec verba. scilicet facere: creare: agere: et ali

Hec verba scilicet facere agere et huiusmodi non dicuntur de deo eam rationem qua dicuntur de creaturis.

unum esse principium et ostendit non plura ut quidam putaverunt.

Unum esse principium ostendit non plura ut quidam putaverunt.

Tribus plato tria esse dixit principia.

Ex qua ratione dicatur creator et quo sit artifex vel quo factor.

creatione

I. Beda

Strab.

BIBLIOGRAPHY

Magistri Petri Lombardi . . . Sententiae in IV Libros Distinctae, ed. I. Brady; M. Colish, *Peter Lombard;* C. de Hamel, *Glossed Books of the Bible and the Origins of the Paris Booktrade;* J. P. Turcheck, 'A Neglected Manuscript of Peter Lombard's *Liber Sententiarum* and Parisian Illumination of the Late Twelfth Century'.

nineteen

Peter of Poitiers, *Five Books of Sentences*

London, British Library, MS Royal 10 A. XIV, fols. 23v–24r
?English; mid-thirteenth century

After the appearance of Peter Lombard's *Sentences,* a number of other, similar collections were made in Paris in the second half of the twelfth century. Almost all depended on Peter Lombard in some way; indeed, his *Sentences* were too important and influential ever to be disregarded by scholastic theologians. By the time it became a set book in the University of Paris, the structure of the *Sentences* had to be closely followed by its tyro commentators; but in this early period of influence, theologians followed its overall framework without necessarily keeping to the Lombard's model exactly.

In such a manner, Peter of Poitiers constructed his *five* books of sentences, closely dependent upon Peter Lombard (more than half of the questions treated by Peter of Poitiers are also in Peter Lombard), but nevertheless still very much a personal exposition of the edifice of Christian theology. His five sections cover: the Trinity; Creation (angelic and human); grace, the virtues and penitence; Christology, including the sacraments and commandments of the Old Law; and eschatology and the sacraments of the New Law. Peter is not interested in questions which involve simply the exposition of doctrine; he only attacks problems where there are issues in dispute—what he calls in the prologue *disputabilia.* He is adamant that he will not discuss those questions sufficiently discussed in other places, those dealt with by canon law, or questions motivated by frivolity or mere curiosity. This delight in the disputable seems to stem from his attraction to the dialectical method. In this he joins two other Peters—Abelard and Lombard—and Gilbert of Poitiers to make up the *Four Labyrinths of France.* This is the title of a polemical attack by Walter of St Victor (d. after 1180), who complained that these masters had subverted the true study of theology into mere logical game-playing.

Like that of many an early schoolman, Peter's life and career is largely a mystery to us. He was probably born in Poitiers or Poitou *c.* 1130. He began teaching theology in 1167, taking over the professorship vacated by Peter Comestor in 1169. In 1193 he was made chancellor of Notre

PARCHMENT: iv (paper) + 120 + v (paper) fols.; page *c.* 250 x 170 mm (variable); text 2 cols., each 190 x 55 mm; 46 lines; ruled in lead-point; written above the top line; one small, ugly hand. Once had bk. nos. as running heads, trimmed by later binder; red title to each question. Catchwords and quire nos. (Roman numerals); incomplete chapter lists for each book. Marginal notes of subject headings or tree diagrams of the contents of questions; occasional references to authorities (e.g., AG = Augustine), chapter nos., NOTA signs and pointing hands; notes by more than one later reader. Blue initial with red flourishing (fol. 1r); plain red or pale blue capitals elsewhere; after fol. 26r space left for blue capitals, not present; paraph signs touched with red.

Owner's note of Clement of Willingham (fol. 120v; ?14th c.); later belonged to John Theyer (1663).

CONTENTS: fols. 1r–120r Peter of Poitiers, *Five Books of Sentences.*

An unpretentious book, with a rather thrown-together feel.

Dame, a position which gave him responsibility for the Paris schools, and in which he continued until his death in 1205. Although he was once thought to be Peter Lombard's pupil, half-a-dozen opinions of *magister meus* (my master) reported in the *Sentences* seem to be at odds with the Lombard's views, suggesting that he had in fact studied in a different school; and, indeed, his rather practical turn of mind (he also wrote allegories, distinctions, and a historical compendium—all primarily *useful* works for students) is reminiscent of the 'biblical moral' theologians of the time, such as Peter the Chanter.

This opening shows bk. 1, chs. 21–22 (note •1• at top of page, and 'xxii' in left margin, fol. 24r). The table on fol. 23v refers to the three persons of the Trinity and their attributes (the subject of chapter 21). Above and below the table are two reference signs (O÷∸) directing the reader to the middle of fol. 24r, by the capital C. These, and the otiose three-line space left at the bottom of the right-hand column of fol. 23v, suggest slavish copying from the exemplar, since there is no reason not to put the references on the same page as the text to which they refer. Note also expunction marks under the word straddling fols. 23v–24r: c'a-ture, changing *creature* to *create.* Within the right-hand column of text, fol. 24r, are four alternative readings, written between the lines and introduced by ł (*vel* = 'or'), e.g., line 19 *alienus* ł *um* (i.e., *alienus* or *alienum*); line 31 *dupliciter* ł *accipitur.*

Ex	Patre	Potente	Uno	Auctore	Operante
Per	Filium	Sapientem	Patri equalem	Natum	Disponentem
In	Spiritu	Benigno	Concordi	Communi	Conservante

From	the Father	Power	One	Originator	Doing
Through	the Son	Wisdom	Equal to the Father	Born	Arranging
In	the Spirit	Bounty	in harmony	Common to both	Sustaining

Ex	patre ·	Potente ·	Uno	Auctore ·	operante ·	origine	Etrna ·	Cuncta ·
Per	filiu ·	sapientem ·	patris equale ·	Naturam ·	disponente ·	perfectissimam pulchritudinem	Speciem	disposita ·
in	spiritu ·	Benigno ·	concordi	communi	conservante ·	beatissima delectatione	usu grat.	conservata ·

Trinitas distinguitur per ea que subdit apostolus ipsi gloria · et dicit significari per Trinitatem et unitatem significari per eternitatem.

BIBLIOGRAPHY

Sententiae Petri Pictaviensis, ed. P. S. Moore and M. Dulong; P. S. Moore, *The Works of Peter of Poitiers.*

twenty

William of Auxerre, *Summa aurea*

London, British Library, MS Royal 9 B. V, fol. 114^{v}
English; Oct. 1231: colophon, fol. 199^{v}

The title 'Golden Summa' gives some insight into the popularity this work enjoyed and the respect in which it was held. Written between 1215 and 1229, it dates from the period when writing a *Sentences* commentary was not yet compulsory for all would-be masters in theology. The usefulness of Peter Lombard's pattern was acknowledged, but nevertheless, the genre was still open to interpretation. William's masterpiece is a kind of hybrid *Sentences* commentary, divided into four books like Peter's work, but not following all of his headings; he manages to include rather more topics than the Lombard—hence, perhaps, the title *Summa*. Unlike Peter Lombard, William likes to introduce specific examples, sometimes near-contemporary, factual instances. For example, he asks if Pope Alexander III was right to release a man from his vow to take the cross and travel overseas? or how it is that the Cistericans can be absolved from paying tithes on land they work themselves? or whether the Hospitallers and Templars can take tithes?

Such questions are fascinating (and sometimes frustrating) to the modern scholar. They signal William's interest in practical moral theology, in which he follows Peter the Chanter, sticking much more closely to the Chanter in his subtle, technical discussion of usury, for instance, than to Peter Lombard, who barely mentions it as a problem. It was the combination of William's clear and precise style and orthodox theology, coupled with his practical interests and examples, that made the *Summa aurea* such a success.

William (1140x50–1231) himself was a secular master, one of a diminishing band of masters in the theology faculty at Paris not affiliated to any religious order. He was archdeacon of Beauvais, proctor for the university at the Roman curia and, interestingly, one of the three-man team papally appointed to correct the 'new' works of Aristotle for use in the schools.

This manuscript of the *Summa*, datable very accurately from its scribal colophon, is a good example of a personal scholar's copy, written up quickly by a team of professional scribes, each

PARCHMENT: ii (paper) + 200 + iii (paper) fols.; page *c.* 300 x c. 245 mm (pages very variable and scrappy; each quire now attached to a separate stubb); text 2 cols., each 250 x 90 mm; 45–80 lines; ruled in lead-point; written above the top line; very compressed, highly abbreviated script; several scribes. Red Roman numerals for quire nos. (often cropped); titles (in red for bks. 1, 3 & 4). Copied in separate sections (gaps at ends of quires). Many marginal notes with references, sub-headings and corrections in the text hand. Fol. 1^r *Summa Magistri Willelmi Antidotensis* (for *Altissiodorensis*) *super Sentencias.* Turquoise and red initials with alternate flourishing, bks. 1 & 4; missing for bks. 2 & 3. Red capitals with slight blue flourishing; red titles and sub-headings; letters touched in red in first quire, and occasionally elsewhere.

Belonged to Worcester Cathedral Priory (fol. 1^r).

CONTENTS: fol. 1r verse: Walther 4685; 1^r–199^v William of Auxerre, *Summa aurea;* 200^{r-v} list of chapters, question numbers and rubrics for bks. 1–3.

An extremely useful, much read book for an individual scholar, though with few reader-aids.

copying separate quires: the gaps between quires testify that the exemplar was not copied in series, but in parallel. Some of the scribes write above the top line of ruling, others write below it, enclosing the text in a kind of ruled box. This move from above to below top line writing was a stylistic change being undertaken by professional scribes at exactly this time; this MS, which contains both sorts, is one of the key early witnesses of the alteration.

This page shows part of the question on giving alms (*elemosina*). Rt col., line 41 [bk. 3, tr. 24, c. 5, q. 2]: 'Queritur post utrum meretrix de acquisitis per meretricium potest facere elemosinam. Videtur quod sic, quoniam suum est, quia dicit auctoritas quod meretrix turpiter acquirit, sed non turpiter accipit; et de suo potest quilibet facere elemosinam.' [Next, we ask whether a prostitute may give alms out of her earnings from prostitution. It seems she may, since it is her own money, because the authority says that a prostitute *makes* money in a shameful way, but she does not *take* the money shamefully; and anyone may give alms from their own money.] The question goes on to compare the position of a merchant, who may make money by lying—a mortal sin just like the 'business' of a prostitute. *He*, however, is allowed to give alms. Eventually, the answer is that a prostitute may give alms in private but not in public. This question was topical because the prostitutes of Paris wanted to contribute to the building of Notre Dame Cathedral.

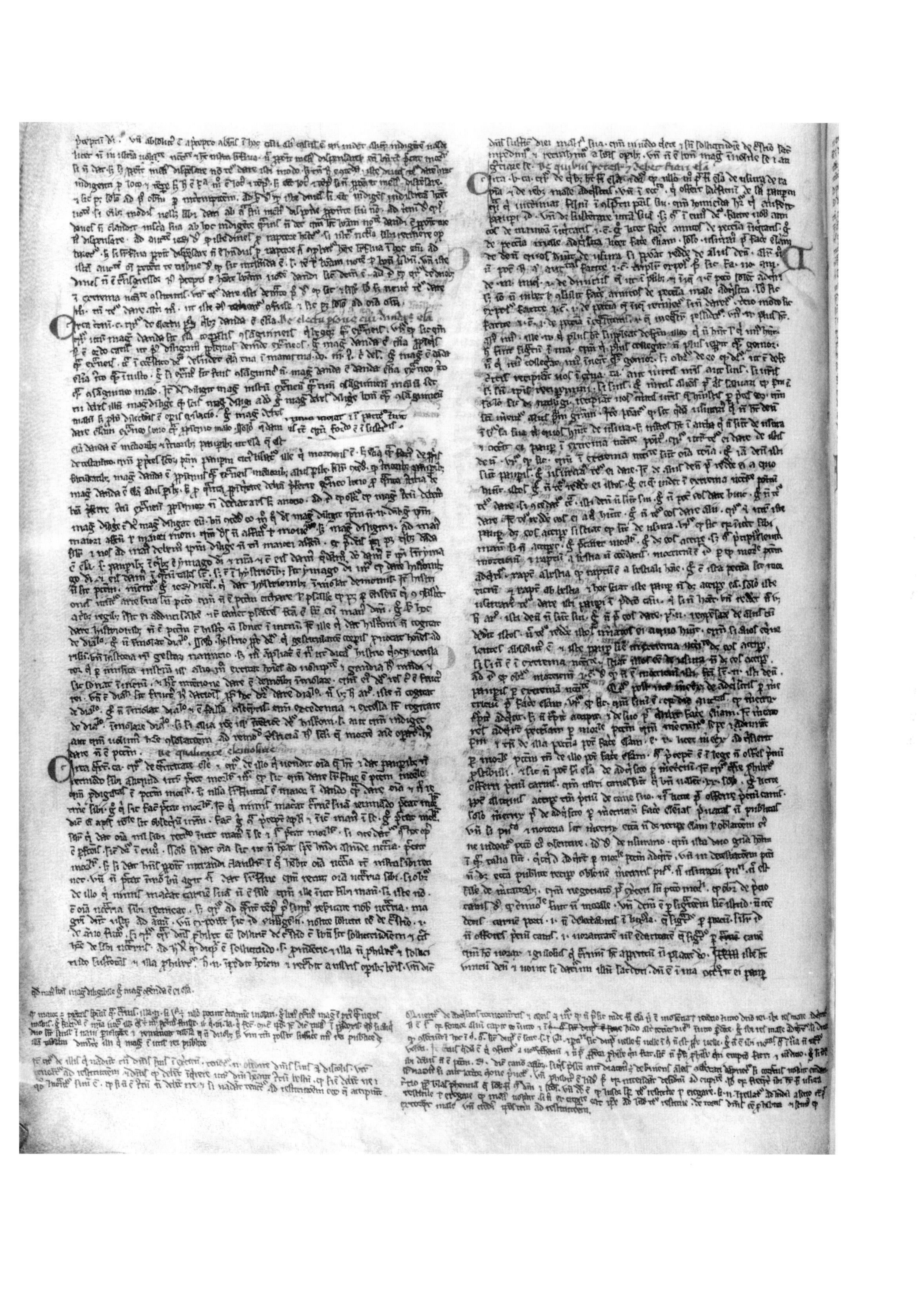

De electu personarum cui danda est elemosina

De qualitate elemosine

De quibus potest et debet fieri elemosina

BIBLIOGRAPHY

Magistri Guillelmi Altissiodorensis. Summa aurea, ed. J. Ribaillier; N. R. Ker, 'From "Above Top Line" to "Below Top Line": A Change in Scribal Practice'; W. H. Principe, *William of Auxerre's Theology of the Hypostatic Union.*

twenty-one

Alexander of Hales, *Disputed questions 'Antequam esset frater'*

London, British Library, MS Royal 9 E. XIV, fol. 83r
?English; mid-thirteenth century

Alexander of Hales (*c.* 1185–1245) is now perhaps best known as the master who first used Peter Lombard's *Sentences*, rather than the Bible, as the base-text for his theology lectures at the University of Paris. A fateful step, it laid the foundation for the *Sentences* commentary becoming a prerequisite for the theology doctorate. In his day, however, Alexander was a famous master who became a *cause célèbre* when, at the height of his career, he joined the fledgling Order of Friars Minor in a magnificent *coup de théâtre*, leaving the pulpit mid-sermon and exchanging his own clothes for a Franciscan habit (1236). As well as publicity, his decision gave the Order its first senior teaching post at the University of Paris—a crucial first step into the scholarly hierarchy.

Few of Alexander's works survive. We know a *Summa theologiae* (finished by a team of Franciscan scholars after his death), his *Gloss on the Sentences*, and these sixty-eight surviving *Disputed questions from before he was a friar*. Disputed questions were a form of teaching peculiar to the new, 'argumentative', university style. Beginning in the 1220s, at regular intervals (perhaps weekly or fortnightly), the Paris theology faculty suspended all normal teaching and held a disputation on a specific question or questions. A regent master presided, aided by bachelors who responded to (*respondens*) or opposed (*opponens*) the question. This session (the *disputatio*) was followed (probably the next day) by the determination (*determinatio*), when the master gave his considered opinions, later written up as edited *reportationes* of the event, as we have here. A second type of question, *quaestiones quodlibeta*, also survive from Paris. In these, instead of the master choosing the topic, questions could be asked by anyone about anything. Although they began in the theology faculty in Paris, such *quaestiones* spread to the other faculties and other universities.

PARCHMENT: ii (paper) + 198 + ii (paper) fols.; once several separate works; page 310 x 235 mm; text 2 cols., each 255 x 80 mm; lines very variable for text and question: here 63 lines; one good scribe for the *Questions.* Modern rebinding with each quire sewn onto separate guards. Fols. 75–133 were once a separate volume, and still bear their original foliation in Arabic numerals, 1–76 (although fols. 9–24 are missing), and a contents list on fol. 75^r (= 1^r). No (surviving) running heads; paraph signs in ink of text. No decoration, except for occasional plain red capitals. The three sets of theological questions (fols. 75–133) have a common indexing system, corresponding to the table of contents on fol. 75^r.

Note of sale, fol. 108^r: 'Richard received three-and-a-half *solidi* for his work on this book. The book of the questions of master Alexander', etc. The MS is known as the *Summa Abendonensis* after the (later) title on fols. 5^r and 198^r.

CONTENTS: fols. 1^r–4^v flyleaves: fragments of 14th-c. antiphonary; 5^r–74^v Robert Courçon, *Summa*; 75^r table of contents; 75^r–82^r anonymous set of theological questions, *inc.* 'Quesitum est de confessione'; 83^r–117^r Alexander of Hales, *Disputed questions*; 117^v–33^r Simon of Hinton, *Questions*; 134^r–41^v Peter of Poitiers, *Sentences* I.1–15; 142^{r-v} misc. theological questions; 143^r–90^r Prepositinus, *Summa;* 191^r–97^v Bernard of Pavia, *Summa on the Decretals* (incomplete).

On this page we may note the original foliation (25) in Arabic numerals (center top margin), along with a barely visible title, trimmed in binding. As well as the hole in the parchment, there is a tear which has been sewn together—the stitching is still visible; this was a common method of repairing defective parchment books. Careful scrutiny of the bottom margin reveals the title which gives this work its attribution: 'Q'est's Hales. anq[a] eet fr' [Questiones Hales antequam esset frater]. Left col. (*Q. xvi*: p. 224 of ed.):

> Queritur de passibilitate anime xpi et ade, et sic membra ordinantur: primo, utrum anima sit passibilis, sive ade, sive xpi; secundo, dato quod paciatur utrum a corporeo vel incorporeo; et de hiis non tangemus ad presens, sed supposito quod anima sit passibilis. Queritur postea utrum anima ade in statu innocentie fuit passibilis, et dato quod fuit passibilis in statu illo, utrum post peccatum fuit addita ei nova passiibilitas, vel eadem quae prius augmentata. [We now inquire about the suffering of the soul of Christ and of Adam, and the questions are ordered thus: first, whether the soul, whether it be Christ's or Adam's, can suffer; secondly, given that it suffers, whether it suffers corporeally or incorporeally; and we do not touch on these now, but assume that the soul may suffer. One may then ask whether Adam's soul could suffer in the state of innocence and, given that it could suffer in that state, whether after original sin a new suffering was added to it, or it was the same suffering increased.]

A. Queritur de passibilitate anime Christi et Ade. Et sic iste ordinandum: primo utrum anima sit passibilis, sive Ade sive Christi. Secundo dato quod patiatur utrum a corpore vel incorporeo. Et de hiis non tangemus ad presens. Sed supposito quod anima sit passibilis queritur [illegible] vera anima Ade in statu innocentie fuit passibilis. Et dato quod fuit passibilis in statu illo, utrum per peccatum fuit addita ei nova passibilitas, ut aliter quam prius angustiata. Et utrum anima Ade secundum omnem portionem vel partem suam fuit passibilis, scilicet secundum inferiorem et secundum superiorem. Quarto si Christus accepit animam cum omni passibilitate, aut cum aliqua et aliqua non. Et loquimur hic de passibilitate que inest ex parte carnis. Post si [illegible] quod fuit secundum partem superiorem, fuit enim comprehensor in via, tollere omnem passibilitatem ut animam Christi non [illegible]. Et si non habet

B. omnem passibilitatem utrum tamen passionem habet. Circa primum procedendo, primo supponenda est differentia inter actum et passionem; post supponende differentie passionis. Dicit enim Damascenus: motus secundum quod fuit ab animalibus secundum se ipsos actiones sunt, secundum vero quod immoderate fiunt et preter naturam, passiones sunt. Dicitur et quod passio dicitur equivoce et quod dicitur de passionibus corporalibus et spiritualibus. Et sic diffinitur: passio est motus ab alio in aliud. Secundum vero quod proprie conveniunt passionibus anime sic diffinitur: passio est motus appetitive virtutis sensibilis in ymaginatione boni vel mali. Item Remigius sic diffinit: passio est motus anime irrationalis per susceptionem boni aut mali. Queritur ergo utrum anima Ade in statu innocentie fuit receptibilis huiusmodi passionum. Videtur quod non. Adam enim dicebatur immortalis secundum corpus. Sed causa est motus immortalitatis circa corpus in eo et impassibilitatis quantum ad animam. Ergo sicut dicebatur immortalis quantum ad corpus in statu innocentie, et dicebatur impassibilis secundum animam. Item quod sic sumitur in ipso de immortalitate corporis et impassibilitate secundum animam probatur. Passio enim que venit in animam venit mediante corpore. Sed ergo corpus Ade in primo statu non fuit subiectum passionibus, nec anima fuit receptibilis mali. Quod autem corpus non fuit subiectum passionibus dicit Aug. xiiii. de civitate: Non igitur vivebant senectute dissoluti vel corruptioni corpore, nec ex corpore nullius intrinsecus morbi, nullius extrinsecus ictus metuebatur. Item ad idem: omne a quo patitur aliquid et quod huiusmodi superius est eo quod patitur, quia potentius est eo quod patitur. Et hoc dicit et Aug. in xii. super Gen. ad litteram. Et in vi. musice dicit quod non potest anima recipere passionem a corpore, quia superior est eo et nobilior. Sed ergo in statu innocentie erat immediate sub Deo, nondum sibi ipso tempore corpore nullo corporali ferior erat. Ergo ut nullius corporis passibilis fuit, et aliter non dicitur passibilis anima, immo receptibilis. Ergo secundum animam fuit impassibilis Adam. Item eiusdem nature fuit in se anima Christi et Ade. Sed dicit Hylarius: Deus verbum caro factus non potuit esse demutabilis anime in patiendo. Ergo si eiusdem nature in spe fuit anima Ade in primo statu, videtur quod non potuit pati. Item ad idem: in primo statu non fuit ad bonum immoderate moveri et corporibus et malis. Ergo secundum sensibilem partem anime non fuit anima mobilis respectu mali et boni. Nec enim sunt perturbationes ut dicit Philosophus: gaudium, dolor, metus et eis oppositum. Ex immoderato enim bono et malo quod movet in presenti gaudium et dolor, ex immoderato bono et malo quod movet in futuro sunt metus et eis opposita. Relinquitur ergo quod anima Ade non fuit ordinabilis ad aliquid immoderate movens, quia perturbaciones enim dicuntur proprie passiones, si non est actuale movens. Ergo anima eius non fuit passibilis, secundum quod passio diffinitur motus

C. appetitive virtutis sensibilis etc. Contra. Dicit Damascenus: omne quod creatum est vertibile est secundum generationem et corruptionem vel alterationem. Ergo cum anima non sit vertibilis secundum generationem et corruptionem, est mutabilis secundum alterationem. Sed omne passibile alterabile est passibile. Ergo anima in statu innocentie fuit passibilis. Item impassibilitas est dos anime una; non enim sunt dotes debende anime glorificate ex parte corporis. Sed illa dos data fuisset anime Ade sive stetisset sive cecidisset, dum modo pervenisset, ergo dos hec non datur nisi post resurrectionem, quod in statu innocentie et in Adam fuit passibilis. Item anima unibilis est corpori, angelus autem non. Hinc enim dicit [illegible] Aug. ostendens animam et angelum, xii. super Gen. Et propter hanc unibilitatem compatitur anima corpori patienti. Unde Damascenus: anima corpore inciso ipsa non incisa condolet et compatitur. Ergo anima fuit passibilis. Si ergo corpus Ade in statu innocentie fuit corpus passibile, hoc non patet, ergo anima habuit potentiam in se patiendi. Item quod corpus Ade fuit passibile et in statu innocentie probatur xi. [illegible] quod ad invicem creati sunt, sed [illegible] passione creati.

ergo sunt ad agendum, ergo in aliud passibile. Cum ergo creati sunt ad agendum in corpus humanum, relinquitur ergo et quod in statu innocentie fuit passibile. Sed hec auctoritas vel melius concludit quod in statu culpe esset impassibilis anima, quia [illegible] non est adhuc de culpa. Ergo si non essent homines in statu culpe non invenirent sibi potestatem agendi in eas. Item quomodo Aug. vult fuit immortalis Adam in statu innocentie et dicit quod immortalitas ista fuit ex ligno vite; alii autem fructus fuerunt ad sustentationem vite. Sed ergo ista immortalitas non fuit in Adam ex se sed ex ligno, ergo de se habebat mortalitatem. Sed sic fuit de immortalitate ex parte corporis, ita fuit de impassibilitate ex parte anime. Ergo de se non fuit impassibilis anima, immo potuit ex extrinseco ~~potuit~~ in ea lesura. Item corpus Ade fuit ex contrariis in quadam equalitate reductis et [illegible] calidum et passiva, calidum ergo et frigidum et quod in eo erant habebant virtutem agendi et patiendi. Et habebat in se virtutem activam et passivam, passibile ergo fuit corpus ab huiusmodi elementis, ergo anima unita ei habuit compassibilitatem. Item si dicas quod corpus Ade quantum est de se fuit impassibile, tamen patet [illegible] intelligamus per impossibile quod non esset lignum vite et quod cum Adam creatus esset in illo statu, vel cum creatus fuit Adam intelligamus quod lignum vite defuerit, esset quod tunc utique defectibilis esset Adam, et tamen quod sic. Ergo in illo statu erat passibilis. Item si dicas quod non esset passio nisi accedente culpa, quia si non comedisset non peccasset, ponamus quod non fuisset ei datum preceptum de non comedendo pomo, adhuc fuit in statu innocentie, constat quod [illegible] Ade [illegible]. Hec autem continuitas fuit divisibilis. Sed ad huiusmodi divisionem sequitur per causam distantia vel solutio. Sed hec est causa doloris. Dolor enim est passio vel solutio vel sic huiusmodi distantie. Ad huiusmodi ergo distantiam sequitur sensus in anima. Ergo passibilitas fuit in ea. Solutio. Dicimus quod anima Ade in statu innocentie uno modo fuit passibilis, alio modo non. Passibile enim multipliciter dicitur. Uno enim modo passibile idest quod receptibile, et sic dicitur anima passibilis in quocumque statu, quia receptibilis est specierum intelligibilium. Species autem in anima sic dicuntur passiones. [illegible] autem dicitur passibile [illegible] informatione que informat eam. Hoc est generalissimo modo passibilis. Secundo dicitur pati recipere aliquid oppositum in receptibili eius, sic receptibile est gaudii et tristitie, que autem [illegible] species intelligibiles recipit, licet sint aliquorum contrariorum, nulla tamen est ibi contrarietas. Recipere autem cum oppositione dicitur duobus modis, quoniam recipit conveniens vel inconveniens; hoc potest esse moderatum vel immoderatum. Si receptum est conveniens moderatum sic dicitur passibile secundo modo. [margin: vel inconveniens si non dicitur sic immoderatum tertio modo.] Quarto modo dicitur passibile quod necessarium est ad passionem immoderatam. Ergo in statu in quo nunc est anima subiecta est necessitati passionis. In statu autem innocentie fuit passibilis secundum primum modum et secundum et receptibilis sive passionis dicitur secundum tertium modum. Sed non recipere non potuit sic [illegible] nisi adveniret culpa, et sic dicitur passio privatio. Quarto modo dicitur passibilitas necessitas ad compatiens. Sic non fuit passibilis anima in statu innocentie, et sic est pena. Iste autem modus probatus est supra. Dico ergo quod anima Ade receptibilis fuit passionum sibi convenientium et [illegible] anime. Potuit enim recipere convenientes moderatas. Etiam immoderatas potuisset recipere, non potuit tamen sic manens in culpa perdente. Rationes ergo quedam probantes esse quodammodo passibilem et quedam probant eam quodammodo impassibilem. Ad primum ergo rationem que probabat animam impassibilem quia corpus fuit immortale, dico quod corpus fuit immortale quia corpus quantum fuit de illo statu non fuit ordinatum ad mortem. Si enim fecisset remansisset in illa vita quousque translatum fuisset a Deo et sic supponitur in immortalitatem gloriosam. Aug. in libro de baptismo parvulorum: Si [illegible] quod per tot annos non [illegible] quod nunc sic homo obedienti eius post tribueret in ale corpus vivere in eo quandam statum quo sine defectu fieret annos temporis quod vellet eum de ad immortalitatem transferre. Item Aug. ix. super Gen.: Sicut Enoch et Helyas in Adam mortui mortis que propaginem gestantes [illegible] vita sunt. [illegible] autem carnis resurrectionem [illegible] corpus animale in spirituale mutentur, non morbo nec senecta deficient. [illegible] hominibus prestatur. Unde solo fructu in angelica forma habebunt

BIBLIOGRAPHY

Magistri Alexandri de Hales. Quaestiones disputatae 'antequam esset frater'; Alexandri de Hales . . . Summma theologica; B. Bazàn et al., *Les Questions disputées et les questions quodlibétiques dans les facultés de théologie, de droit, et de médecine;* P. Glorieux, 'Autour de la "Summa Abendonensis"'; F. Pelster, 'Die Quaestionen des Alexander von Hales'.

twenty-two

Albert the Great, *De unitate intellectus contra Averroem*

Paris, Bibliothèque nationale de France, MS lat. 14557, fol. 24[r]
Paris (St Victor); late thirteenth century

Some medieval controversies and problems come down to us with all the force they mustered in their own time. Diverse issues, from the mystery of the Incarnation to the proper use of money and goods, are still the subject of lively debate. Other questions have lost their context—they no longer fit into our metaphysical schema. It's not that the problems have necessarily been solved, but rather that their solution is not now a key piece in our cosmic jigsaw. Such is the argument over the unity of the intellect, an issue that served to divide the greatest theological minds of the thirteenth century and vividly to expose the problems attendant on applying Greek and Arabic learning to traditional theological debates.

Put simply, the question was whether there is only one intellect in which everyone shares, or whether each person has their own. This was not a query that would have worried Augustine. His theology was largely biblical, where such questions are not asked. But the introduction of Aristotle into the arts syllabus brought new Greek metaphysical ideas of ordering the world into currency. The terms in which questions were posed changed; new words and language were deemed necessary: Aristotle not only required consideration of the intellect, he further divided it into 'passive' or 'possible' and 'active' or 'agent'. Aristotle's ideas were mediated through two Islamic theologians: Avicenna (Ibn Sina: 980–1037) and Averroes (Ibn Rushd: 1126–1198). In this, as in other cases, what was commonly thought of as Aristotle's solution was really that of Averroes, and the title Albert gave the work he wrote (between 1256 and 1263) at the request of Pope Alexander IV, *On the Unity of the Intellect, in Opposition to Averroes*, reflects this.

For Christians, the issue had really to be decided on the side of particular individual intellects, for without a part of each person which was incorruptible (i.e., immortal) how else could everyone be individually resurrected at the Day of Judgment? But a crucial problem

PARCHMENT: iv + 366 fols.; page 315 x 235 mm; text 2 cols. each 250 x 85 mm; 53 lines; one scribe, writing a typical highly abbreviated university hand. 3 booklets bound together. Running heads with title and bk. nos. Red and blue initials with contrasting penwork; red and blue paraph signs; *tituli* in red. Colophon: 'hanc questionum disputavit in curia Romana', fol. 32^r^.

CONTENTS: A: fols. 1^r^–23^v^ Robert Kilwardby, *De conscientia;* 24^r^–32^r^ Albert the Great, *De unitate intellectus contra Averroem;* 32^r^–162^v^ several disputed and quodlibetal questions, mostly by Gerard of Abbeville; 163^r^–82^v^ Thomas Aquinas, *In Boetium de Trinitate.*

B: fols. 183^r^–249^r^ John Damascene, *De fide orthodoxa;* 249^v^–59^v^ theological misc.

C: fols. 261^r^–366^r^ Henry of Ghent, *Summa theologica.*

remained: how we can understand anything, unless we somehow participate in it, through a common intellect? Albert, and his pupil Thomas Aquinas, sought a synthesis of Christian and Aristotelian ideas that would satisfy both sides. The Aristotelians were led in Paris by Siger of Brabant (*c.* 1240–*c.* 1284) who is known (erroneously) for the double-truth doctrine, that there was one truth for faith and another for reason. Even to consider this as a possibility was desperately damaging to Christian orthodoxy: God is One, and all knowledge must be unified and simple, in reflection of God; the idea that a separate system of knowledge might exist outside theology was inadmissible. Not until Thomas (*De unitate intellectus contra Averroistas*) was the matter settled, temporarily at least, though the debate raged until the Reformation, when other issues seemed more pressing.

For Albert to write against Aristotle is ironic, since this German Dominican teacher's main interest was natural science; Aristotle was his obvious master. Albert commented on most of Aristotle's works, writing on everything from minerals to weather, and attempted to fill in gaps where he saw them. His trust in experiment developed over time, as he became more willing to rely on the evidence of his eyes. Nevertheless, although his heart was in nature, his motivation for knowing the world was not 'purely scientific' in our terms. He saw nature as a mirror held up to God; and his desire to know the Creation was in order better to know its Creator. He was clear that revelation remained superior to natural philosophical investigation; but a theologian could and should use all means to find out more about God. A prolific writer of genuine humility, Albert is the only man of the High Middle Ages to be known as 'Great' during his lifetime.

This page shows his preface, which gets straight down to business: 'Quia apud nonnullos eorum qui philosophiam se profitentur scire dubium est de anime separatione a corpore, et si separatur, quod ex ea (altered from a) remaneat, et si manere concedatur secundum intellectum.' [According to some of those who claim to know philosophy there is doubt about the separation of the soul from the body and, if it is separated, about what lives on from it; and if the soul lives on then it must be conceded that the intellect does too.]

[illegible]

BIBLIOGRAPHY

Albertus Magnus. Opera omnia: 17(i) *De unitate intellectus contra Averroem,* ed. A. Hufnagel; *Albert the Great,* ed. F. Kovach and R. Sahahn; P. Mandonnet, *Siger de Brabant et l'averroisme latin au XIIIe siècle;* P. Mazzarella, *Il 'De unitate' di Alberto Magno e di Tommaso D'Aquino; Albertus Magnus and the Sciences,* ed. J. Weisheipl.

twenty-three

Thomas Aquinas, *Summa theologiae*

Oxford, Bodleian Library, MS Lat. th. c. 27, fol. 4r
Probably English; mid- to late thirteenth century

Thomas is the only medieval theologian whose ideas command an active following in the twentieth century. The symmetry of his methodical synthesis of traditional Christian (Augustinian and Platonist) theology with Aristotelian methods and categories may be thought of at once as the zenith of medieval scholastic thought and its downfall. His apparently comprehensive, even-tempered certainties, the product of method and reason, continue to attract those seeking answers to the problems of faith.

Thomas (*c.* 1224–1274) was the youngest son of Count Landulf of Aquino, who was a relative of the emperor and the king of France. Schooled at the famous Benedictine abbey of Monte Cassino, where his family hoped he would become abbot, and later studying arts at Naples, Thomas nevertheless wished to join the Dominican Order. His family strongly opposed his becoming a Mendicant, when the wealth of the Benedictines beckoned; but join he did, and was sent to Paris to study theology with Albert the Great. His subsequent teaching career took him to Cologne, Anagni, Orvieto, Rome, Naples and Paris. He died at Fossanuova, on 7 March 1274.

Thomas is renowned for his massive output. He was said to dictate seamlessly to several secretaries at once, each taking down a different work. He wrote biblical commentary, at least one commentary on the *Sentences*, commentaries on much of Aristotle and the *Liber de causis*, and disputed and quodlibetal questions, as well as short tracts in answer to specific questions, for instance, in opposition to the Averroists or Avicebron, or about government in reply to the duchess of Brabant. Aware of the inadequacy of western knowledge of Aristotle, he had William of Moerbecke translate or retranslate many of his works, leaving a valuable legacy for later scholars. But Thomas' name is almost synonymous with his *Summa theologiae* or *theologica*, which, together with the earlier *Summa contra Gentiles* is a massive statement of the whole of Christian theology. The *Summa* is in three parts, the first (*prima*) dealing with God,

PARCHMENT: Parchment; iii (parchment) + 138 + ii (parchment) fols.; page 310 x 220 mm; text 2 cols., each 215–255 x 70–85 mm; *c.* 48–58 lines; ruled in lead-point, with wide margins left for notes; four similar hands, heavily abbreviated. Running heads with question nos. in Arabic numerals; top outer corners give question no. and subject in brief; catchwords. Many marginal additions, notes, subject headings, cross-references, textual corrections and additions, article nos., pointing hands etc. Original binding of alum-tawed (white) leather on boards. Blue and red initial (fol. 1^{r}) with red and blue infilling and flourishing. Elsewhere, blue capitals with red flourishing; red and blue paraph signs.

Bought at Sotheby's on 12 June 1963, lot 146.

CONTENTS: fols. 1ra–135rb Thomas Aquinas, *Summa theologiae*, part 1; 135rb–37^{vc} list of questions and articles of *Summa;* 138^{ra-va} three theological questions of 'brother R. Minor', Robert of Winchester and 'Master T of Teford'.

A typical theological schoolbook.

the second dealing first (*prima secundae*) with God's relations with humanity and secondly (*secunda secundae*) with humanity's relations with God, and the third (*tertia*) with Christ and the sacraments as the path for the human return to God (i.e., planned as Peter Lombard's *Sentences* but in three unequal books, rather than four.)

The parts of the *Summa* circulated both together and, as here, separately. The *secunda secundae*, dealing with moral instruction, was the most popular single piece. The number of extant MSS of Thomas' works, although only exhaustively catalogued (in alphabetical terms) as far as Paris, is nevertheless 2,591. Three autograph MSS are extant in eight codices or fragments.

This page shows the beginning of question 3: on the simplicity of God. It exhibits many typical features of a schoolbook: running head with *quaestio* no. (3: top center), and subject (*q. 3. de simplicitate divina*: top right); pointing finger; faces drawn down left margin; careful corrections (mostly insertions) in left- and right-hand margins; shield-shaped lozenge with subject of text (*Deum non esse corpus tripliciter ostenditur:* bottom right). Question two (left col.) refers to several ways (*viae*) of proceeding, and these are marked in the outer margin: *2ª via, 3ª via* etc. The three books of the *Summa* are divided into questions, themselves divided into articles. Each article has been numbered by this MS, and an Arabic 14 (|ℒ) can be seen in the right margin.

Although Thomas' place in the pantheon of philosopher-theologians was secure, he was not without his critics. Some of his positions were condemned by Stephen Tempier and Robert Kilwardby in 1277, and by John Peckham in 1284; but his opinions were officially imposed on the Dominican Order in 1278. The Roman Catholic Church considers his teaching an authentic expression of doctrine, and canon law makes study of his works the accepted basis for theology.

moueri. si igitur id a quo mouetur moueatur, oportet ipsum ab alio moueri
et illud ab alio. hic autem non est procedere in infinitum quia sic non esset aliquod primum mouens
et per consequens nec aliquod aliud mouens, quia mouentia secunda non mo-
uent nisi per hoc quod sunt mota a primo mouente, sicut baculus
non mouet nisi per hoc quod est motus a manu. ergo necesse est de-
uenire ad aliquod primum mouens quod a nullo mouetur, et hoc omnes intelli-
2a uia. gunt deum. Secunda uia est ex ratione cause efficientis. Inuenimus enim
in istis sensibilibus esse ordinem causarum efficientium, nec tamen inuenitur, nec est
possibile, quod aliquid sit causa efficiens sui ipsius, quia sic esset prius se
ipso, quod est impossibile. Non autem est possibile quod in causis efficientibus procedatur in infinitum,
quia in omnibus causis efficientibus ordinatis, primum est causa medii, et medium est
causa ultimi, siue media sint plura siue unum tantum. remota
autem causa remouetur effectus. Si igitur non fuerit primum in causis efficientibus,
non erit ultimum nec medium. Sed si procedatur in infinitum in causis efficientibus, non erit prima causa efficiens, et sic non erit nec effectus ul-
[illegible]

[illegible]

BIBLIOGRAPHY

Sancti Thomae de Aquino. Summa theologiae; H. F. Dondaine and H. V. Shooner, *Codices manuscripti operum Thomae de Aquino;* L. E. Boyle, *The Setting of the* Summa theologiae *of Saint Thomas;* J. A. Weisheipl, *Friar Thomas d'Aquino, His Life, Thought and Works.*

D

Theology Made Accessible

twenty-four

Peter the Chanter, *Verbum abbreviatum*

Oxford, Bodleian Library, MS Bodl. 373, fol. 2r
English; second half of the thirteenth century

The office of *cantor* or chanter at the Cathedral of Notre Dame in Paris was, in the late twelfth century, filled by a theologian teaching at the cloister school. Peter (d. 1197), from a knightly family of Hodenc-en-Bray, near Reims, where he was educated, was one of the greatest figures of Paris theology. Primarily a biblical scholar, Peter's learning was nevertheless wide, and his writings included a set of *distinctiones* 'defining' and illustrating biblical words according to various senses of Scripture, a *Summa on the sacraments*, a Gospel harmony, a technical manual of grammar and, particularly, the *Verbum abbreviatum*, known after its opening words, 'Verbum abbreviatum fecit dominus super terram' (Rom. 9:28). The work is a 'popular manual of ethics' (Baldwin), centered around the vices and virtues. Although not always organizationally easy to follow, since he attempts to include under each heading a comprehensive collection of scriptural, patristic and classical references, as well as contemporary stories, *exempla* and even occasional *questiones*, all bound together with his own analysis and comment, the work was a smashing success. Peter's view was that *any* source with correct opinions, be it Christian or pagan, could be used by theologians to fight against vices and commend virtues, and so the *Verbum* became a treasure-trove of references and arguments for scholars and preachers.

In an academic world becoming known for its prolixity (which was to get worse), it may have been Peter's unfavorable comments on the proliferation of glosses and stated aim of being brief that made the work popular. It is ironic, then, that the more than ninety extant manuscripts of the *Verbum* exist in two main versions, long and short, where it seems likely that the more popular, shorter text (probably complete by 1197) is an abbreviation of an earlier, longer form (written *c.* 1191–92). Nevertheless, there remain various forms of short text, some with no marginal notes, as here, others with marginalia outlined in boxes outside the main text, and yet more where the marginalia have been incorporated into the main text.

PARCHMENT: Parchment; i + 125 fols.; page 340 x 230 mm; text 2 cols., each 230 x 70 mm; 40 lines; ruled in crayon; written above the top line; one scribe. Chapter headings in red; rubrication of first letter of sentence, up to fol. 110v; catchwords. 14th-c. NOTA signs. English, 15th-c. leather binding on boards with two clasps. Red and blue initial with green highlighting of infill and flourishing (fol. 1v); minor initials in red or blue with blue or red penwork flourishing.

Given by the dean and canons of Windsor in 1612.

CONTENTS: fol. 1r–120v Peter the Chanter, *Verbum abbreviatum* (short version), with capitula list (fol. 1r–v); ending imperf., 'tetigit ut' (*PL* 205:356B); 121r–24r part of a moral treatise, *inc.* 'Vanitas vanitatum . . . hoc auctoritas ita insinuat'.

Peter's general tenor was intensely practical, earning him a place in Grabmann's 'biblical moral school' of masters. Unlike most of his contemporaries, he was not particularly interested in speculative theology; instead, he was probably the single most important source for discussions of practical ethics in the schools. He addressed questions which fascinate the modern reader by their contemporary significance: can teachers take money for teaching the word of God? Can a cathedral accept money given by prostitutes? Can moneylenders charge interest? Are some weapons too horrible to be used in warfare? His answers lead the reader to a man of integrity and wisdom, steeped in biblical reading, and yet fully aware of the dilemmas posed by life. Indeed, as chanter, he was the second ranking dignitary in Notre Dame, after the dean, and his life was filled with practical ecclesiastical duties. His unusual interests leave us uncertain who his own teachers may have been, but he himself was the center of a wide circle of influence, working for church reforms.

This extract (left col., line 12) contains one of Peter's most famous *dicta*, that the student of sacred Scripture needs to pass through three levels:

> In tribus igitur consistit exercicium sacre scripture, circa lectionem, disputationem et predicationem, cuilibet istorum inimica est prolixitas, mater oblivionis et noverca memorie. . . . Post lectionem igitur sacre scripture et dubitabilium per disputationem inquisitionem et non prius, predicandum ut sic cortina cortinam trahat. [Training in sacred scripture consists of three parts, reading, disputation, and preaching; and prolixity, the mother of forgetfulness and stepmother of memory, is inimical to them all. . . . Therefore, after reading sacred scripture and examining doubtful questions through disputation, and not before, one may preach 'as curtain draws on curtain' (Hildebert of Lavardin, *Sermons*).]

uiamus. breuitatemque imitantes. colligamus utiliora capitula sumpta. tum ex corpore sacre scripture. tum ex benedictis aliarum scripturarum. Quicquid enim ubicumque bene dictum est: ut meum initium est. inquid theologus ad singulorum uiciorum redargutionem. et ad uirtutum et morum commendationem. optimeque uerborum directionem. negociorumque in ecclesia emergentium decisionem.

Quod sacra scriptura est quasi domus.

In tribus igitur consistit exercicium sacre scripture. circa lectionem. disputationem. et predicationem. cuilibet istorum inimica est prolixitas. mater obliuionis. et nouerca memorie. Lectio autem est quasi fundamentum. et substratorium sequentium quia per eam cetere utilitates comparantur. Disputatio quasi paries est. in hoc exercitio et edificio. quia nichil plene intelligitur: fideliter ue predicatur: nisi prius dente disputationis frangatur. Predicatio uero cui subseruiunt priora. quasi tectum est tegens fideles ab estu et a turbine uiciorum. Post lectionem igitur sacre scripture et dubitabilium per disputationem inquisitionem et non prius: predicandum ut sic cortina cortinam trahat. et cetera. De breuitate lectionum.

Gregorius autem breuitatem lectionis commendans ab eaque prolixitatem et superfluam expositionem resecans: ait. Lectio ista. Exiit qui seminat. et cetera. Non indiget expositione: sed ammonitione. Ammonitoria igitur quia per se patent: seorsum in loco priuato legantur: expositoria uero et difficilia in scolis audiantur. Ad hec inquid terenda sunt magistrorum limina. Item Ieronimus. Cum dominus ante offensam ydolatrie illi populo tantum decalogum commisisset. sufficientem ad salutem: post illam multiplices contulit cerimonias: quibus minus eorum exigentibus honerati sunt et afflicti. eorum exemplo nos uereri deberemus. Quod cum deus tantummodo textum mathei ecclesie primitiue commisisset omnia necessaria saluti continentem. minus nobis exigentibus putatiuis exercitationibus et inquisitionibus superfluis. et prolixis aliis glosarum multitudine. lectionum superfluitate et prolixitate honerati sumus. in quibus est tantus labor et afflictio spiritus. puta in glosis illis que non intra sed circa textum locantur. Item ysaias. centesimo sexagesimo quarto. Quare argentum uestrum appenditis non in panibus: in refectione. scilicet spiritualium eloquiorum sacramentum et necessariorum. et laborem. id est studium uestrum non in saturitate: sed in foliis uerborum et multitudine. que autem prouolant. et animam non saciant. Item idem nonagesimo. Ubi est litteratus ubi est uerba legis ponderans. scilicet scriba et phariseus. legem superflua expositione honerans. Item ieronimus textum per textum exponit aliam glosam super uacaneam indicans. Idcircoque nobis difficiliorem ad intelligendum. Item sicut ieronimus et origenes asteriscos et obelos illuminandis et confodiendis. et delendis apposuerunt: ita et nunc magis opus esse uidetur: ut hec poneremus ad explanationem difficilium et iugulationem delectationemque prolixitatis et superfluitatem glosarum. Item sicut in templo candelabro erant instrumenta infusoria. extinctoria. et emunctoria. sic in sacra scriptura infusores fuerunt. ut qui eam exposuerunt. Ieronimus et Gregorius extinctores qui hereses extinxerunt. scilicet ualidi mallei hereticorum. Augustinus et hylarius

BIBLIOGRAPHY

Petrus Cantor, *Verbum abbreviatum;* idem, *Distinctiones Abel,* ed. J. B. Pitra; *Pierre le Chantre. Summa de sacramentis et animae consiliis,* ed. J. A. Dugauquier; J. W. Baldwin, *Masters, Princes and Merchants. The Social Views of Peter the Chanter and His Circle.*

twenty-five

Bible moralisée

Vienna, Österreichische Nationalbibliothek, MS 2554, fol. 16r
Paris; 1220–30

The *Bible moralisée* is the only exception to this book's rule of showing only the typical—books that would have been found in any decent theological library in the thirteenth century. But this small group of volumes, produced in Paris between *c.* 1220 and *c.* 1248, represents 'the first truly spectacular creations in the thirteenth century' (Branner, p. 32), and as such, surely earn their place. There are four extant moralized Bibles from the first half of the thirteenth century. In chronological order these are 1) Vienna, ÖN, MS 1179; 2) this MS; 3) the Toledo cathedral Bible (3 vols) + NY, Pierpont Morgan, MS 240; 4) Oxford, BL, MS Bodl. 270b + Paris, BnF, MS lat. 11560 + London, BL, MSS Harley 1526–27. Ten other, later MSS survive, but of greatly inferior quality.

Although marvelously illustrated, these moralized Bibles are more than giant picture books. Indeed, it is the confluence of text and image on such a large scale that makes them unique. Beginning at Genesis and working through both Testaments, the books present selected biblical verses illustrated first 'literally', then coupled (in the roundel below) with a 'spiritual' interpretation in both words and picture. Three of the Bibles have text in Latin; this MS uses French. Although closely related, the conception of texts and images is unique to each copy, although there is evidence of tracing (and of misunderstanding) between copies.

Both text and image are carefully planned, produced, it seems, under the direction of an 'iconographer'. Where the text is Latin, it is the version of the Vulgate used in the schools of Paris—the so-called 'University' or 'Paris Bible', following the Vulgate order of books. The texts and interpretations seem to follow the *Ordinary Gloss* (no. 1), perhaps through the medium of the *postillae* of the Preacher Hugh of St Cher (no. 8) and linking the books with Hugh or his school. This, coupled with Branner's belief that some of the painters of the Oxford/Paris/London copy also appear in the Great Bible of St Jacques—Hugh's convent base—perhaps points to a Dominican provenance. Certainly, at just this time the Dominicans were experimenting with the production of new types of book and study aids, although usually of a humbler sort. The patronage of the copy now in Toledo by Blanche of Castille, mother of St Louis of France, suggests that the Preachers may have successfully produced a high-class

PARCHMENT: i + 66 (fol. 64 missing) fols.; page 340 x 260 mm; text frame 280 x 210 mm; 8 compass-drawn roundels in 2 cols., per page; apparently one scribe for text. Full-color miniatures, with gold backgrounds and highlights.

Sometime between 1567 and 1783 it came to the library of the canonesses of Hall (Tyrol); thence (1783) to the Imperial Library in Vienna.

CONTENTS: fol. i^v full-page miniature of God as creator, with compasses; 1^r–65^v *Bible moralisée*, Gen. to 2 Sam. 4 (ends incomplete); 66^r six armorial drawings.

teaching tool which combined theological and moral content with luxury artwork—guaranteed to appeal to the religious French monarchy. But in fact, we have virtually no hard evidence about for whom these books were made, or how they were used.

This Vienna Bible has more than 1,000 scenes, but it is compressed in comparison to Toledo, which has *c.* 5,500. Its text is a paraphrase of the Bible, not a straight translation, and much of the painting appears to have been done by just one artist. The pictures contain many fascinating references to contemporary issues, including (fol. 37^r: 1 Sam. 13: 19–20) a moralization of 'bad scholars' leaving theology to go to Bologna to study laws and decrees. The roundels are read in vertical pairs. The lower two pairs on this page illustrate Ex. 2:3–4: Moses abandoned in the bulrushes. Moses in his cradle becomes Jesus cradled in the Gospel book, a splendidly 'literal' allegorization of Christ as the Word of God, and a very uncommon image. The lowest right-hand roundel reads: 'Ce qe Marie plora por son frere moyses qi estoit en l'eue descoverz senefie qe la synagogue plora et mena grant duel de iesu crist qant ele le vit el munde descovert en la devinitei.' [Miriam weeping over her brother Moses, who was placed uncovered in the water, signifies Synagogue weeping, in great distress over Jesus Christ, when she sees him in the world in his uncovered divinity.]

The rather anti-judaic tone of this passage is characteristic of the moralized Bible, which takes a polemical stance against all unorthodox groups. In the lower left-hand roundels, Moses in the bulrushes becomes Jesus surrounded by 'thorns'—here clearly Jews.

Ici uienent li
seriant pha
on ⁊ tolent
as meres lor
enfanz ⁊ les
ocient toz.
Ce qe pharaons
commanda
les enfanz de la t̄
re a tuer fors moy
ses ocirre autresi
senefie herode qi
comanda qe tuit
li enfant fussent
tue ⁊ de tenchi
a tens qe iesu criz
fu nez.
Ici ors prenent
lenfant ⁊ le
mettent en
un bercuel
de uergel ⁊ puis
le gietent en une
eue corant ou il
auoit glaiolois
⁊ il le mistrent en
tre les glagieus.
Ce qe moyses
fu mis el ber
cuel des chices sene
fie iesucrist senefie
qi fu mis en la cra
che as bues. ce qil
fu botez en leue
entre les glagieus
senefie ihucrist
qi fu botez en le
ue del munde
entre les espines.
Ici nest moyses
del uentre sa
mere ⁊ la uen
triere le recoit.
⁊ li peres se de
mente qil en porra
fere.
La natiuitei
moyses senefie
la natiuitei ie
sucrist. la uentriere
qi receut moysen se
nefie la pucele sain
te anastaise qi recut
iesucrist. ce qe li peres
se dementa senefie
ioseph qi se dementa
qi porroit fere de ie
sucrist.
Ici plore marie
por moyse son
frere qe le uoit
en leue descouert.
Ce qe Marie
plora por son
frere moyses qi estoit
en leue descouerz se
nefie qe la synago
gue plora ⁊ mena
grant duel de ihucrist
qant ele le uit el
munde descouert
en la deuinitei.

BIBLIOGRAPHY

Bible moralisée, ed. R. Haussherr; A. de Laborde, *La Bible moralisée conservée à Oxford, Paris, et Londres;* R. Branner, *Manuscript Painting in Paris during the Reign of St Louis. A Study of Styles;* J. Lowden, *The Making of the* Bibles Moralisé*es.*

twenty-six

Anonymous, Sermon *exempla*

Vatican City, Biblioteca Apostolica Vaticana, MS Ottob. lat. 522, fol. 172^{v}
?France; late thirteenth century

Stories are the basis of the Christian faith. The Bible proceeds not by creeds or, by and large, lists of laws, but by stories of the work of God in creation. So it is natural that sermons have always included stories; and as aids for preaching became increasingly common from the thirteenth century onward, medieval preachers and teachers made collections of illustrative and edifying stories called *exempla* (or *similitudines*), referenced thematically or alphabetically for easy use. Although, as here, most are anonymous, some collections were the work of known masters: the earliest surviving purpose-made collection is credited to the Dominican Etienne de Bourbon (d. 1261); but Jacques de Vitry (d. 1240), Vincent of Beauvais (d. 1264) and Humbert of Romans (d. 1277) were also associated with popular sets of tales, sometimes culled from sermons themselves. Some stories appear again and again; all purported to be factual, though many are too good to be true.

Judged on the quantity of written evidence, it might be thought that Christian preaching only began in the thirteenth century, especially after the Fourth Lateran Council of 1215. But preaching had always been integral to Christianity. The surge is not in preaching but in aids for preachers: books of *distinctiones* (interpreting words and ideas according to the various senses of Scripture), collected sermons, and books of *exempla* all begin to appear in profusion. Paris masters produced handbooks for their confrères in the field—scholars like William of Auvergne or John of La Rochelle wrote on *The Art of Preaching* (both written in the 1230s–40s), and practitioners like William Peraldus published books of model sermons (no. 29). Although Christian doctrine was the creation of academic theologians, few masters thought of themselves as inhabiting an ivory tower. Henry of Ghent (d. 1293) sums this up when he reminds his pupils that a teacher's audience is not simply the listeners in his classroom, but all those outside the schools whom *their* words will reach (*Quodlibet* 10, q. 16). In particular, with the coming of the friars and their street ministry, manuals for preaching

PARCHMENT: i (paper) + 321 (missing fols. 210–19) + i (paper) fols.; page 160 x 110 mm; text 120 x 80 mm; 38 lines; drypoint ruling; several scribes. Made up of at least 11 booklets, the latter part of which (bklets. G-K, fols. 142–321) was once consecutively foliated (1–162). Some marginal notes to fols. 142–321 with names of people and places. Decoration: poor; major initials and capitals sometimes touched in red.

CONTENTS: fols. 1^r–4^v former flyleaves.

A-F: fols. 5^r–141^v 6 bklets. containing a miscellany of Franciscan texts including John Pecham, *On poverty*.

G: fols. 142^r–94^v *Liber exemplorum;* 95^r–202^v misc. *exempla* material.

H: fols. 203^r–69^v specifically Franciscan *exempla* collection.

I–K: fols. 270^r–321^v misc. Franciscan material, including (295^r–304^v) a spiritual treatise, 'Hec que tibi mitto' and (314^r–17^v) later alphabetic index of examples in G–K.

A typical Franciscan *vade mecum* book.

and penitence were greatly in demand from those dealing firsthand with the cure of souls. Preaching aids had been known before—famously, the *Regula pastoralis* of Gregory the Great (no. 10); what made the difference was the steady improvement in clerical education, particularly among the new Franciscan and Dominican Orders, which produced men well enough trained to make use of them. Consequently, preaching aids are generally written in Latin, although the sermons themselves would have been preached in the vernacular.

Exempla cover all sorts of themes and types, from everyday events, to re-workings of fables, tales of famous people, or miracle stories. They are too varied and colorful to be summed up simply. In this MS, they appear to have been written down without a discernible internal logic. (Schmitt thinks Dominican collections tended to have more of a logical order than Franciscan ones which were, if anything, alphabetical.) Those which are localizable tend to be about either Paris or Assisi. A few have punchlines in Old French. They are written in a 'chatty' Latin, often tricky to understand, but they take us directly into medieval life. This story (fifth item down), which relies on an auditory pun, refers to Francis of Assisi: 'Nota de beato Francisco a quo cum quidam peteret verbum hedificationis respondit: frater agnus non dicit nisi be; cogita ergo bene, loquere bene, et fac bene et salvaberis.' [Remember blessed Francis who, when a certain man asked him for edifying words, answered: brother lamb says nothing but *beh*; therefore think *be*nignly, speak *be*nignly and act *be*nignly, and you shall be saved.]

¶ Sl'o Si medicine potio sua maneret nullus sumeret pecca d'tali potio. Sic nullus
d; placitum sed in mal'. 7c. s. d. ¶ Semel lapsus e' in peccatum. 7c. s. s.
¶ Sl'o Stipes exter d'incendio promior e' ad comburendum. Sic ho' peccata
13 ¶ Sl'o dr ys. b. peccata ducet e' pl'us ms captiuus q' n' hnt scam. 7c.
Sl'o q' pisces 7 aues 7 bestie captiuant' 7 capiunt' pp' dformi sete. Si e' piscis
saret sb' ame hamum. 7 auis sb' gno laqu. 7 bestie sb' ramis 7 foliis
fouea n'q' caperent'. Sic n' ho' si saret 7 cogsceret q'nta latz pena sb' culpa
¶ Sl'o q'd sic ueteres statue itm pigi solent. s' qda' uetule maledce
facies suas ung'e 7 depinge studnt. Ill' aut q' facuit s' alia' ymagyne
q' illa' q' fecit ds ill'. dicet ad iudicio. no' noui uos. hac facie no'
feci ego. bn. ps. ymagiem ipor ad nichilum redigetis. 7c. s. d.
¶ Sl'o d' bto' Francisco a q' e' qda' petet ubi hedificatois. ps. frat. dgn
n' d' n' be. cogita q' bn. loque bn. 7 fac bn. 7 saluabis.
¶ Sl'o q'd asini l; sit stolid' anab' cu' dfacrnt exhonati fimo q' ptat.
stolidiores q' s' peccatores q' fimo fendissimo peccator suor exhonati
nolunt. l' q' fimo dicitur onati s' n' exhonati appetunt. 7c. s. d.
¶ Ex. Cu' dyas p' os cuidam demoniaci loquens dicet q' peccatum miro m' eis fecit
dix' ei qdam. e' q' nusq' in studio se hoies ad peccat' alliciens. q' ps. pp'
luc' aurum q' ind' habentur. na' 7 q' mdat latrias fetore suum; pp' luc' q' ind' hi
¶ Ex. Legit' in uita sci. Jo. elary sil' 7 patriarche constant. q' consuetudo erat
apud illos q' electo aliq' imperatore. ipo die coronatois ei afferebat
cora' eo diuisas spes marmoris ut s' eliget d' q' uelet s' sepulcri
hedificari. ut q' h' amoneret se sep' cogitare mortale ne extolet d' gla' tpali
¶ Ex. Jd' Jo. patriarcha effect'. fecit sibi fieri sepulcr' ipsum 7 statuit qda'
q' ei i magnis festis b' e' cet' i loco honoris dicet i aure. q' recordaret
d' pficiendo sepulcr'. ut s' haret mortis memoria. 7 humiliaret. 7c. s. s.
¶ Ex. Dr' q' cu' papa elect' e'. i eminenciori loco i oclis ei stuppa i cedit'
7 ei acclamatur. sic transit gla mundi. ut q' h' humiliet. 7c. s. d.
¶ Sl'o q'd ho' q' flagellat' a d'o d; e'de q' pp' duo ad med' iumti fla
gellat' ul' q' forte erit ex uia ut ad uia' redat. l' q' erit i uia. s;
lente ibat. Si e' ex uia erit p' pecc' 7 mortale. d; redire ad uia
pecc' d'serendo. Si i uia erat s; lente i cedbat pauca bona agendo
d; accellerare gssu pla bona faciendo. ps. multe sr' infirmi' tes eor p'. 7c.
¶ Qda' sci' pr' i ueit' dya' premere faciat mag' ad collu' suu' 7 q'siuit
ab eo q'd e' uellet face ille. q' ps. i isto facto pono capita 7 cruda' 7
medullas i usu' h's s'r s'r fuerunt p' magistraui sepe replou illu' 7 reposita
d'on' tp's uarie ostendendi. 7c.

BIBLIOGRAPHY

L. Oliger, 'Liber exemplorum fratrum minorum saeculi XIII'; C. Brémond, J. Le Goff, and J.-C. Schmitt, *L'"Exemplum"*; Th.-M. Charland, *Artes praedicandi;* A. Lecoy de la Marche, *Anécdotes historiques, legendes et apologues tirés du recueil inédit d'Étienne de Bourbon;* J.-C. Schmitt, 'Recueils franciscains d'"Exempla" et perfectionnement des techniques intellectuelles du xiiie au xve siècle'; J.-Th. Welter, *L''Exemplum' dans la littérature religieuse et didactique du moyen âge.*

twenty-seven

Thomas Chobham, *Summa confessorum*

Oxford, University College, MS 119, fol. 50r
Probably English; mid-thirteenth century

The literature of penance was not new to the thirteenth century, but tighter parochial organization, a desire for greater guidance for the clergy, the strength of canon law and a strong streak of practical moral theology in the Paris schools combined to produce a resurgence of pastoral manuals for parish priests. The practical tone of these manuals was a reflection and distillation of the academic theologians. One branch of these handbooks, such as Robert of Flamborough's *Liber poenitentiale*, was firmly legal; another, exemplified by the *Summa confessorum*, stressed the needs of everyday life over the letter of canon law. The Fourth Lateran Council, held by Pope Innocent III in 1215, dealt with many matters of pastoral care, although Thomas betrays no knowledge of its specific decrees.

Thomas (d. after 1233) was an Englishman educated at Paris (possibly as a student of Peter the Chanter); he returned to pursue an ecclesiastical career in London and Salisbury, where he was subdean until 1217. It is possible that he then returned to Paris. The *Summa* was probably completed and in circulation by 1216. Over one hundred surviving manuscripts and two early printings (Cologne 1485; Paderborn 1486) testify to its great popularity, rivaled only by the *Speculum iuniorum* (*c.* 1250) and William of Pagula's *Oculus sacerdotis* (*c.* 1320–1328).

The work is straightforward, divided into seven sections dealing with the nature of penance, the different types of penance, sin, sacraments, the priesthood, priestly behavior in the confessional and, finally, specific penances for specific sins. It is a comprehensive work, ranging from everyday sins like lying to extraordinary incidents such as a mouse eating the eucharistic bread. In all cases his approach is more practical than dogmatic.

PARCHMENT: Parchment; i (paper) + 69 + i (paper) fols.; page *c.* 245 x 170 mm (very variable); text 2 cols., each *c.* 200 x 65 mm; 44–55 lines; ruled in lead-point; small schoolhand, at least two scribes. Red titles; letters occasionally touched with red; occasional marginal tree diagrams. Marginal subject headings, usually in ink of text, but in red on fols. 6ʳ–7ʳ. Red and blue initials with some alternate-color flourishing; red and blue plain capitals. Bound in limp parchment with two ties, now lost.

Once belonged to Thomas of Billingham (fol. 68ʳ: late medieval); earlier owner's name erased.

CONTENTS: fol. 1ʳ tree diagram of the effects on sin of various sorts of doing good; 1ᵛ repeat of fol. 1ʳ; 2ᵛ proverbial sayings (Walther nos. 1062, 4580, 18341), list of the seven sacraments, questions on the power of priests, list of the major divisions (*articuli*) of the *Summa*'s text, in later hand; 3ʳa–68ʳa Thomas of Chobham, *Summa confessorum*, followed by a list of *articuli* as on fol. 2ᵛ.

A cheap, useful (and used) personal reference volume.

The page reproduced shows part of the section on the sins associated with gluttony and drunkenness. Where possible, subject headings such as *De bona ira* (The good side of anger) and *De tribus gradibus ire* (The three levels of anger) are written in the right- or left-hand margin beside the text; but where the space is too small, reference letters (d-h) are given, and linked to headings written in the top or bottom margin. The small d on the right-hand side is a guide-letter for the scribe who inserted the red capitals after the text was written. The left margin shows an alteration by expunction of the number of days of penance from *x* (10) to *xl* (40).

Also in the left margin, a reader has added a NOTA sign, marking a passage of special interest. The eminently sound penance begins: 'Unde si quis pronus est ad ebrietatem, debet ei iniungi in penitentia quod non intersit publicis potationibus, et quod non bibat nisi in hora vespertina antequam ingrediantur lectum.' [So if anyone is disposed to drunkenness, a penance should be imposed that he not be present at public drinking, and that he not drink except in the evening before he goes to bed.]

¶ de bona ira

¶ de ira mala

¶ de tribus gradibus ire

·e· ¶ de penit. appellantis hominem iebrium

·f· ¶ de vomitu eukaristie

g ¶ quam detestabilis est ebrietas h notat

BIBLIOGRAPHY

Thomae de Chobham. Summa confessorum, ed. F. Broomfield, with extensive bibliography; *Thomas de Chobham. Summa de arte praedicandi,* ed. F. Morenzoni; J. J. F. Firth, *Robert of Flamborough. Liber poenitentialis;* A. Frantzen, *The Literature of Penance in Anglo-Saxon England;* J. T. McNeil and H. M. Gamer, *Medieval Handbooks of Penance.*

twenty-eight

Robert Grosseteste, *Templum Dei*

Oxford, Bodleian Library, MS Bodl. 36, fols. vi^{v}–vii^{r}
Probably English; mid-thirteenth century

Although his early life is largely unknown, it seems that Robert Grosseteste's initial education was in arts and science; he came late to theology and may have been to a great degree self-taught. Certainly, although he became the first chancellor of the newly organized university of Oxford (*c.* 1214), archdeacon (1229) and then bishop (1235) of Lincoln, and lecturer to the Oxford Franciscans (1229/30), Grosseteste's writings are always out of the ordinary, never following the common run of structure and sources found in contemporary Paris masters. So when he chose to put together a quick reference manual for clerics with the cure of souls (whether monks, friars or parish clergy), Grosseteste produced innovations in both structure and layout—a manual composed almost entirely of diagrams and tables, covering penitential examination, vices and virtues, sacraments, beatitudes, the commandments, and canon law.

Robert of Flamborough's *Liber poenitentialis* provided the basis for Grosseteste's work, but little else. Beginning by defining human beings as the spiritual temple of God (1 Cor. 3:17), Grosseteste first describes the structure of the corporeal temple, producing a spiritual allegory of the body, and then goes on to the spiritual temple, which has foundations, walls and a roof made of faith, hope and love, respectively. In the second part of the work he reveals how we may build up and preserve the temple, using the bricks of confession and the other sacraments, particularly advising clerics on the practice of penitence. The *Templum* demonstrates Robert's characteristic regard for 'real life' as opposed to theory; he considers the circumstances of sin, as well as the sin itself, humanely taking note of mitigating and redeeming features. He leaves the penances themselves to be found elsewhere.

Probably written sometime between 1220 and 1230, the straightforward character and handy format of the *Templum* gave it wide popularity. More than ninety manuscripts survive, with production stretching well into the fifteenth century, and in English, French and German as well as Latin.

PARCHMENT: (very thin, 'onion skin' quality): iii (paper) + vii (parchment) + ii (paper) + 144 (131 double) + iii (paper) fols.; page 145 x 100 mm; text 105 x 70 mm; 58 lines; ruled in lead-point; tiny bookhand, heavily abbreviated; fols. 131ʳbis–44ᵛ a separate booklet, in a different, but similar, hand. No heads or titles; letters touched in red; red paraph signs.

Belonged to Carmarthen Franciscans (fol. vᵛ: mid-15th c.); given to Bodleian by John Davies of Lincoln College, Oxford, 14 March 1615.

CONTENTS: fols. viʳ–xʳ Robert Grosseteste, *Templum Dei;* 1ʳ–46ʳ Raymond of Peñafort, *Summa de penitentie;* 46ʳ–50ᵛ Robert Grosseteste, *De confessione;* 51ʳ–55ᵛ Hugh of St Victor, *De arrha anime;* 56ʳ⁻ᵛ Anon., *De beatitudine;* 58ʳ–60ʳ Anon., *De caritate;* 60ʳ–65ᵛ Bernard of Clairvaux, *Letters* (extracts); 66ʳ–67ᵛ Hugh of St Victor, *De laude caritatis;* 67ᵛ–69ᵛ Anon., *De virgine Maria;* 70ʳ–73ʳ Aelred, *Meditations;* 75ᵛ–76ʳ Thomas Gallus, *De septem fructibus contemplationis;* 78ʳ–93ʳ William of St Thierry, *De contemplando Deo, De natura amoris;* 93ʳ–98ʳ Bernard of Clairvaux, *De laude nove militie;* 99ʳ–115ʳ Richard of St Victor, *Benjamin minor;* 115ᵛ–23ʳ Hugh of St Victor, *De amore,* bk. 2; 123ʳ–27ʳ eight sermons; 128ʳ–31ʳ notes, incl. diagram of soul and emotions; 132ʳ–35ᵛ two sermons; 135ᵛ–40ᵛ Cyprian, *De xii abusivis;* 140ᵛ–43ᵛ Anon, *De triplici tabernaculo.*

Typical theological setting for the *Templum Dei;* a preacher's pocketbook.

The page shown here includes the ten commandments, which are part of the temple's spiritual roof of love. The writing is not merely tiny, but heavily abbreviated, occasionally giving only the first letter of the word. The parchment of fol. viiʳ has been patched before use (top right), but this patch has at some time become detached and been reinserted askew. The smaller holes are evidence of bookworm.

'Hoc sunt decem precepta decalogi quae hoc precepto continet: Dilige dm̄n̄ dm̄ .t. ex tᵒ. cᵉ. tᵒ. ex tᵃ. mᵉ. tᵃ. ex tᵃ. aᵃ tᵃ.' : i.e., 'Dilige dominum deum tibi. ex toto corde tuo. ex tota mente tua. ex tota anima tua.' [These are the ten commands of the Decalogue which are contained in this command: love the Lord your God with all your heart, with all your mind, and with all your soul].

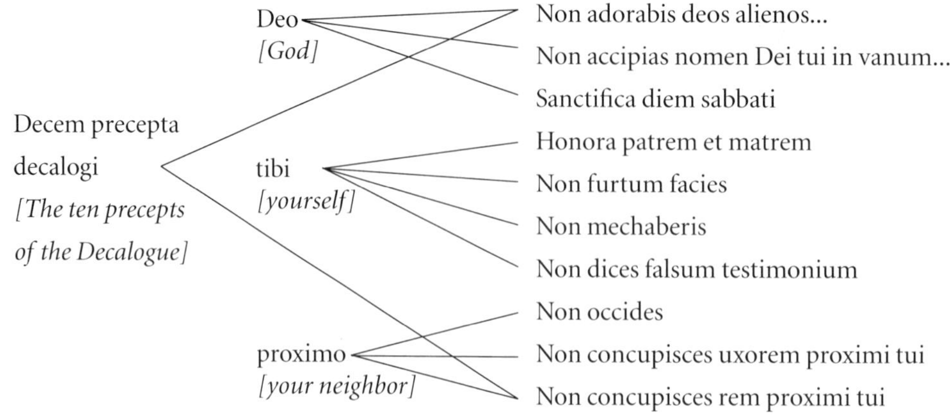

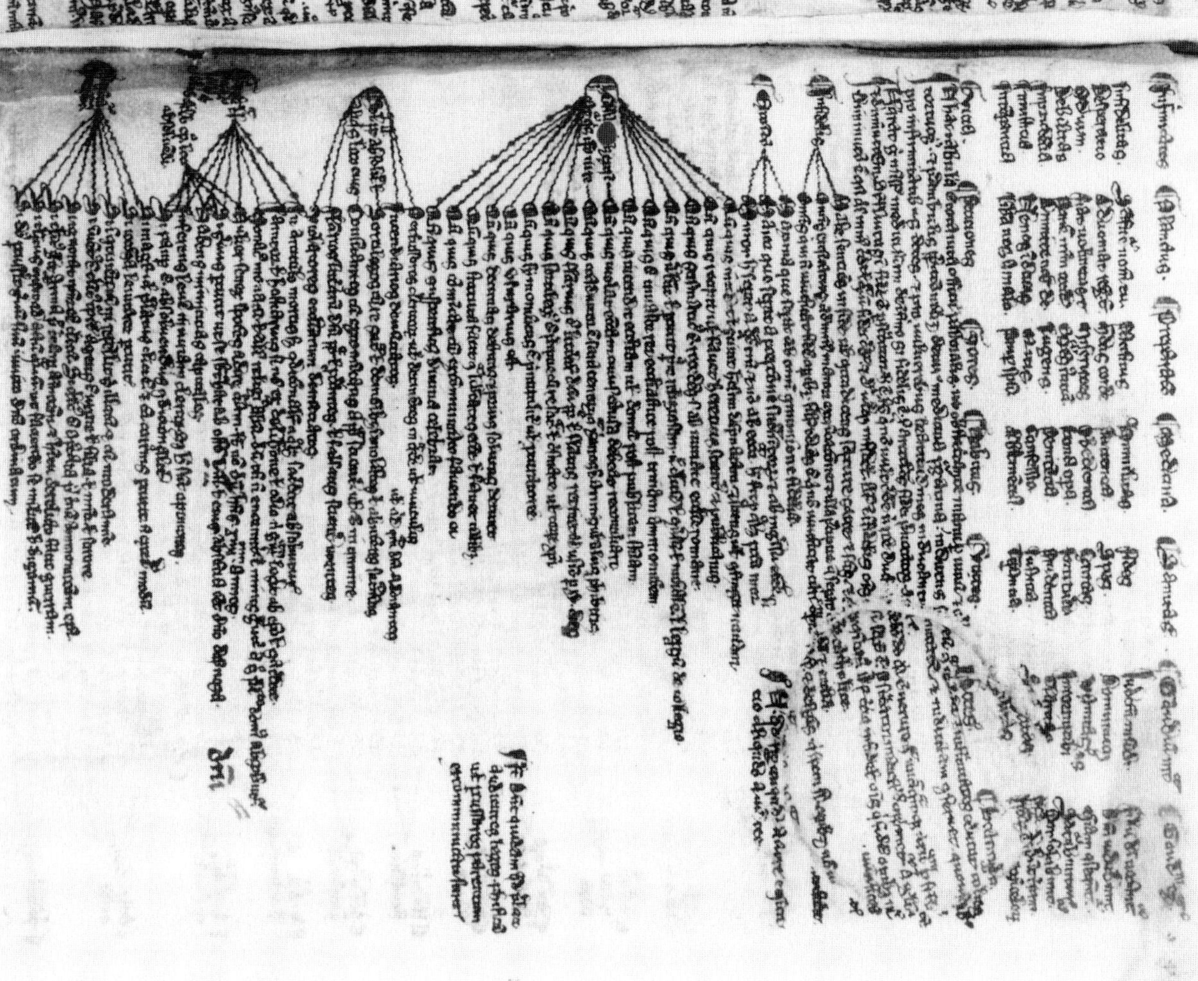

BIBLIOGRAPHY

J. W. Goering and F. A. C. Mantello, *Robert Grosseteste. Templum Dei;* R. W Southern, *Robert Grosseteste; Robert Grosseteste*, ed. D. A. Callus; S. Wenzel, 'Robert Grosseteste's Treatise on Confession *Deus Est*'.

twenty-nine

William Peraldus, *Sermons on the Sunday Epistles*

Oxford, Trinity College, MS 79, fols. 12^{v}–13^{r}
English; mid- to late thirteenth century

'Peu d'ouvrages, dans toute l'histoire littéraire, connurent un aussi brillant succès'. Thus does Fr. Dondaine sum up the remarkable life of the *Summa of Vices and Virtues* by William Peraldus. Immensely popular, surviving in hundreds of MSS, the *Summa* was an international best-seller for centuries after its composition. Scarcely less well known were his sermon collections—collections on the Sunday Epistles, on the Gospels and on various feasts and saints' days. Schneyer's magisterial *Repertory* attributes almost 600 sermons to William; his collections were without doubt the indispensable medieval preaching aid. Yet we know almost nothing of their author, and what we do know is a salutary reminder that Paris theologians were by no means unchallenged in the practical business of taking theology from the schools to the streets.

It is not impossible that William studied at Paris, but the focus of his life and ministry are the French south. He was well established as a preacher in the Dominican house at Lyons by 1249, and by 1261 he was prior. Although Paris was the center of distribution for sermon aids, Lyons was the center of much of the writing, perhaps because, although it had a *studium* and some decent teachers, it was not a 'research university' in the way that Paris was, but rather a center for preparing friars for practical ministry. As well as these, the most influential sermon collections of all, Lyons produced the first collection of sermon *exempla* (no. 26) by Stephen of Bourbon, sermons, an *exemplum* collection and a preaching manual by Humbert of Romans (later Dominican Master-General).

These are not fully prepared sermons; rather, this is a collection of sermon models, giving themes, outlines and hints for each preacher to expand (and translate from Latin to the ver-

PARCHMENT: ii (paper) + i (parchment) + 159 + ii (paper) fols.; page 165 x 110 mm; text 2 cols., each 120 x 38 mm; 40–44 lines; ruled in lead-point; one very small, practiced hand. No general running heads, but sprinkled throughout with titles, marginal headings, subject headings, reference signs, cross-references and short notes; much evidence of subdivision, using words, signs and (Arabic) numbers. Text has been corrected. Occasional marginal faces and pointing hands. Red or pale blue initials with alternate color flourishing beginning each sermon. First sermon has red title, but none elsewhere; very occasional red or blue paraph signs.

Received by Ralph Vawdrey (chaplain of Magdalen College, Oxford; d. 1478), from his uncle, to keep him well occupied and to pray for his uncle's soul. Ralph is in turn to bequeath the book to 'another honest priest and preacher' who will pray for them both (fol. 1^r). Donated to Trinity by Richard Bull (d. 1645). A few indecipherable Hebrew words (fol. 153^r).

CONTENTS: fol. 1^r donation note; 1^v anon. sermon on *Exite obviam ei* (Matt. 25:6); 2^v–5^v alphabetical index of sermons by topic; 6^r–152^r William Peraldus, *Sermons on the Sunday Epistles*; 152^v–57^v assorted sermon notes in later hands.

A very typical pocket-sized friar's sermon collection.

nacular) for himself, adapting the basics to suit his intended audience, clerical or lay. The *Sermons on the Sunday Epistles* were written between 1240 and 1245, after the writing of the *Summa of Vices* (*c.* 1236) but before William had finished the *Summa of Virtues* (before 1248).

In the model sermon shown here, for the third Sunday in Advent (fol. 12^v, col. 1, line 21), William refers his readers to his other famous work: 'Si vis dilatare materiam istam, respice in tractatu de viciis in capitulo de otio'. [If you wish to expand this material, look in the treatise on vices, in the chapter on idleness.] Clearly, model sermons were no good without the reference tools to go with them! This page also shows marginal (Arabic) numbering of points in the argument and (top right, fol. 13^r) a running head: *doa 3a* [*domenica tertia*: third Sunday]. The sermon text is 1 Cor. 4:1, 'Think of us this way: as servants of Christ', and William elaborates on the theme of Christian service.

The *Sermons on the Epistles* remind us of just how professional the Paris book distribution system had become, for they appear on the first list of so-called *pecia* books, produced by the university stationers in 1248. Popular books were advertised for rent in quires (*peciae*), so they could be taken away and copied by scholars or their hired scribes. The system meant that dozens of standardized copies of a text could be made, relatively cheaply and quickly, and that several copies, at different stages of completion, could be made at once. William's Epistle sermons were advertised in sixty-five *peciae*, costing 2 *solidi*, 6 *denarii* (*CUP*, I, p. 647).

citum esse ne sit servus inutilis ocio tor-
pendo. Vel infidelis servitium quod Christo debent a-
liis solvendo. Sed potius bonus et fidelis ei suum
servitium exhibendo, ut mereatur a Christo
audire in futuro. l. c. xxv. Euge bone et fidelis etc. Circa primum nota quod sola
inutilitas ministrorum Christi sufficit iram ei(us)
promereri. Iuxta illud Prov. xv. a. [...]
xiiii. c. Iracundiam eius inutilis sustinebit.
Item maledictionem dei habent tales
secundum capitulum suum. Iuxta illud Matth. xxi. De male-
dictione ficulnee non facientis fructum.
Item merentur mortem temporalem et eter-
nam. De primo habes Luc. xiii. De ficulnea
fructum non ferente. Succide illam. Ut
quid etiam terram occupat. De secundo Matth.
xxv. Et inutilem servum proicite in tene-
bras exteriores. Illic erit fletus et stri-
dor dentium. De utroque Matth. iii. et vii. Omnis
arbor que non facit fructum bonum exci-
detur et in ignem mittetur. Si vis dilatare materiam istam, respice in tractatu
de viciis in capitulo de ocio. Contra secundum
nota quod tria genera hominum sunt qui ser-
vicium quod Christo debent aliis solvunt. Unde
servi infideles sunt. Primi sunt
1ᵐ voluptuosi, de quibus legitur ad Ro.
ult. Huiusmodi non serviunt Christo sed ventri. Ad Phi-
lipp. iii. Quorum deus venter est etc. Isti fece-
runt de ventre suo deum suum. Sed ignis in-
fernalis devorabit eum. I. Cor. vi. Esca ventri et
venter escis. Deus autem et hunc et has
2ᵘ destruet. Secundi sunt ambiciosi, ser-
vicium quod debent Christo solvere in pauperibus
potius volunt solvere canibus, scilicet ven-
toribus ne moveant eos vel ad lucrandum
canibus, sicut patet in illis qui vacant
venationi. Tales non attendunt quod dicit
dominus Matth. xv. Non est bonum sumere panem
filiorum et mittere canibus. De talibus le-

gitur Osee xii. Effraim pascit ven-
tum etc. et sequitur: et oleum in Egyp-
tum ferebat. Effraim interpretatur [...] Egyptus [...]
dat filius diaboli. Unde debuit facere elemosinas filiis dei. De apostolo legitur ad Ro. xv. quod
elemosinas tulit in Ierusalem. Sed tales episcopi aufe-
runt eas illis de Ierusalem, et dant eis qui sunt
in Egypto. Subtrahunt ora dei in pauperibus quod canibus et porcis dant. Fili-
os enim diaboli dilatant invitando ut de
suo accipiant. Filii vero dei vix post lon-
gas preces ad portam extorquere ab eis [...]
vari [...] porigi. Multi sunt qui se fa-
cerent pro [...] quod faciunt pro minuto lar-
giores elemosinarum esse quam beatus
Martinus. Cum enim ipse divisit pallium
quod dedit, isti pro minuto totum pallium
et alias vestes expendunt. Tercii sunt
cupidi et avari qui servitium quod Christo debe-
tur expendunt, quos ydolatras esse constat ex illo verbo ad Eph. v. Avaricia est
ydolorum servitus. Unde dicit glossa. Avari de num-
mis [...] et ex eo quod dicit glossa super i. Matth. Non potes-
tis deo servire et mamone. Mamo-
na est Syra lingua divicie quibus servire deum
negare est. Tales tyranni corde adorant
et quasi deificant quem incessanter in pedi-
bus conculcant. Hoc enim ab homine colitur quod
pre ceteris diligitur, ut dicit glossa August. super i. ad Phi-
lipp. Quorum deus venter est. Circa tertium no-
ta quod triplici ratione Christo debemus adherere ad servi-
endum ei. Primo quia nulli [...] sed quia ad hoc
de nichilo nos fecit ut ei serviamus.
Unde nisi hoc faciamus digni sumus ad nichilum
2 redigi. Secundo quia ipse servivit. Luc. xxii.
Ego in medio vestrum sum sicut qui ministrat et attende modum serviendi. Servivit enim
in humillimo officio, scilicet in pedum a-
blutione, de quo Io. xiii. Servivit
et nobis preciosissimo ferculo dum se ipsum

expendit in servitio nostro. Bernardus. Boni ministri
qui carnem suam in cibum, sanguinem in potum,
animam ministravit in precium. [...]
[...]
Iuste sibi vendicat vitam meam qui pro mea posuit suam. Non refugias [...]
[...] non timeas facere expensas in servicio
eius qui se ipsum expendit in servitio tuo.
Dicas cum B. Duo minuta habeo domine
Ihesu, scilicet corpus et animam. Hec digne et offe-
ram cum vidua muliere. Tertio quia angelis suis ipse mandavit ut nobis ministrent.
Unde ad Heb. i. Nonne omnes administrato-
rii sunt spiritus in ministerium missi propter eos qui here-
ditatem capiunt salutis. Psalmus. Angelis suis
mandavit de te etc. Circa quod ut ne sis ingra-
tus de tanto beneficio, diligenter attende quis
mandavit, quia deus, et quibus, quia angelis, et de quo, quia de putredine [...]
et quid, ut scilicet custodiant te, et non tantum in uno
loco sed in omnibus viis tuis, nec uno die sed
anno, sed a nativitate usque ad finem vite.
Sic pro hoc beneficio serviret homo toto
tempore vite sue, satis non esset hoc nimis.
Quarto quia ipse ministraturus est nobis. Luc. xii. Et transiens ministrabit e-
is. Si aliquis mille annis ministraret ei
ut unica hora ministraret ei in celo, non
esset hoc nimis. Et tamen pro singulis diebus horis
quibus ei debito modo ministrabimus, si in bono perseveremus, ministrabit ipse nobis plus quam
c. m. annorum. Hec ministratio est faciei
eius ostensio, de qua in Psalmo. Saciabor cum
apparuerit gloria tua. Et Ieronimus. De torrente
voluptatis tue potabis eos. Fideli et utilius servi-
ent cum servientibus se regnum largiatur eternum. Unde cantat ecclesia. Ecce advenit domi-
nator dominus et regnum in manu eius. In-
tellige ad dandum. Mira cecitas hominum
qui illis cum tanta diligentia serviunt cum quibus

nec villam nec castrum lucrari possunt,
creatori vero suo non pro regno et tali regno servire volunt. Fideli et honesti servientes
cum ei servire regnare honestissimum [...]
est quod requirit ut quis mundare se. Iuxta illud: Hec est
voluntas dei sanctificatio vestra. I. Thess. iiii. Se
floribus se ornare virtutum et similia. Hic
potes descendere ad singula vicia et virtutes.
[S]ic nos existimet homo
[ut] ministros Christi. Cum quilibet christianus minister
Christi sit, et pro ministerio suo si debito modo fuerit, regno celorum remunerandus sit, si vero non
fuerit debito modo, in infernali patibulo affi-
gendus, valde sollicitus debet esse quomodo sic Christo
serviat ut Christus ei servitium gratum habeat.
Si enim tanto labore et sollicitudine ad-
discat aliquis artem aliquam, ex qua lucretur
victum suum, cum quanta sollicitudine debet ad-
discere ministerium illud, circa quod ipsi potest accidere
tantum periculum vel tantum lucrum. Necesse autem habet cog-
noscere quilibet christianus qualiter velit Christus ut
debito modo serviat sibi, et quale velit esse
ministrum suum et qualia velit sibi ministrari.
Primum non docet ipse Christus. Io. xii. Qui michi ministrat me sequatur. Similitudo morum dilectionem requirit. Eccl. xiii. Omne animal diligit
simile sibi, sic et omnis homo proximum suum.
Ideo familiari amore dilexit Christus Iohannem
evangelistam quia virgo erat sicut et ipse. Unde
Io. ult. vocatur discipulus quem diligebat Ihesus.
B. Beatus est domine Ihesu qui te hominem inter homines
conversantem diligenter observans, pro viribus
se probat imitatorem tui. Si autem vis scire magis specialiter qualiter Christus velit ministros suos esse, sex sunt que ipse requirit in
eis. Primum est intelligencia vel pru-
dentia. Prov. xiiii. Acceptus est regi minister
intelligens. Iracundiam eius inutilis sustinebit.
Quasi non debuit dicere non intelligens, dixit inutilis.
Non intelligentem enim ministrum Christus inutilem reputat

R̃ quare debemus Christo servire

BIBLIOGRAPHY

Dondaine, 'Guillaume Peyraut. Vie et Oeuvres'; L.-J. Bataillon, 'Approaches to the Study of Medieval Sermons'; D. L. d'Avray, *The Preaching of the Friars;* idem and N. Bériou, *Modern Questions about Medieval Sermons;* J. Destrez, *La Pecia dans les manuscrits universitaires du xiii*^{e} *et xiv*^{e} *siècle;* J. B. Schneyer, *Repertorium der lateinischen Sermones des Mittelalters für die Zeit von 1150–1350.*

thirty

Bonaventure, *Apologia pauperum*

Florence, Biblioteca Medicea Laurenziana, MS Plut. 27 dext. 9, fol. 79r
?Paris; late thirteenth century

Perhaps it is not surprising that at the beginning of the thirteenth century two men, Francis and Dominic, should have perceived the problems of the Church so similarly and imagined such similar solutions, each gathering around him a group of men to live, in poverty, a replica of the life of Jesus and his Apostles. But it is surely extraordinary that fifty years later each of their bands of brothers nurtured a theologian of brilliance, whose different styles and concerns combined magisterially to address every major issue of the times. Thomas Aquinas and Bonaventure, Dominican and Franciscan respectively, were remarkable contemporaries. While Thomas' rigidly logical progression through the speculative theological debates of his day cut through thorny problems with the strength and regularity of a machine, Bonaventure followed a more mystical and contemplative, though no less rigorous, path toward knowledge of God.

Born around 1217, John of Fidanza, from Bagnoregia near Viterbo, followed the middle-class son's career path and studied arts at Paris. On graduating, he entered the Franciscan Order and spent the next ten years studying theology, becoming a teaching master in 1253–1255, although his inception as a master (like that of Thomas Aquinas) was held up by the row already brewing with the secular masters of the University of Paris over the place of the Mendicants. His exceptional gifts, both intellectual and spiritual, were recognized early, and he was made Minister-General of the Order in 1257, holding the post until his death at the Second Council of Lyons in 1274.

From 1257 onward, Bonaventure's writing was largely in the service of the Order, and the Order needed his skill. Almost before Francis' death, the brothers had divided into those who believed they must stay utterly faithful to the manner of the founder's life, living in complete poverty and shunning education or ecclesiastical office, and others who believed that God had called them to wider possibilities in the service of the Church, which required them to live in

PARCHMENT: 190 fols. (blank sheet after fol. 25; fol. 61 doubled); page 290 x 210 mm; text 2 cols., each 245 x 65 mm; 50 lines; one scribe for *Apologia.* Running heads with book and chapter numbers; pecia mark, fol. 103v. Old foliation suggests texts originally in MS now missing. Red and blue initials with contrasting penwork.

Belonged to Franciscan convent of Santa Croce, Florence.

CONTENTS: fols. 1^r–25^v Bonaventure, *Breviloquium;* 26^r–59^r idem, *Apologia pauperum;* 59^r–100^v idem, two works on the Franciscan Rule; 101^r–43^v Robert Kilwardby, *De ortu scientiarum;* 143^v–45^v anon. treatise on music; 146^r–75^v Albert the Great, *On Aristotle De mineralibus;* 176^r–88^v Aristotle, *Ethics.*

houses, undertake university study, and even become church dignitaries. Most of all, this difference of interpretation caused them to clash on the issue of poverty. Francis had embraced Lady Poverty in the manner of Christ and the Apostles, so it was said, owning nothing and using no more than he needed to sustain life. As scholars or bishops, Franciscans found this life impossible. Moreover, the phenomenal growth of the Order (from 12 brothers in 1209 to about 30,000 in 1250) doubtless reduced the quality of men applying to join: some simply wanted an easier life.

In the meantime, as the Order became fashionable, lay patrons donated increasing amounts of money, land and goods for its use. Dissenting voices began to sniff hypocrisy, as Franciscans proclaimed their close imitation of Christ's poverty, while building up surpluses. The papal bulls *Quo elongati* (Gregory IX, 1230) and *Ordinem vestrum* (Innocent IV, 1245) sought to solve the problem by making the popes technical owners of Franciscan property, but the situation remained uneasy.

Bonaventure was thus faced with dissension over property both within the Order and without, and he wrote several treatises on the question, both for his brothers and the outside world. The middle-way *Apologia pauperum* of 1267 was directed at the external audience. It became the classic Franciscan statement of the doctrine of poverty and was adopted by later popes. Bonaventure defines poverty as the way of life followed by Christ and the Apostles, which involved the restrained use (*usus*), but not ownership (*dominium*), of goods. He defends his position on two fronts, legal and biblical, and although his addressing of the legal questions of poverty is a little shaky, his biblical defense is an exegetical tour de force. He aims to justify three practices: disavowal of money, begging and renunciation of ownership. His biggest problem is to explain the Apostles' possession of a common purse, which he does by a theory of condescension: Christ did not need or want this shared money, but allowed it so that anyone who was unable to face a life of utter poverty would not be discouraged from following him.

The initial letter on this page begins chapter 7, on cupidity.

adamantinum uocant nullo facile igne consumi quia in-
positus focis igne sentit. uiget scintilla deflammata cum
quasi aque infusione madida resplendet. Talia erant
hebreorum puerorum corpora; que de ieiunio in adamantinam
consistentiam transierant. nam per ignis non ad dispendium sui
sed ad gloriam mutabantur. Daniel quoque quem cum eiecissent
inedia ieiunio, leones docuit ieiunare et insuper
[illegible]; in adamantinam soliditatem abstinentie
rigore membra duratus non patitur ulterius. Sic
enim constrinxerant ieiunia ut eius corpore ferinis
morsibus locus esse non possit. Clausa tenebant leones ora, que abstinentia prophete scientes compuerebant; ut
aufere aptum non possent [illegible] quibusdam uinculis
alligata. Et hiis igitur et aliis potest colligere quod cum
per ieiunium obtineat perfectio scientie, sapientie et uirtutis. per que mens humana purgatur illuminatur et perficitur.
misteria sacretue celestis ab omnibus quidem, sed maxime [illegible]
ei; sed maxime ab hiis qui cupiunt esse perfecti. Unde
etiam [illegible] expedit uniuersis [illegible] illa [illegible]
[illegible] quod dicit corporali ieiunio uitia comprimit.
mentem eleuat. uirtutem largitur et premia. Et augustinus
in quodam sermone. ieiunium mentem purgat uirtute sub-
leuat sensum; carnem spiritui subicit. cor facit contritum et
humiliatum. quod dicit non spernit. concupiscentie nebulas disper-
git, libidinum ardores extinguit. castitatis
lumen accendit. ebrietatem non amat; diuitias superfluitatem uidetur. superbiam calcat. humilitatem commen-
dat. Ambrosius. [illegible] ieiunium continentie ma-
gisterium est. pudicitie disciplina. humilitatis uitalis
castigatio carnis; forma sobrietatis. uirtutis [illegible]
[illegible] aue. [illegible] expensa. leuitatis
[illegible] castitatis origo; tempus gratie; custodia
iuuentutis. Hec de ieiunii laude diffusius
diximus; ut carnalis sapientes homines et intellectu
instruamur et inflamemur affectu. quatinus sibi recog-
noscentes errorem, in ieiunio et fletu et planctu
conuertantur ad dominum. Quoniam que pro misericordias sa-
crificium deuote preces offerimus; non sic decipi; [illegible]
[illegible] uenditur. [illegible] in possimus et
gaudeamus. Tertius uersus [illegible] septem; in
in quo uoluntaria et penitiosa paupertas
fundamentum euangelice perfectionis astruitur;
et quam nunc uideri possimus [illegible] dissoluunt.

Christiane religionis fundamentum esse Christum
Ihesum sapiens ille architectus et apostolus Paulus ad Cor. asserit; dicens fundamentum
aliud ponere nemo potest preter id quod positum est. Christus Ihesus.
Hec quoniam in uno [illegible] collocantur [illegible]
[illegible] ad Ephesios dicat esse [illegible] [illegible]. in
[illegible] uero [illegible] de quo uero ad Ephesios le-

bitur. In caritate radicati et fundati. Fundamento quippam
comparatur et radici. Ut igitur hec duo iungantur simul.
Christiane religionis fundamentum et radix est fides que
per caritatem operatur. Sic et glossa super id. fundamentum
aliud et cetera. dicens fidem que per dilectionem operatur, in fundamento ponitur; uerumtamen fidei pertinet. Huic autem fundamento siue radici directe aduersatur cupiditas.
ut quod scribit ad Thimotheum. Radix omnium malorum est
cupiditas. quam quidam appetentes errauerunt a fide.
Ex hac uero radice tamquam amara scilicet superbia; immundi
mala originem fomitum et incrementum susceperunt. Atque
quod cum ciuitatis babilonice fundamentum ab augustino esse
perhibetur. Omnium namque bonorum origo. et noue ciuitatis
Ierusalem fundamentum et fundator Christus Ihesus. qui in hoc apparuit
ut diaboli solueret opera. Huius cupiditatis oppositum
summe debuit affectu complecti. ut omnino carebo [illegible]
re. Et enim cupiditatis uitium [illegible] radicatur
in affectu uitalis. Ideo non et [illegible] a rebus exterius possessis;
non necesse est. quod perfectum radicalis illius auulsio utrique re-
spiciat. ut auaritie rubiginosa affectio et hec terre-
ne illecebrosa possessio, tam spiritualiter quam corporaliter ab-
dicetur. Unde super illud Matthei. Petrus simon petrus
ad Ihesum. ecce nos reliquimus omnia. dicit. Bernardus.
[illegible]; et non ad insipientiam quod scilicet [illegible] tantum
acupia eius; et relinquere hoc magis expedit. quam ab
[illegible] [illegible]. Et si fugiendarum diuitiarum [illegible]
est. quod autem [illegible] [illegible] sui amore ualeant possidi.
Si igitur [illegible] abdicatio indicit. et [illegible] eius
que in paupertas [illegible]. ipsa est quasi radix omnium malorum perfecte [illegible] et babilonis fundamentum ciuitatis
[illegible] conueniant. quod perfectionis euangelice per
Christo [illegible] et complementum [illegible] eius efficiunt.
ipsa paupertas [illegible] secundum quandam analogiam et coheren-
tiam ad priora; radix est et fundamentum. Propter
quod Christus cum ad perfectionem discipulos informaret in monte. cum que noue Ierusalem descendentis de celo fundamen-
ta perfectionis uidelicet euangelice iam in montibus sanctis
[illegible] apostolis collocaret. [illegible]
sa [illegible] a sede paupertatis excellentia sumit ini-
tium. dicens. Beati pauperes spiritu. quoniam ipsorum est regnum [illegible].
Deinde conuersus de perfectionis aggressione [illegible]
[illegible] ad hanc suo instruit exemplo dicens. Si uis perfectus
esse. uade uende omnia que habes. et da pauperibus; et ueni
sequere me. Quem locum exponens Ieronimus. ad Demetriadem
ait. Apostolica fastigia est perfecte que uirtutis. omnia uendere
et pauperibus distribuere. et sic leuem atque expeditum cum
Christo ad celestia subuolare. Cum uero duo circa temporalium bonorum possessionem considerare contingat, dominium uidelicet
et usum; sitque usus necessario annexus uite presenti. con-
gelice paupertatis est. possessiones terrenas quantum ad domini-

BIBLIOGRAPHY

S. Bonaventurae . . . Opera Omnia, vol. 8: *Apologia pauperum contra calumniatorem;* J.-G. Bougerol, *Introduction à saint Bonaventure;* D. Burr, *Olivi and Franciscan Poverty;* E. Gilson, *La philosophie de saint Bonaventure;* M. Lambert, *Franciscan Poverty;* L. Little, *Religious Poverty and the Profit Economy.*

Glossary

Canon
Greek: 'a straight rod'. In a theological context, the canon is the term for the group of biblical books which the Church (in the form of a General Council) regarded as inspired by the Holy Spirit, the 'canon of Scripture'.

Canon Tables
Comparative tables of passages found in each of the four gospels, based on a division of the texts into numbered sections.

Carolingian
Relating to the reign of Charlemagne (Latin: 'Carolus magnus') and the intellectual revival stimulated by it.

Catchword
The word or phrase beginning a quire (*q.v.*) written in the bottom margin of the *previous* quire of a manuscript, so that the two could be linked in the correct order. As an alternative to using catchwords, quires could be consecutively numbered.

Caution Note
A note in a book recording its use as a pledge or security for a loan of money.

Eadem
Latin: 'the same woman'.

Exegesis
From the Greek meaning 'to narrate or explain'. The act of explaining and interpreting a text, usually a text of Scripture.

Explicit
Latin: 'it ends'. The last word or phrase of a text or manuscript.

Fathers
I.e., Fathers of the Church. A group of Latin and Greek authors from the Early Church period, whose writings on doctrine were deemed to be especially important. Membership in the group is somewhat open-ended, especially in the Eastern Church; but Basil, Gregory of Nazianzus, Cyril of Alexandria and Theodoret are always recognized to be among the Greek Fathers, and Ambrose, Gregory the Great, Augustine and Jerome among the Latin.

Flourishing
Intricate, meandering decoration made with pen and ink. In manuscripts where the decoration is commonly in red and blue, a red initial will have blue flourishing, and vice versa.

Historiated
Description of an initial which illustrates a text or story pictorially, as opposed to an initial 'decorated' with abstract patterns.

Ibid. (Ibidem)
Latin: 'the same place'.

Idem
Latin: 'the same man'.

Incipit
Latin: 'it begins'. The first word or phrase of a text or manuscript.

Lemma
Greek: 'a thing assumed'. A word or short phrase taken from a text on which a gloss is based, usually placed at the beginning of the gloss, and often underlined in red (pl. *lemmata*).

Nota (Bene)
Latin: 'take note' (take careful note). A phrase often written in the margin of a manuscript to alert the reader to a particularly interesting passage of text. Often abbreviated to a sign or monogram.

Pandect
A collection of related texts in one volume. Although usually applied to the Bible, from the twelfth century it is also used for the books of civil and canon law.

Patristic
see *Fathers*

Penwork
see *Flourishing*

Postill
Postilla(e): a lemmatized commentary on a biblical text.

Quadrivium
see *Seven Liberal Arts*

Quire
A booklet usually made by folding a folio-sized sheet of parchment or paper in four, giving eight folios (= sixteen sides; other numbers are, however, possible) for writing. A series of quires were sewn together to make a codex.

Sacrament
'An outward and visible sign of an inward and spiritual grace.' A sacrament is a place where God (in the form of the Holy Spirit) is guaranteed to be present to the believer. Each sacrament has an outward form which signals and symbolizes the presence of the Spirit (such as the water used in baptism), but which does not restrict it. From Peter Lombard (d. 1160) onward, the Church has commonly agreed on seven sacraments: baptism, confirmation, penance, the eucharist, ordination, marriage, and extreme unction.

Sacramental
An action or situation which may function like a sacrament but where, as opposed to the canonical seven sacraments, there is no guarantee that God will be present.

Scholastic
A product of the medieval schools, from the mid-twelfth century onward.

Seven Liberal Arts
The traditional subjects of Roman education, divided into the *trivium*: grammar, rhetoric, and dialectic (logic), based on words; and the *quadrivium:* arithmetic, geometry, astronomy, and music, based on numbers.

Signature
see *Quire*

Summa
A comprehensive text attempting to cover the whole of a specific subject.

Targum
Hebrew: 'translation'. A series of Aramaic interpretive translations of the books of the Hebrew Bible (Old Testament) made during the period in which Hebrew had ceased to be the common language of speech among Jews. The Targums are written versions of oral explanations used in conjunction with the synagogue biblical readings.

Trivium
see *Seven Liberal Arts*

Bibliography

Alan of Lille. *De fide catholica contra haereticos*. 1.30. *PL* 210: 305–430.

Albert the Great. Edited by F. Kovach and R. Sahahn. Norman, Okla., 1980.

Albertus Magnus. Opera omnia, 17.i: *De unitate intellectus contra Averroem*. Edited by A. Hufnagel. Aschendorff, 1975.

Albertus Magnus and the Sciences. Edited by J. Weisheipl. Toronto, 1980.

Magistri Alexandri de Hales, Quaestiones disputatae 'antequam esset frater'. 3 vols. Quaracchi, 1960.

Alexandri de Hales . . . Summa theologica. 4 vols. Quaracchi, 1924–48.

St Ambrose. Letters. Translated by M. Beyenka. Fathers of the Church, vol. 26. New York, 1954.

Sancti Ambrosii Opera, 10: *Epistulae*. Edited by O. Faller and M. Zelzer. 3 vols. CSEL 82. Vienna, 1968–90.

Andreae de Sancto Victore. Opera. 7 vols. Vol. 6: *Expositionem in Ezechielem*, edited by M. A. Signer. CCCM 53. Turnhout, 1986–.

Augustine of Hippo. *De doctrina christiana*. Edited by J. Martin. CCSL 32. Turnhout, 1962.

———. *De doctrina christiana*. Edited by G. M. Green. CSEL 80. Vienna, 1963.

———. *On Christian Doctrine*. Translated by D. W. Robertson. Indianapolis, 1958.

Baldwin, J. W. 'Masters at Paris from 1179 to 1215: A Social Perspective'. In *Renaissance and Renewal*, edited by R. L. Benson and G. Constable, pp. 138–72. Cambridge, Mass., 1982.

———. *Masters, Princes and Merchants. The Social Views of Peter the Chanter and His Circle*. 2 vols. Princeton, 1970.

Baron, R. *Science et sagesse chez Hugues de St.-Victor*. Paris, 1957.

Bataillon, L.-J. 'Approaches to the Study of Medieval Sermons'. *Leeds Studies in English*, n.s. 11 (1980): 19–35.

———. *La prédication au xiiie siècle en France et Italie*. Aldershot and Brookfield, Vt., 1993.

Bazàn, B., Fransen G., et al. *Les Questions disputées et les questions quodlibétiques dans les facultés de théologie, de droit, et de médecine*. Turnhout, 1985.

Bede. *Historia ecclesiastica*. Edited with English translation by B. Colgrave and R. A. B. Mynors. Oxford, 1969. Historical notes, commentary, and bibliography by J. M. Wallace-Hadrill. Oxford, 1988.

Benson, R. L., and Constable, G., eds. *Renaissance and Renewal*. Cambridge, Mass., 1982.

St Bernard of Clairvaux, His Life as Recorded in the Vita prima Bernardi, by William of St Thierry. Translated by G. Webb and A. Walker. London, 1960.
Bernard of Clairvaux, On the Song of Songs. Edited by K. Walsh and I. Edmonds, Cistercian Fathers Series 4, 7, 31, 40. Shannon, Ireland and Kalamazoo, Mich., 1971–80.
Bernard of Clairvaux: Selected Works. Translated by G. R. Evans. New York, 1987.
Bible moralisée. Faksimile-Ausgabe im Originalformat des Codex Vindobonensis 2554 der Österreichischen Nationalbibliothek. Edited by R. Haussherr. 2 vols. Graz and Paris, 1973.
Biblia latina cum glossa ordinaria. Facsimile reprint of the first edition printed by Adolf Rusch of Strassburg, 1480/81, with introduction by K. Froehlich and M. T. Gibson. Turnhout, 1992.
Biblioteca rerum Germanicarum. Edited by P. Jaffe. 6 vols. Berlin, 1864–73.
Bischoff, B., and M. Lapidge. *Biblical Commentaries from the Canterbury School of Theodore and Hadrian.* Cambridge, 1994.
[Bodleian Library]. *A Summary Catalogue of Western Manuscripts in the Bodleian Library at Oxford.* Edited by F. Madan, H. H. E. Craster, et al. and vol. 1 by R. W. Hunt. 7 vols. Oxford, 1895–1953.
Boethius. The Theological Tractates. The Consolation of Philosophy. Translated by H. F. Stewart, E. K. Rand, and S. J. Tester. Cambridge, Mass., and London, 1973.
———. *In topica Ciceronis. PL* 64: 1039–1174.
S. Bonaventurae . . . Opera omnia. 10 vols. Vol. 8: *Apologia pauperum contra calumniatorem,* pp. 233–330. Quaracchi, 1882–1902.
Bougerol, J.-G. *Introduction à saint Bonaventure.* Paris, 1988.
Boyle, L. E. *Pastoral Care, Clerical Education and Canon Law 1200–1400.* London, 1981.
———. *The Setting of the* Summa theologiae *of Saint Thomas.* Toronto, 1982.
Brady, I. 'Manducator and the Oral Teachings of Peter Lombard'. *Antonianum* 41 (1966): 454–90.
Branner, R. *Manuscript Painting in Paris during the Reign of St. Louis. A Study of Styles.* Berkeley, Los Angeles, and London, 1977.
Brémond, C., J. Le Goff, and J.-C. Schmitt. *L''Exemplum'.* Turnhout, 1982.
Brown, D. *Vir trilinguis. A Study of the Biblical Exegesis of St. Jerome.* Kampen, 1992.
Brown, P. *Augustine of Hippo.* London, 1967.
Brown, S. 'Key Terms in Medieval Theological Vocabulary'. In *Méthodes et instruments du travail intellectuel au moyen âge,* edited by O. Weijers, pp. 82–96. Etudes sur le vocabulaire intellectuel du moyen âge 3. Turnhout, 1990.
Brundage, J. A. *Medieval Canon Law.* London, 1995.
Burr, D. *Olivi and Franciscan Poverty.* Philadelphia, 1989.
Cartulaire de l'Eglise de Notre-Dame de Paris. Edited by B. Guérard. Paris, 1850.
Cassiodorus. *Institutiones. Divine and Human Readings.* Translated by L. W. Jones. Columbia, N.Y., 1946.
Catto, J. I., ed. *The History of the University of Oxford, 1: The Early Oxford Schools.* Oxford, 1984.
Chadwick, H. *Augustine.* Oxford, 1986.
Charland, Th.-M. *Artes praedicandi.* Paris and Ottawa, 1936.
Châtillon, J. 'L'heritage littéraire de Richard de Saint-Victor'. *Revue du Moyen âge latin* 4 (1948): 23–52, 343–64.

Chenu, M.-D. *Introduction à l'étude de St Thomas d'Aquin.* Montreal and Paris, 1950. Translated by A.-M. Landry and D. Hughes under the title *Toward Understanding Saint Thomas.* Chicago, 1964.

———. *La théologie au douzième siècle.* Paris, 1957. Excerpted and translated by J. Taylor and L. K. Little under the title *Nature, Man, and Society in the Twelfth Century.* Chicago, 1968.

———. *La théologie comme science au xiii*[e] *siècle.* Paris, 1957.

Clanchy, M. T. *Abelard: A Medieval Life.* Oxford, 1997.

Cobban, A. B. *The Medieval English Universities.* Cambridge, 1988.

Colish, M. *Peter Lombard.* Leiden, 1994.

Collinson, R. L. *Encyclopaedias: Their History throughout the Ages.* London and New York, 1966.

Contreni, J. J. *Carolingian Learning, Masters and Manuscripts.* Aldershot, 1992.

———. *The Cathedral School of Laon from 850 to 930: Its Manuscripts and Masters.* Munich, 1978.

———. *Education and Culture in the Barbarian West, from the Sixth through the Eighth Century.* Columbia, S.C., 1978.

Contreni, J. J., and P. P. O Niill. *Glossae divinae historiae: The Biblical Glosses of John Scottus Eriugena.* Florence, 1997.

Courtenay, W. J. *Schools and Scholars in Fourteenth Century England.* Princeton, 1987.

———. *Teaching Careers in the University of Paris in the Thirteenth and Fourteenth Centuries.* Texts and Studies in the History of Medieval Education, no. 18, edited by A. L. Gabriel and P. E. Beichner. Notre Dame, Ind., 1988.

Coxe, H. O. *Catalogus codicum MSS qui in collegiis aulisque Oxoniensibus hodie adseruantur.* Oxford, 1852.

Dahan, G. *Les intellectuels chrétiens et les juifs au moyen âge.* Paris, 1999.

Daly, S. 'Peter Comestor: Master of Histories'. *Speculum* 32 (1957): 62–73.

d'Avray, D. L. *The Preaching of the Friars.* Oxford, 1985.

d'Avray, D. L., and N. Bériou. *Modern Questions about Medieval Sermons.* Spoleto, 1994.

de Hamel, C. *Glossed Books of the Bible and the Origins of the Paris Booktrade.* Woodbridge, 1984.

Decrees of the Ecumenical Councils. Edited by N. P. Tanner. 2 vols. London and Washington, D.C., 1990.

Defensor Locogiacensis monachi. Liber scintillarum. Edited by H. M. Rochais. CSEL 117. Turnhout, 1957.

Defensor's Liber Scintillarum *with an interlinear Anglo-Saxon version.* Edited by E. W. Rhodes. EETS. London, 1889.

Destrez, J. *La Pecia dans les manuscrits universitaires du xiii*[e] *et xiv*[e] *siècle.* Paris, 1935.

Dondaine, A. 'Guillaume Peyraut. Vie et Oeuvres'. *Archivum Fratrum Praedicatorum* 18 (1948): 162–236.

Dondaine, H. F., and H. V. Schooner. *Codices manuscripti operum Thomae de Aquino.* 3 vols. in progress. Rome, 1967–.

Duke Humfrey's Library and the Divinity School 1488–1988. Exhibition catalogue. June-August. Oxford, 1988.

Dunbabin, J. *France in the Making 843–1180.* Oxford, 1985.

Einhard and Notker the Stammerer. Two Lives of Charlemagne. Translated with introduction by L. Thorpe. Harmondsworth, 1969.

[Engelberg]. *Catalogus codicum manu scriptorum . . . Engelberg.* Edited by B. Gottwald, O.S.B. Freiburg-im-B., 1891.
Ferruolo, S. *The Origins of the University. The Schools of Paris and Their Critics, 1100–1215.* Stanford, Calif., 1985.
———. 'Parisius-Paradisus: The City, Its Schools, and the Origins of the University of Paris'. In *The University and the City: From Medieval Origins to the Present,* edited by T. Bender, pp. 22–43. New York, 1988.
Firth, J. J. F. *Robert of Flamborough. Liber Poenitentialis.* Toronto, 1971.
Fontaine, J. *Isidore de Séville et la culture classique dans l'Espagne wisigothique.* Paris, 1983.
Ford, G. B. *The Letters of Isidore of Seville.* Amsterdam, 1970.
Fournier, P., and G. Le Bras. *Histoire des collections canoniques.* 2 vols. Paris, 1931–32.
Frantzen, A. *The Literature of Penance in Anglo-Saxon England.* New Brunswick, N.J., 1983.
Friedmann, A. *Paris, ses rues, ses paroisses du moyen âge a la révolution.* Paris, 1959.
Gabriel, A. L. 'The Cathedral Schools of Notre-Dame and the Beginning of the University of Paris'. In *Garlandia. Studies in the History of the Mediaeval University,* pp. 39–64. Frankfurt, 1969.
———. 'English Masters and Students in Paris during the Twelfth Century'. In *Garlandia. Studies in the History of the Mediaeval University,* pp. 1–37. Frankfurt, 1969.
———. 'The Ideal Master of the Mediaeval University'. *Catholic Historical Review* 60 (1974): 1–40.
———. *Student Life at Ave Maria College, Mediaeval Paris.* Notre Dame, Ind., 1955.
Ghellinck, J. de. *La mouvement théologique au xiie siécle.* Bruges, Brussels, and Paris, 1948.
Gibson, M. *The Bible in the Latin West.* Notre Dame, Ind., 1993.
Gibson, M., T. Heslop, and R. Pfaff. *The Eadwine Psalter.* Philadelphia, 1992.
Gilson, E. *The Mystical Theology of St. Bernard.* London, 1940.
———. *La philosophie de saint Bonaventure.* Paris, 1943.
Glorieux, P. 'Autour de la "Summa Abendonensis"'. *RThAM* 6 (1934): 80–84.
———. 'L'enseignement au moyen âge. Techniques et méthodes en usage à la Faculté de Théologie de Paris, au xiiie siècle'. *AHDLMA* 35 (1968): 65–186.
———. *La littérature quodlibétique.* 2 vols. Paris, 1925–35.
Goering, J. W. *William de Montibus c. 1140–1213. The Schools and the Literature of Pastoral Care.* Toronto, 1992.
Goering, J. W., and F. A. C. Mantello. *Robert Grosseteste. Templum Dei.* Toronto, 1984.
Grabmann, M. *Die Geschichte der scholastischen Methode.* Freiburg-im-B., 1911. Reprint, Darmstadt, 1957.
Grandjean, M. *Laïcs dans l'Église.* Paris, 1994.
Gratian, *Decretum.* In *Corpus iuris canonici,* edited by A. Friedberg, 1. Leipzig, 1979.
S. Gregorii magni. Moralia in Iob libri I–X. Edited by M. Adriaen. CCSL 143, 143A, 143B. Vienna, 1979–85.
Grégoire le Grand. Morales sur Job. Edited by A. de Gaudemaris and R. Gillet. SC 32. Paris, 1974.
Gregory the Great. *Morals on the Book of Job.* Translated by C. Marriott. Library of the Fathers, 18, 21, 23, 31. Oxford, 1843–50.
Gross-Diaz, T. *The Psalms Commentary of Gilbert of Poiters.* Leiden, 1996.
Magistri Guillelmi Altissiodorensis. Summa aurea, Edited by J. Ribaillier. 4 vols. Paris and Rome, 1980–87.

Hailperin, H. *Rashi and the Christian Scholars.* Pittsburgh, 1963.
Hallam, E. *Capetian France 987–1328.* London, 1980.
Häring, N. *The Life and Works of Clarembald of Arras. A Twelfth-Century Master of the School of Chartres.* Toronto, 1965.
[Harleian collection]. *A Catalogue of the Harleian Manuscripts in the British Museum.* 4 vols. London, 1808–12.
Haskins, C. H. 'The Life of Medieval Students as Illustrated by Their Letters'. In *Studies in Medieval Culture,* pp. 1–35. Oxford, 1929.
———. *The Renaissance of the Twelfth Century.* Cambridge, Mass., 1927. Reprint, New York, 1958.
Hugh of St Victor. On the Sacraments of the Christian Faith. Edited by R. J. Deferrari. Cambridge, Mass., 1951.
Hugh of St Victor. *De scripturis et scriptoribus sacris.* In *Opera Omnia.* Venice, 1588.
Hugo de Sancto Caro. Postilla super Totam Bibliam. Paris, 1533–39; Paris, 1545.
Isidori Hispalensis episcopi. Etymologiarum sive originum. Edited by W. M. Lindsay. Oxford, 1911. Reprint, 1985.
Ivo of Chartres. *Panormia. PL* 161: 1045–344.
James, M. R., and F. Taylor. *A Descriptive Catalogue of the Latin Manuscripts in the John Rylands University Library.* Manchester and London, 1921. Reprint, Munich, 1980.
Jerome. *Catalogus de catholicis scriptoribus De viris inlustris.* Edited by E. C. Richardson. Leipzig, 1896.
———. *Liber de nominibus hebraicis. PL* 23: 771–858.
John of Salisbury. *Metalogicon.* Edited by C. C. J. Webb. Oxford, 1929.
Kelly, J. N. D. *Jerome, His Life, Writings and Controversies.* London, 1975.
Ker, N. R. 'From "Above Top Line" to "Below Top Line": A Change in Scribal Practice'. In *Books, Collectors and Libraries. Studies in the Medieval Heritage,* edited by A. G. Watson, no. 7. London, 1985.
Kibre, P. *The Nations in the Mediaeval Universities.* Cambridge, Mass., 1948.
———. *Scholarly Privileges in the Middle Ages.* London, 1961.
Kuttner, S. *Harmony from Dissonance: An Interpretation of Mediaeval Canon Law.* Latrobe, Penn., 1960.
———. *History of Ideas and Doctrine of Canon Law in the Middle Ages.* London, 1992.
Laborde, A. de. *La Bible moralisée conservée à Oxford, Paris, et Londres.* 5 vols. Paris, 1911–27.
Lacks, S. 'The Source of Hebrew Traditions in the *Historia Scholastica*'. *Harvard Theological Review* 66 (1973): 385–86.
Lambert, M. *Franciscan Poverty.* London, 1961.
Landgraf, A. 'Recherches sur les écrits de Pierre le Mangeur'. *RThAM* 3 (1931): 292–306, 341–72.
Lanfranc. *De corpore et sanguine Domini. PL* 150: 407–42.
Leclercq, J. *The Love of Learning and the Desire for God.* London, 1978.
———. *Recueils d'études sur S. Bernard.* 3 vols. Rome, 1962–69.
Lecoy de la Marche, A. *Anécdotes historiques, legendes et apologues tirés du recueil inédit d'Étienne de Bourbon.* Paris, 1877.
Leff, G. *Paris and Oxford Universities in the Thirteenth and Fourteenth Centuries.* New York, 1968.

Light, L. *The Bible in the Twelfth Century: An Exhibition of Manuscripts at the Houghton Library.* Cambridge, Mass., 1988.

———. 'French Bibles c. 1200–30: A New Look at the Origins of the Paris Bible'. In *The Early Medieval Bible*, edited by R. Gameson. Cambridge, 1994.

———. 'Versions et révisions du texte biblique'. In *Le Moyen Age et la Bible,* edited by P. Riché and G. Lobrichon, pp. 55–93. Paris, 1984.

Little, A. G. 'The Franciscan School at Oxford in the Thirteenth Century'. *Archivum Franciscanum Historicum* 19 (1926): 803–74.

Little, L. *Religious Poverty and the Profit Economy.* London, 1978.

Lottin, O. *Psychologie et morale aux xiie et xiiie siècles.* 5 vols. Louvain-Gembloux, 1942–60.

Lowden, J. *The Making of the* Bibles Moralisées. 2 vols. University Park, Penn., 2000.

Lubac, H. de. *L'Eucharistie et l'Église au Moyen Age.* 2nd ed. Paris, 1949.

———. *Exégèse médiévale: Les quatre sens de l'Ecriture.* 4 vols. Paris, 1959–64. Translated by M. Sebanc under the title *Medieval Exgesis.* Grand Rapids, Mich., and Edinburgh, 1998.

Luscombe, D. E. *The School of Peter Abelard.* Cambridge, 1969.

Macy, G. *Theologies of the Eucharist in the Early Scholastic Period.* Oxford, 1984.

Mandonnet, P. *Siger de Brabant et l'averroisme latin au XIIIe siècle.* 2 vols. Louvain, 1908–11.

Marenbon, J. *The Philosophy of Peter Abelard.* Cambridge, 1997.

Markus, R. A. *Gregory the Great and His World.* Cambridge, 1997.

———. *Speculum: History and Society in the Theology of St Augustine.* Cambridge, 1988.

Marrou, H. *S. Augustin et la fin de la culture antique.* Paris, 1938.

Martin, H. *Catalogue général des manuscrits des bibliothèques publiques de France. Paris, bibliothèque de l'Arsenal.* 9 vols. Paris, 1885–99.

Matter, E. A. *The Voice of My Beloved. The Song of Songs in Western Medieval Christianity.* Philadelphia, 1990.

Mazzarella, P. *Il 'De unitate' di Alberto Magno e di Tommaso D'Aquino.* Naples, 1949.

McClure, J. 'Gregory the Great. Exegesis and Audience'. Ph.D. diss., Oxford, 1978.

McKitterick, R. *Carolingian Culture: Emulation and Innovation.* Cambridge, 1994.

McLynn, N. B. *Ambrose of Milan.* London and Berkeley, Calif., 1994.

McNeil, J. T., and H. M. Gamer. *Medieval Handbooks of Penance.* New York, 1938. Reprint, 1990.

Minnis, A. J. *Medieval Theory of Authorship: Scholastic Literary Attitudes in the Later Middle Ages.* London, 1984.

Minnis, A. J., and A. B. Scott, with D. Wallace. *Medieval Literary Theory and Criticism c. 1100–c. 1375: The Commentary Tradition.* Oxford, 1988.

Moore, P. S. 'The Authorship of the *Allegoriae super vetus et novum testamentum*'. *New Scholasticism* 9 (1935): 209–25.

———. *The Works of Peter of Poitiers.* Washington, D.C., 1936.

Munk Olsen, B. 'The Production of the Classics in the Eleventh and Twelfth Centuries'. In *Medieval Manuscripts of the Latin Classics: Production and Use*, edited by C. A. Chavannes-Mazel and M. M. Smith, pp. 1–17. London and Los Altos Hills, Calif., 1996.

Neaman, J. S. 'Magnification as Metaphor'. In *England in the Thirteenth Century. Proceedings of the 1989 Harlaxton Symposium*, edited by W. M. Ormrod, pp. 105–22. Stamford, 1991.

Nelson, J. *Charles the Bald.* London, 1992.

Noonan, J. T. 'Gratian Slept Here: The Changing Identity of the Father of the Systematic Study of Canon Law'. *Traditio* 35 (1979): 145–72.

Oliger, L. 'Liber exemplorum fratrum minorum saeculi XIII'. *Antonianum* 2 (1927): 203–76.
O'Meara, J. J. *Eriugena*. Oxford, 1988.
Pain, N. *The King and Becket*. London, 1964.
Paré, G., A. Brunet, and P. Tremblay. *La renaissance du xiie siècle. Les écoles et l'enseignement*. Paris and Ottawa, 1933.
Paschasius Radbertus. De corpore et sanguine Domini cum appendice epistola ad fredugardum. Edited by B. Paul. CCCM 16. Turnhout, 1969.
Pelster, F. 'Die Quaestionen des Alexander von Hales'. *Gregorianum* 14 (1933): 401–22, 501–20.
Peter Abelard. 'Historia calamitatum'. In *The Letters of Abelard and Heloise*, translated with introduction by B. Radice, pp. 57–106. Harmondsworth, 1974.
Magistri Petri Lombardi . . . Sententiae in IV libros distinctae. Edited by I. Brady. 2 vols. Grottaferrata, 1971–81.
Sententiae Petri Pictaviensis. Edited by P. S. Moore and M. Dulong. 2 vols. Notre Dame, Ind., 1943–50.
Petrus Cantor. *Distinctiones Abel*. Edited by J. B. Pitra in *Spicilegium Solesmense*, vol. 3, pp. 1–308. Paris, 1855.
———. *Pierre le Chantre. Summa de sacramentis et animae consiliis*. Edited by J. A. Dugauquier. Analecta medievalia Namurcensia, vols. 4, 7, 11, 16, 21. Louvain/Lille, 1954–67
———. *Verbum abbreviatum*. *PL* 205: 21–554. Short version.
Petrus Comestor. Historia scholastica. *PL* 198: 1053–1644 and *Acts* 198: 1645–1722.
Post, G. 'Alexander III, the *Licentia docendi* and the Rise of the Universities'. In *Anniversary Essays in Medieval History by Students of C. H. Haskins*, edited by J. L. LaMonte and C. H. Taylor, pp. 255–77. Boston, 1929.
———. 'Masters' Salaries and Student Fees in the Mediaeval Universities'. *Speculum* 7 (1932): 181–98.
———. 'Parisian Masters as a Corporation, 1200–1246'. *Speculum* 9 (1934): 421–45.
Principe, W. H. *Hugh of St Cher's Theology of the Hypostatic Union*. Toronto, 1970.
———. *William of Auxerre's Theology of the Hypostatic Union*. Toronto, 1963.
Randall, L. C. *Medieval and Renaissance Manuscripts in the Walters Art Gallery*. 2 vols. Baltimore, 1989.
Rashdall, H. *The Universities of Europe in the Middle Ages*. New ed. Edited by F. M. Powicke and A. B. Emden. 3 vols. Oxford, 1936. Reprint, 1997.
Richard of St Victor. Liber exceptionum. Edited by J. Châtillon. Paris, 1958.
Richard of St Victor. Selected Writings on Contemplation. Translated by C. Kirchberger. London, 1957.
Richard of St Victor. The Twelve Patriarchs, the Mystical Ark, Book Three of the Trinity. Translated by G. Zinn. London, 1979.
Riché, P., and G. Lobrichon. *Le Moyen Age et la Bible*. Paris, 1984.
Rijk, L. M. de. *Logica modernorum*. 2 vols. Assen, 1962–67.
Robert Grosseteste. Edited by D. A. Callus. Oxford, 1955.
Rochais, H. M. 'Contribution à l'histoire des florilèges ascétiques du haut moyen âge latin: le "Liber scintillarum"'. *Revue bénédictine* 63 (1953): 246–91.
Fr. Rogeri Baconis. Opera quaedam hactenus inedita. Edited by J. S. Brewer. Rolls Series 15. London, 1859.

Rouse, R. H. 'The Early Library of the Sorbonne'. *Scriptorium* 21 (1967): 42–71, 226–51.
Rouse, R. H., and M. A. Rouse. 'Biblical Distinctions in the Thirteenth Century'. *AHDLMA* 41 (1974): 27–37.
———. 'The Book Trade at the University of Paris, ca. 1250–ca. 1350'. In *Authentic Witnesses: Approaches to Medieval Texts and Manuscripts*, pp. 259–338. Notre Dame, Ind., 1991. Originally published 1988.
———. 'The Commercial Production of Manuscript Books in Late-Thirteenth Century and Early-Fourteenth Century Paris'. In *Medieval Book Production: Assessing the Evidence. Proceedings of the Second Conference of the Seminar in the History of the Book to 1500. Oxford, July 1988*, edited by L. Brownrigg, pp. 103–15. Los Altos Hills, Calif., 1990.
———. *Manuscripts and Their Makers: Commercial Book Producers in Medieval Paris 1200–1500*, 2 vols. (Turnhout, 2000).
———. *Preachers, Florilegia and Sermons: Studies on the* Manipulus florum *of Thomas of Ireland.* Toronto, 1979.
———. 'The Verbal Concordance to the Scriptures'. *Archivum Fratrum Praedicatorum* 44 (1974): 5–30.
Rud, T. *Codicum manuscriptorum ecclesiae cathedralis Dunelmensis.* Durham, 1825.
Saenger, P. *A Catalogue of the pre-1500 Western Manuscript Books at the Newberry Library.* Chicago and London, 1989.
Savage, E. A. *Old English Libraries.* New York and London, 1911. Reprint 1970.
Schmitt, J.-C. 'Recueils franciscains d' "Exempla" et perfectionnement des techniques intellectuelles du xiiie au xve siècle'. *Bibliothèque de l'École de Chartes* 135 (1977): 5–21.
Schneyer, J. B. *Repertorium der lateinischen Sermones des Mittelalters für die Zeit von 1150–1350.* 11 vols. Münster, 1969–90.
Shailor, B. A. *Catalogue of Medieval and Renaissance Manuscripts in the Beinicke Rare Book and Manuscript Library, Yale University.* 2 vols. Binghampton, N.Y., 1984.
———. 'The Scriptorium of San Pedro de Cardeña'. *Bulletin of the John Rylands Library* 61 (1978–79): 447–73.
Shereshevsky, E. 'Hebrew Traditions in Peter Comestor's *Historia Scholastica*'. *Jewish Quarterly Review* 59 (1969): 268–89.
Smalley, B. *The Becket Conflict and the Schools.* Oxford, 1973.
———. 'Ecclesiastical Attitudes to Novelty c. 1100–c. 1250'. In *Church Society and Politics*, edited by D. Baker, pp. 113–31. Oxford, 1975. Reprint in B. Smalley, *Studies in Medieval Thought and Learning*, edited by B. Smalley, pp. 97–115. London, 1981.
———. 'Glossa Ordinaria'. *Theologische Realenzyklopädie* 13 (1984): 452–57.
———. *The Gospels in the Schools c. 1100–c. 1280.* London, 1985.
———. '*Prima clavis sapientiae:* Augustine and Abelard'. In *Studies in Medieval Thought and Learning*, pp. 1–8. London, 1981.
———. 'The Quaestiones of Simon of Hinton'. In *Studies in Medieval History presented to F. M. Powicke*, edited by R. W. Hunt, W. A. Pantin, and R. W. Southern, pp. 209–22. Oxford, 1948.
———. 'Some Thirteenth-century Commentators on the Sapiential Books'. *Dominican Studies* 2 (1949): 318–55.
———. *The Study of the Bible in the Middle Ages.* 3rd ed. Oxford, 1982.

Southern, R. W. 'Lanfranc of Bec and Berengar of Tours'. In *Studies in Medieval History Presented to F. M. Powicke*, edited by R. W. Hunt, W. A. Pantin, and R. W. Southern, pp. 27–48. Oxford, 1948.

———. *Robert Grosseteste.* Oxford, 1992.

———. *Scholastic Humanism and the Unification of Europe, 1: Foundations.* Oxford, 1995.

———. 'The Schools of Paris and the Schools of Chartres'. In *Renaissance and Renewal*, edited by R. L. Benson and G. Constable, pp. 113–37. Cambridge, Mass., 1982.

Spicq, C. *Esquisse d'une histoire de l'exégèse latine au moyen âge.* Paris, 1944.

Stephen of Tournai. *Epistulae. PL* 211.

Swanson, R. N. *The Twelfth-Century Renaissance.* Manchester, 1999.

Taylor, J. *The Didascalicon of Hugh of St. Victor.* Reprint, New York, 1991.

Sancti Thomae de Aquino. Summa theologiae. Rome, 1962.

Thomae de Chobham. Summa confessorum. Edited by F. Broomfield. Analecta Mediaevalia Namurcensia 25. Louvain and Paris, 1968.

Thomas de Chobham. Summa de arte praedicandi. Edited by F. Morenzoni. CCCM 82. Turnhout, 1988.

Thorndike, L. *University Life and Records in the Middle Ages.* New York, 1944. Reprint, 1975.

Thurot, Ch. *De l'organisation de l'enseignement dans l'Université de Paris.* Paris, 1850.

Turcheck, J. P. 'A Neglected Manuscript of Peter Lombard's *Liber Sententiarum* and Parisian Illumination of the Late Twelfth Century'. *Journal of the Walters Art Gallery* 44 (1986): 48–69.

Van Engen, J., ed. *Learning Institutionalized.* Notre Dame, Ind., 2000.

Wagner, D. *The Seven Liberal Arts in the Middle Ages.* Bloomington, Ind., 1983.

Walter of St. Victor. *Contra quatuor labyrinthos Franciae.* Edited by P. Glorieux in *AHDLMA* 27 (1952): 187–335.

Warner, G. F., and J. P. Gilson. *Catalogue of Western Manuscripts in the Old Royal and King's Collections.* 4 vols. London, 1921.

Weisheipl, J. A. *Friar Thomas d'Aquino, His Life, Thought and Works.* New York, 1974.

Welter, J.-Th. *L''Exemplum' dans la littérature religieuse et didactique du moyen âge.* Paris and Toulouse, 1927.

Wenzel, S. 'Robert Grosseteste's Treatise on Confession *Deus Est*'. *Franciscan Studies* 30 (1970): 218–93.

Wilmart, A. *Bibliothecae apostolicae Vaticanae. Codices reginenses latini.* 2 vols. Vatican City, 1937.

Index

Index of Manuscripts

Index of Early Printed Books